Mt. Elbrus - Russia
18,510 ft.
August, 1991

Mt. Everest - Nepal
1st: 21,000 ft.-May, 1990
2nd: 24,000 ft.-May, 1992
3rd: 27,500 ft.-May, 1993

Mt. Kilimanjaro - Tanzania
19,341 ft.
August, 1989

Mt. Kosciusko - Australia
7,310 ft.
March, 1991

ISBN: 978-1-57833-707-1 (Soft)
        978-1-57833-706-4 (Hard)
Library of Congress Control Number: 2018959475

First printing February 2019

Book Design: Crystal Burrell, **Todd Communications**
The body typeface for this book was set in ITC Cheltenham

Published by:
Miracle Mile Publishing Co.
611 E. 12th Ave., Anchorage, AK 99501

Distributed by:

Todd Communications
611 E. 12th Ave. • Anchorage, Alaska 99501-4603
(907) 274-8633 (TODD) • Fax: (907) 929-5550
with other offices in Juneau and Fairbanks, Alaska
sales@toddcom.com • **WWW.ALASKABOOKSANDCALENDARS.COM**

Cover portrait of Mike Gordon by Ken Kennell.

Dedication

In Memory of Ruben Gaines

Alaska State Poet Laureate

1973-1978

What others say about
Learning the Ropes

*"In **Learning the Ropes**, Mike Gordon masterfully chronicles a raucous time in Alaska's history, from the turbulent '60s to the freewheeling '70s, the hard-knock '80s and beyond. He's done it all: raised a family, held office, faced down thugs and gangsters, and climbed mountains the world-over—all while running the world famous Chilkoot Charlie's. Everyone I know in Anchorage has a story of a wild night (or two or three) spent at Koot's. Alaska wouldn't be the same without Mike."*

Dave Onofrychuk
Writing Professor,
Alaska Pacific University

"This book is a fascinating read and important to the cultural history of Anchorage. Mike's writing skills capture the characters inhabiting the underbelly of Spenard (Anchorage's most notorious neighborhood) and the challenges of creating and operating the world famous nightclub, Chilkoot Charlie's.

Mike and I were blessed to grow up in the new state of Alaska with rich experiences in scouting/outdooring, entrepreneurial opportunities and the trans-Alaska pipeline boom, where working hard made success an obtainable goal—if you could navigate the pitfalls!

I enjoyed the read because I learned a lot about what Mike had been doing with his life that I didn't know, and the candor of his thoughts regarding the issues he confronted."

Norm Rokeberg,
Friend since 1955,
Alaska House Member (1995 – 2007),
Commissioner, Regulatory Commission of Alaska (2013 –)

*"**LEARNING THE ROPES** is a raw, revealing, humorous memoir by a man who struggled with addiction, waded through local politics and battles with a motorcycle gang, the founding and running of his world-famous bar, Chilkoot Charlie's, and climbing the highest summits of the seven continents. Later in life and restless, he returned to the University of San Francisco to complete his bachelor's degree in political science then went on to earn a master of arts in writing at Alaska Pacific University in Anchorage.*

Mike Gordon is as much a part of Alaska's history as anyone who has ever written about it."

Jan Harper Haines,
*Author of **COLD RIVER SPIRITS***

*"Some people are born on top, some are carried there, and then a few find the inner strength and fortitude to reach the top of a peak on their own. In **Learning the Ropes**, Mike Gordon takes you on an inspirational and poignant journey of a spirited child in an epidemic quarantine camp in the South to a budding young entrepreneur who gets his start shining shoes of servicemen in Alaska and goes on to create Alaska's hallmark saloon - Chilkoot Charlie's. This is a wild and crazy glimpse into old school Alaska, where fists, guns, cash and cocaine ruled. Gordon's tale is a powerful reminder of the importance of love and how we can turn to nature to save ourselves. The peaks and valleys of life can make or break you, but if you learn the ropes and put in the hard work, you can survive anything."*

Don Rearden
*Author of **The Raven's Gift***

"Mike Gordon is a man's man and a better friend than you could ever have. And, he is nothing like you would expect from someone who has climbed the Seven Summits, built a multi-million dollar business from nothing, traversed the good, the bad and the ugly and come out on the other side a hero to many.

No. You'd be hard-pressed to find a better man, much less gifted author, unless you've been privileged to know Mike as I have now for the last forty-seven years. He certainly could be legitimately pretentious, but he is not. He always has been and remains, definitively, an extraordinary human being. He appears perfectly normal - and he is for sure a wonderfully cordial, humble, humorous, charitable and very likeable guy. But, beneath these wonderful traits are hidden the ability to delve deeper and realize more meaning and convey those otherwise normal life experiences in a very special and unique way. He makes those sorts of seemingly mundane things… meaningful. He gives them weight and somehow sucks his reader into his vortex of insightfulness.

You put down Mike's work for a little break… and you find yourself thinking about what he has just given you, without even realizing that he has just snared you. He makes normal life experiences and some incredible adventures in life… well… spellbinding."

Jack Kent
Friend and Chilkoot Charlie's entertainer

TABLE OF CONTENTS

Foreword

It would be an exaggeration to say that *Learning the Ropes* is my life's work, but not by much. I have been working on this memoir off and on since I first began writing on the north side of Mt. Everest in the spring of 1990. I couldn't possibly calculate the number of hours devoted to the project; suffice it to say that the sum total would eclipse any other single effort with the exception of Chilkoot Charlie's. Midway, I used it as my project for my master's degree in writing at Alaska Pacific University when my academic mentor, Timothy M. Rawson, PhD, suggested rather than writing a scholarly work on history or philosophy, I write a book "no one else could write."

I have tried to shed some light on the history of the Anchorage I grew up in, including the Wild West early days in which I operated Chilkoot Charlie's, as well as the pipeline days and the '80s decade of riches-to-rags. I've tried to be fair and honest in my presentation of others with no intention to harm anyone. I've tried to do justice to some remarkable personalities and changed the names of a few to protect their anonymity. I have tried to be forthright about my family and forthcoming about myself. Mostly, I've tried to write an honest memoir, which is hard to do, and I apologize to anyone I might not have mentioned or who might take offence at how I have presented them. All the recollections are mine alone.

Initially, I was reluctant to write about my cocaine addiction. I was ashamed. Another writing mentor at APU, David Onofrychuk, said, "Just write it, Mike. If you're uncomfortable with it you can always remove it later." What great advice that was. I found that just the writing of it was cathartic. Once on paper it was no longer something about which I was ashamed. After all, I did overcome my addiction, which is central to the story. Unlike many, I recognized that the party was over and fortunately I was married to a woman who stuck with me in spite of my challenges and shortcomings, for which I am eternally grateful.

My life has been blessed in many ways. I've certainly had my share of problems, but I've always been a survivor. The bar business is a tough and competitive environment and Chilkoot Charlie's was a wild ride. It was not always fun, but it was never boring. I am proud to know that my employees and I created an iconic landmark unarguably known around the world. It gave me a canvas upon which to express my creativity. It allowed me to attempt the Seven Summits and I would not trade those climbing adventures for anything. The effort added years to my life. I stayed in superb shape, made a lot of great friends, many for life, and saw much of the world I would never otherwise have seen.

Many people have contributed to the writing of **Learning the Ropes**, by editing, reading early manuscripts and offering suggestions, or simply by way of encouragement they gave me along the way. I owe a debt of gratitude to Ruben Gaines, Timothy M. Rawson, PhD, David Onofrychuk, Don Rearden, Jonathan Bower, Jan Harper Haines, Nick Coltman, Jack Toman (Kent), Peter Coyote, Chuck Becker, Ali McCart, Svaja V. Worthington, Rachel Epstein, Rosanne Pagano, Dan Bigley, Lisa Maloney, Jana Ariane Nelson, Rick Fischer, Norman Rokeberg, Art Hackney, David White, Tom Laret, Reidun (Lilla) Paxton, Walter John, Sharon Richards, Joe and Gena Columbus, Charlie McAlpine, Nate Baer, Stu and Maureen Aull, my publisher, Flip Todd, and all of the many avid readers of my short stories in the *Anchorage Press*. Last, and foremost, I would like to thank my wife, Shelli, for her excellent editing and proof-reading, her encouragement and support, but mostly for her love, without which this book would never have been completed.

Mike Gordon

When my publisher told me his Hong Kong contact said the News and Publication Agency of China had asked about two photos in this book that were taken in Tibet, one of the Tibetan family and one of me with Jim Whittaker, I said, "If they read what I've written about China and Tibet, they're not going to like it." I was right.

The next communication from the Hong Kong contact read under the heading "Learning the Ropes" URGENT!

"The verdict came out today. And as expected, the book is not cleared. In fact, the Authority has said that not just 5 pages, but pages from 84-101 (the entire chapter on my attempt of the north side of Everest) have content that is politically inappropriate for production in China..."

I said, "I'm not omitting anything or rewriting anything for the benefit of the Chinese Communist government. Everything I have said about China and Tibet is true, and I could say so much more!"

Ever since Communist China's brutal military invasion of Tibet in 1959, and displacement of the Dalai Lama, they have systematically engaged in what can only be called "ethnic cleansing." They have destroyed Buddhist monasteries and sacred monuments, uprooted entire cities for their hydro-electric projects, imported large numbers of ethnic Chinese and prohibited the teaching of the Tibetan language in schools. They would like the rest of the world to naively view their efforts as humanitarian and applaud them. Trust me. Everything the Chinese do in Tibet is at the point of a rifle.

FREE TIBET!

Introduction

Whenever I read a story that seems too grand to be true, or meet a person who seems larger than life, I have to stop and ask myself whether the story could possibly be true or if the person could possibly be real. *Learning the Ropes* is such a story and Mike Gordon is such a person. The author was my roommate in college and I've known him for over 50 years. We have swapped stories and shared photos of our exploits many times. When this occurs, I find that the images of my own life experiences seem to fade away as I hear about his most recent trip or view photographs taken from the top of the world.

Although I thought I knew Mike Gordon well, *Learning the Ropes* is like traveling through time and meeting an entirely new person. The book opens with fascinating glimpses of life in the rural South of the 1950s and then introduces you to the challenges of living in Alaska before statehood. I not only enjoyed reading about the many experiences; I also found myself fascinated by the author's nearly total recall of events that occurred decades earlier.

As much as I enjoyed the historical cruise through the first few chapters, I was totally riveted by the descriptions of Mike Gordon's first ascent of Mt. Denali in 1989. The narrative was so clear and vivid I actually thought I could hear the wind and feel the cold as I "climbed" with Mike to the top of the mountain. I felt like I was experiencing the same psychological and emotional challenges of the climbing team. I also felt the thrill of survival as we descended from the mountain peak to safety. Although I have done some climbing of my own over the years, I never fully appreciated the life-threatening risk of climbing until I read *Learning the Ropes*.

In contrast, I loved Mike's description of his ascent on Mt. Kilimanjaro as more of a rugged hike than a serious climb, and yet I have experienced Mt. Kilimanjaro myself, and that mountain is still the highest on the African continent. Since I have spent seven weeks on two safaris in Africa, I could relate to the author's statement that Africa moved him emotionally and filled him with wonder. I thoroughly enjoyed his description of his experiences in the Masai Mara, which mirrored my own memories of that fascinating wilderness area.

My idea of a good book is one that I cannot put down. *Learning the Ropes* is that kind of book. For example, I was totally captivated while reading about Mike's ascent of Mt. Aconcagua. Again, I could feel myself climbing the mountain with Mike. I could see the terrain and enjoy the views through his eyes even though I have never been to that part of the world. Mike's imagery made this possible with statements like, "...we could hear the wind coming like a colossal locomotive through canyon after canyon until it finally and abruptly slammed into us with tremendous force." At that moment I had to gasp for air, because I could actually feel that same force. The book also introduces humorous as well as fascinating historical vignettes as when, following his descent from Aconcagua, he describes how he celebrated and sang all night with three German climbers as the Berlin wall was being torn down.

I also enjoyed the history of Chilkoot Charlie's, and its relationship with the Alaskan pipeline. I have heard about Koot's often and even visited Koot's on a couple of occasions, but *Learning the Ropes* provides a far greater appreciation of the history and challenges of that institution and of pipeline-era Alaska. I also enjoyed the story of Mike applying Chilkoot Charlie's decals to Chinese trucks near the Nepal border. That description had a special meaning to me because I have traveled with Mike and seen him apply those decals surreptitiously to many surfaces, always with a devious grin on his face. Having also traveled through Alaska with Mike, I loved his comments about his home state, like his reference to Mr. Whitekeys lyrics about Fairbanks: "It's not the end of the world, but you can see it from there."

The imagery of the views from some of the mountain peaks described by Mike was so vivid I felt I could see the very same views. The statement, "It was a crystal-clear day and everyone was visiting and photographing the spectacular array 8,000 meter peaks," enabled me to imagine those same peaks; the same for his statement that standing on top of Mt. Vinson was "beyond exhilarating. It was unbelievable. I felt like an astronaut." How can one not emotionally experience those pristine vistas through words such as these?

The ultimate high, however, was reading the description of Mike's multiple attempts on Mount Everest. I have talked with Mike about those climbs, and I've seen the photos taken during those ascents, but *Learning the Ropes* provides a much more granular perspective of the hardscrabble effort that very few people have the courage to attempt. In a word, this read is simply amazing.

In a much more personal way, I read and enjoyed the description of Mike's return to the University of San Francisco and his graduation from college 48 years late. It provides what amounts to a very special epilogue to a larger-than-life book authored by a larger-than-life person. And, since I shared that special occasion, I can attest to the fact that the USF graduation meant as much, if not more, to Mike than all of the other thrilling experiences described in *Learning the Ropes*.

L. Richard Fischer
Senior Partner, Morrison & Foerster LLP
Washington, DC

Denali

The first rope line to head down was Henrik, me and Wayne, in that order. Henrik Jones, a brainy kid in the MBA program at Harvard Business School, went over the edge as I eased my way closer to it, waiting for him to go lower, keeping the line taut lest he fall. I waited; and waited. The second line was impatient for us to move over the ridge. Gordy walked up to me and shouted over the gale, "Mike, what's going on?"

"I don't know. I'm waiting for Henrik to move lower," I said.

Gordy walked over to the edge and there stood Henrik on the rim of the abyss. He was waiting for me—afraid of pulling me over if he continued lower.

Gordy bellowed, "Henrik, get your ass moving!" and down we went.

Fine snow swirled around me and larger chunks of ice and snow fell on my head from above, down the vertical wind tunnel of an avalanche chute, where I dangled in space on the multi-colored rope. We were enshrouded in cloud; couldn't see anything beyond the rock and ice face, that pinkish pastel rope and each other—not a bad thing.

I had not cut sufficiently large air holes in the bottom of the bandage covering my frostbitten nose. I felt like I was suffocating, and Wayne, despite my hollering up at him, continually allowed too much slack in the line causing it to get dangerously entangled in my crampons.

Arriving back at Camp III, Scott Wollems, another Denali guide said, "If I had been your guide, you would never have summited."

"What do you mean?" I asked.

"I don't do nighttime summits," he said.

Early Years

More than four decades earlier—long before I'd ever heard of Denali, or even seen snow—polio stalked the streets, homes and schools of my childhood. Survival was uncertain even at sea level. Epidemics were common when I was a five or six year old in the small Central Florida town of Fort Meade, noteworthy solely because Stonewall Jackson was stationed there a decade before the Civil War began. No one had a clue what caused the disease and, of course, everyone was terrified when it sauntered into town. I was warned never to drink cold water after exerting myself.

I suffered through measles, chicken pox, whooping cough and scarlet fever, but somehow I managed to dodge the mumps and polio bullets. To combat the inevitable fever associated with the maladies I did get, my parents were instructed to "sweat it out." Mine dutifully complied with layers of heavy blankets. It's a wonder any of us survived.

My dad was a high school coach and, during the summers, a counselor at a boy's camp in the woods of North Carolina named Camp Highland Lake, so we traveled up there two or three times. These trips were grand family adventures. I recall driving on narrow mountain roads with my parents up front, my sister and me in the rear, singing along together for miles. We sang old standards like, "I've Been Working on the Railroad," "Way Down Upon the Swanee River" and a version of "Someone's in the Kitchen with Dinah." Those were gloriously happy days for me.

When we arrived in North Carolina one summer the state of Florida was experiencing another polio epidemic; so our family and others on their way north were quarantined in a very remote part of the mountains for two whole weeks. The living conditions were crowded and the environment was nothing to sing about. There was no outhouse. It was like a refugee camp. My mother may have been the only grown woman there. Our source of drinking water and where we bathed was a nearby stream with overhanging branches. To alert everyone to the danger of water moccasins—or to be herpetologically correct, cottonmouths, for their white mouth lining—my dad would go to the stream at dawn, lop off the snakes' heads with a machete, and drape their bodies on the overhanging branches—*Agkistrodon piscivorus*, the world's only semi-aquatic viper, can be aggressive and delivers a potentially fatal bite.

I was the youngest kid in the group. There were lots of older boys around, either trying to pick on me or get me into trouble of some sort, but I was pretty feisty and never, ever, let anyone push me around. My first day at school in Fort Meade, my parents were walking the school grounds and saw a knot of kids cheering on a fight. Pulling out enough children to get to the center of the ruckus, they discovered their own son. I remember that other kid well. He had blond, curly hair and freckles, and went around with one leg of his jeans rolled up higher than the other. He was a bully and had thrown dirt and ants on my brand new smallpox vaccination. When my parents finally got to us, I had just picked him up and dashed his body onto one of the big oak tree roots sticking up out of the dirt. The older kids in the quarantine camp had not found themselves a cherry.

One day at the camp my mom and dad had been off on an errand. Returning to the shack we occupied, they discovered me backed into a corner with half a dozen older boys held at bay. In my hands was the camp honey bucket. I swung it threateningly at the bigger boys, shouting, "I'll 'fo' it on you!" as some of the unsavory contents sloshed menacingly out onto the rough-cut, wooden floor.

When we finally arrived at Camp Highland Lake, I became pals with the son of another couple on the staff. The older boys involved both of us in various pranks, like peeing in the gas tank of the camp director's car. They also coaxed me into leaping off the high dive into the pool. "Mike! Jump! You can do it!" And I did.

Dad organized a treasure hunt one night for all the boys. One of the chores they had to fulfill was to enter an old abandoned barn, climb up a ladder into the hay-loft and gather some article or other. Dad was in the loft waiting for them. One of his hands was completely covered with phosphorous paint that glowed green in the dark, but he kept it hidden behind his back. When those boys got to the top of the ladder the hand would appear seemingly out of nowhere—very slowly—and the fingers would part their hair, passing ever-so-lightly over their skulls.

Years later, he chuckled as he said, "I could actually feel the hairs on their heads standing straight up on end before they screamed, fled down the ladder and out the barn doors like their asses were on fire." The dad of those early years is the dad I remember most fondly.

We did a lot of moving when I was growing up and, being small for my age, no one was ever the least bit intimidated by me. In every new place we moved I had to prove myself by fighting someone. It happened when we moved three times in Mississippi and twice more when we moved to Alaska. Not long after we moved out to Spenard—now a neighborhood in Anchorage—from Government Hill, a group of three kids called me out from my front porch. My mom told me later that my little back got rigid as a board and the hair on the back of my neck stood out straight like porcupine spines. She said to those boys, "Why does it take all three of you to call out my son? Are you too cowardly to do it alone?" Pound for pound, I was a pretty tough kid. I had to be tough because neither my mom, nor that honey bucket were always close at hand.

Boid

My first pet was a dog—a pointer; in other words, a "boid" dog. He followed me home from school one day. My mother stood on our porch in Fort Meade, Florida and watched as, with a rope around its neck, I drug the hapless critter, paws digging little creases of useless resistance, down the dirt road toward the house, hollering from afar, "Mom! Look what I found!" We soon moved way out into the country, and Boid came along.

Boid and I became pals in the way only a dog and a seven-year-old-boy can be, but he had a couple of interesting idiosyncrasies. For one, he was terrified of thunder and lightning.

We lived on a long, straight, two-lane macadam country road with no shoulders. You could literally see the road until it disappeared into the horizon, distorted by the shimmering heat waves and the occasional large slow-moving tortoise, which we called gophers. Boid had plenty of freedom to roam when we were not doing things together. I have a vivid memory of him appearing on that distant, blurry, razor's edge of a horizon, hell-bent for home when the heavens of sub-tropical Florida began to pound out their thundering chorus, accompanied by a flashing lightshow of strident, stabbing, erratically aimed bolts of lightning.

That dog was visible from a mile off, making a bee-line for the front porch. It was no doubt during one such experience that he figured out how to let himself into the porch, which had a screen door that opened outwards, not inwards. The door had a conveniently located diagonal wire on the outside of the bottom half to lend structural support. Boid could insert one of his paws behind that wire and pull the screen open just enough to skirt around it and make his entrance. Once inside, he hid under the couch and would not come out until the heavens had settled their arguments, and then some. It was not unlike a marmot believing that his puny little network of tunnels is going to protect him from a hungry grizzly bear, or the belief that anything—like an amulet—is going to protect any of us from the vagaries of the world or our own fate. The protections many seek from parents, siblings, friends—the government—or whatever, might more appropriately and beneficially come from that fading American tradition called self-reliance.

Boid would not enter the house proper, either. Though I had managed to drag him home in Fort Meade, neither I nor anyone else could cajole or physically force him into the house. His previous owner had branded into his canine brain that he was an outside dog, not an inside dog.

While other kids wanted to be firemen or policemen, or whatever, I only wanted to be a big game hunter. That was all there was to it. I loved watching that era's black and white thirty-five millimeter movies that showed an intrepid couple, Osa and Martin Johnson, facing hostile lions and rhinos on the plains of Africa or ducking flying snakes in Borneo. My parents would watch from the window as I walked off into the orange grove with my BB gun over my shoulder, Boid on point, as if we were venturing into the African savannah in search of big game. Dad would tell my mother, "Ruth, come over here. You've got to see this."

Of course, there were no lions, rhinos or flying snakes in the orange grove, though there were plenty of snakes that slithered across the ground. I carried around a harmless pet garden snake for the longest time, but one had to be ever-watchful for the other kind. My very first childhood recollection is of seeing a beautifully multi-colored coral snake wiggling across the kindergarten lawn and instinctively knowing, even as a pre-school child, that it was dangerous. When I moved to Alaska a few years later, I was told there were no snakes. I didn't believe that for a second, but what a relief it was when I eventually realized it was true. Of course in Alaska we have Yogi to deal with.

My Florida focus was on birds, and Boid's was on retrieving the fallen ones. If I'd ever been caught and the awful carnage brought to light, I'd probably still be working off the money I'd owe in fines to the state of Florida for decimating the ranks of mockingbirds, the Florida state bird. Today it pains me and when bad things happen in my life, I sometimes think it's the result of bad bird karma. While commiserating with my wife, Shelli, about some misfortune, I'll just look at her and say, "It's the birds."

My sister, five years my senior, was in junior high at the time. She was taking alto saxophone lessons and whenever she would start practicing, Boid would start to howl. He was a natural vocalist and everyone but my sister thought it was hilarious. Not being exactly what you would call a musical prodigy and taking advantage of the accompaniment, she felt, with a fair amount of justification, that Boid's behavior was disruptive.

Mom and Dad both taught at the grade one-through-twelve Fort Meade school. Mom taught English and Dad was the coach. The school had never had a coach until Dad arrived and set about organizing a football team. Many of the kids on the team lived great distances from the school and there were no "soccer moms" or "soccer dads" in those days. Dad drove all over the countryside shuttling kids to and from their homes to practice and games, sometimes arriving home well after dark. The first season the team did not win a single game, but by the end of the second year they were playing larger schools like Kissimmee and Orlando—and beating them. When I attended my dad's funeral in Anchorage, Alaska in 1976, I was never more touched than by the large wreath placed before his coffin from the Fort Meade "Class of '49." He must have been awfully important in the lives of those kids because they never forgot him.

All in all, it was a very pleasant experience living out there in the country, though I remember that my parents were having marital and financial problems at the time. As I understand it, my dad went to his father-in-law in Daytona Beach to ask for assistance and was told to buzz off. My grandfather had not approved of the marriage in the first place, he being a wealthy businessman and my dad being a "jock" and a high school coach. It was a moment in time when it occurred to me that security in this life is not a given and that adults are imperfect, as when my dad decided to show me how to light the gas hot water heater.

He put a match to it and it lit. He then turned the gas off and handed me the matches with instructions to turn the dial a certain direction, light another match and insert it into the opening at the bottom of the heater. When I did, it blew up in my face. I was not wearing a shirt and was seriously burned from the waist up. Fortunately, I carry no external scars from the experience. Why a father would want to show a seven-year-old how to light a hot water heater is one of those unanswered and mildly disturbing questions in my life.

All things come to an end, as did our sojourn in the country in Central Florida. Teaching hardly paid a living wage there at the time, I was told, so my dad went to work for the American Red Cross and they moved us to Mississippi, where he became the Field Director at Keesler Air Force Base in Biloxi. Since Clara Barton founded the American Red Cross during the Civil War, the organization has always had a very close relationship with the military. My dad said he held a civilian rank equivalent to that of a major in the military and I remember the guards would always salute our car as we entered or left the base.

Boid did not make the journey with us, and I am not privy to his fate. But with his musical background, natural talent and enthusiasm he might well have ended up singing lead in a mongrel blues band.

The Black Mark

We moved right into Biloxi proper and I proceeded to get myself into a bit of trouble. I'm not sure exactly how it happened. It was probably the old story of the kid moving from the country to the big city and falling in with the wrong crowd. First, I got caught stealing a yo-yo from a variety store. Then I skipped school and stayed home all day with a friend smoking Kool cigarettes that I stole from my mother. My older sister, Pat, a regular Sherlock Holmes, ratted me out.

Next thing I knew I was sitting in the principal's office at school with both of my parents. The principal chastised me for skipping school and held before me my school record with a very big black mark next to my name. He said, "Michael William Gordon, this black mark will be next to your name for the rest of your life. You need to mend your ways now, before it's too late." Now, that'll get an eight-year-old's attention.

Soon thereafter we moved from Biloxi down the road to Gulfport. During a fight with my sister while Mom and Dad were at work, she locked me out of the house and I stood on the lawn swearing at her at the top of my lungs. A neighbor told my mom I had the foulest mouth of any little boy she had ever heard. Mom never spoke to her again.

Another time in Gulfport I got a spanking for punching my sister in the stomach.

"You're not supposed to punch a girl in the stomach," my parents chimed in together.

It was apparently of no consequence that she was older and bigger than me and had both hands clasped tightly around my neck—my eyes popping out, gasping for breath—when I punched her. Soon we moved even further out into the country to Orange Grove. I felt like the family was seeking a safe haven—and I was the reason—though there were no doubt other issues in play.

The move to Orange Grove was just what I needed. We were in the middle of nowhere. I made wooden traps for catching flying squirrels. When I caught one I'd take the trap into the bathroom, close the door, release the squirrel into the tub and, wearing leather gloves, grab the little critter and tie one end of a string around its neck, the other around a loop in my jeans. I'd put acorns in my pocket and take the squirrels to school with me. They were easily tamed. Mom taught at the one-and-only school in Orange Grove, and loved to tell the story of how one of the other teachers cautiously approached her and asked her if she could stop her son from bringing squirrels to school in his pocket because he was disrupting the class.

When my mother did my laundry she never knew what she was going to find in those jean pockets: squirrels, "twags" (Mississippi-little-boy-speak for frogs), garden snakes, whatever. All I can say is I must have come by it naturally. My dad killed moccasins and rattlesnakes and preserved them for display in jars full of formaldehyde, though I had (nor have) no idea for what purpose.

Playing and acquiring marbles was a big deal during school recess. I was pretty good at marbles, but I devised a better method of accumulating them. I took a one-pound coffee can, cut a round hole in the bottom of it, turned it upside down—being careful to have the hole just the right size and the bottom pushed up just the right amount—and would pay two marbles for every one that was dropped into the hole from waist height.

We had the only television for miles around and my friends would come over to our house on Saturday mornings to watch *Buster Brown's Circus* and *No School Today*, which featured famous radio show characters Big Jon and Sparkie and the theme song "Today's the Day the Teddy Bears Have their Picnic." Sparkie was an elf who wanted nothing more than to be a real boy; he was created by Jon Arthur, who also played Big Jon and provided the voices for a number of other characters.

Another program we watched, and probably the first science fiction series, was *Captain Video and His Video Rangers*. The captain had a teenage sidekick referred to only as the Video Ranger. Popular with adults and kids alike, the series featured the Video Rangers fighting for truth and justice in a distant future, working from their secret mountaintop base. It also had the first robot to be seen on TV. But, radio programs like *The Fat Man*, a detective series based on a Dashiell Hammett character, were still more popular than anything on television.

Two of my young friends lived farther out along the dirt road on which we lived. They were brothers and their names were Effort and Johnnie. Effort was my age. Johnnie was a little bit older, but mentally challenged. Back then we called it retarded.

We three had all kinds of adventures together, even "discovering" a small lake in which we used to go skinny-dipping. It had cottonmouth moccasins swimming lazily in the current of the stream running out of one end of it. One day, when Effort and Johnnie and I were on one of our adventures out in the woods, Johnnie announced that he had to take a crap, which he did. To his dismay and our horror, it had a huge worm sliding around in it. I vividly remember the squiggler. It was not a flat, white tape worm. It was a big, round worm, like an earthworm, and more than a foot long.

We all ran back to Effort and Johnnie's house, where their father was sitting on the porch in a rocking chair. Effort and I both chimed in together, "Johnnie's got a worm in his crap!" I assumed his dad would want to take Johnnie to the hospital, but Johnnie's father thought it was the funniest thing he had ever heard. He started rocking wildly back and forth in his chair, slapping his legs and hollering at the top of his lungs, "Why, you wormy sapsucker!"

My family only lived in Orange Grove for about a year before the military rotated us to Elmendorf Air Force Base in Anchorage, Alaska, where I was to spend the rest of my childhood. I took a lot of razzing about my Southern accent at first, but I cannot think of a better place to have grown up than Anchorage in the fifties and sixties. I was raised on hunting, fishing and the Boy Scouts of America. I became an Eagle Scout, an accomplishment I am proud of to this day. When some people—astonished—say, "You were an Eagle Scout?" I always reply, "No. I *am* an Eagle Scout." My interest in Boy Scouts kept me out of a lot of trouble. I also played alto saxophone—a hand-me-down from my sister—in the high school band and was a starting defenseman on the Anchorage High School hockey team.

Years later, while still in high school, I had a chance to visit Effort and Johnnie in Mississippi. The house where we had run to tell their dad about the worm was a tar paper shack. I was so grateful that my family had moved to Alaska when we did, thinking that had we not, I would still be walking around barefoot, with a perpetually stubbed toe. There is nothing that hurts worse than a stubbed toe, other than re-stubbing a toe that has not completely healed from a previous stubbing. I also reflected on the freedom riders going down to Mississippi in their buses and I could see Effort and Johnnie's father sitting out there on his porch with a shotgun in his lap, rocking back and forth saying, "Yankee sapsuckers!" waiting for his chance to even the score.

A few years ago I found myself overnighting in Jackson, Mississippi. When I got up the next day to drive to Biloxi I asked for a map at the ho-tel desk and searched in vain for that little country community of Orange Grove, which I knew was somewhere outside of Gulfport. I asked the desk clerk if she knew where Orange Grove was and she did not, so she asked an elderly man walking by if he knew where it was.

He said, "Sure," and pointed to the area north of Gulfport saying, "This area here is all Orange Grove. It's really grown up the last few years."

That was an understatement. Orange Grove was now suburbia

and part of greater Gulfport. I was able to find the grade school I had attended and the road my family had lived on, but it sure didn't look anything like it had looked forty years earlier. Now it was full of large, Southern-style houses with sprawling, manicured lawns.

Later in the day, as I drove through Biloxi reminiscing about my childhood, I found myself thinking I'd better not get a traffic ticket because if the cop looked me up in his computer, no doubt the first thing he'd see would be my grade school record with that big black mark next to my name.

The Entrepreneur

My dad was already in Alaska during the summer of 1953 when my mother, my sister and I boarded the Greyhound bus that was to be our home for the next week, traveling from Mississippi through the Texas and New Mexico deserts, and the redwood forests of California and Oregon. The bus was my idea and by the time we arrived in Seattle, both my mother and my sister wanted to kill me. But come on; when you take the advice of a ten-year-old about life-changing travel decisions you need to be grown-up enough to own the consequences.

All I remember about Seattle, our embarking point for Seward, is how many shots we received. Alaska was considered an overseas military move, so we were inoculated against everything under the sun. We felt like human pin cushions, and I thought, "We're leaving America!"

We traveled north to Seward on an old gray tub named the *U. S. S. Funston*, after the colorful Teddy Roosevelt era general that had nearly single-handedly captured a fabled Philippine guerrilla leader on his own turf during America's "pacification" of that archipelago. Years later, he would order the destruction of the buildings along Van Ness Avenue in San Francisco during the great earthquake and fire of 1906, thus saving the buildings beyond, all the way to the Pacific Ocean. There is a street named after him in the City by the Bay.

Of course I couldn't have cared less about history at the time, and my ten-year-old brain simply wasn't capable of imagining all the implications and possibilities of a move to Alaska, which was as alien to me as if I were on a freighter headed for King Kong's uncharted volcanic island home in the old black and white movie. Then, sure enough, as if on cue, while I was busily watching whales spouting and playing shuffleboard on the open deck, a rumor circulated aboard that a huge volcanic eruption had just turned our destination, Anchorage, into another Pompeii. I thought, "Wow! How cool is that!" A sentiment not shared by my mother.

Once we docked in Seward we boarded the Alaska Railroad for the ride to Anchorage. I marveled at the herds of moose on either side of the tracks going through the Portage flats. Up to that point, the largest wild animal I'd ever seen was a raccoon.

Upon arrival in Anchorage, though the sun was visible again, the place was in fact covered in an inch or two of fine volcanic ash from the recent Mt. Spurr eruption. It got into everything. If you were too lazy to scoop it up yourself, you could buy it by the labeled jar for years afterward in souvenir shops around town—some enterprising person's attempt to make a quick buck.

I was soon to realize that, at the tender age of ten, I had landed in the middle of an enterprising opportunity of my own. We lived in a part of Anchorage called Government Hill, aptly named because it was contiguous with the military base where my father was stationed. Government Hill was one huge apartment complex of mostly one and two bedroom apartments filled to the brim with military and civil service people, all transient, so just going through the Dumpsters was like dredging for gold. My friends and I fashioned a couple of sleds out of perfectly good corrugated metal sheets and slid down the steep gravel cliffs next to Ship Creek, scrambling back up to the WW II pill boxes we fancied as forts, decorated with a treasure trove of Dumpster furnishings.

Then, of course, there was the military base right next door with the rows of huge barracks filled with enlisted men. My dad made me a shoeshine box and I would cruise the barracks shining shoes for fifty cents, shooting the bull with the guys. What responsible parent today would allow their ten-year-old son to wander, at will, around a five-hundred-man barracks? Times have changed.

Sooner or later it came to my attention that there were a lot of pop bottles lying around those barracks. A pop bottle was worth ten cents at the Piggly Wiggly on Government Hill. All one needed was a grocery cart to haul them from the barracks to the store. No problem. It was an early recognition that making money wasn't difficult. The essential components were just lying around; all a person had to do was put them together. Of course, I was too young to have any long range plans—I was just having fun and learning to look for opportunities.

Next I acquired a paper route—a pretty big one. A buddy of mine had an adjacent route and we would alternate not delivering our papers every Friday. Instead, we would take them to the base gate at the end of the day, when everyone was in line in their cars on the way home from work, the majestic Chugach Mountains in the background, and sell them for ten cents apiece. I even had the foresight to save a few in case of complaints from people on my route.

At that time, my sister was a freshman in high school and a real knockout—the living embodiment of the word "pulchritude." I had a school picture of her posing very seductively in a tight sweater, showing off two of her more significant attributes. In order to increase circulation on my newspaper route I wandered through the barracks with that picture of my sister. The pitch went like this: "You sign up for one month of the *Anchorage Times*, pay in advance and I'll give you my sister's phone number." *What a bonanza.* That is, until the phone started ringing.

Wall Street knew nothing that I did not know intuitively. Sex sells and I had the perfect setup. The only problem was my sister, who liked getting calls from guys—but not every Tom, Dick and Harry on Elmendorf Air Force Base, practically twenty-four hours a day. Could be we had to change our phone number. I don't remember. But I do remember my sister's plaintive cry, "Daddy, make him stop!" and the subsequent licking I got.

That was the last licking I ever received from my dad and the phone number scheme was, perhaps because of said licking, the last good business idea I had for the next fifteen years. When the next idea did arrive it was a whopper, and the world famous Chilkoot Charlie's nightclub was born in the heart of Spenard—then a seamy part of Anchorage, full of nightlife and characters and advertised as "The Miracle Mile."

Shame

It was in my sixteenth year that it happened, on the same trip during which I visited Effort and Johnnie in Mississippi. I remembered from earlier years the "White" and "Colored" bathrooms, and segregated drinking fountains, and the sting of peoples' reactions when I innocently befriended a black boy my own age. But there was an incident on this trip from which I just turned heel and walked away. It is my last memory of the Old South.

Both of my parents were teaching school again, this time in Anchorage. Taking advantage of their summer break of 1958, we drove down the Alcan Highway. Driving the Alcan in those days was an adventure in itself. We visited friends and relatives in Chicago, Pittsburgh, Philadelphia and Florida. When we weren't staying with friends or relatives we stayed, at my insistence, in motels with swimming pools because I was practicing my diving techniques. Getting creative, I dove off the board backwards one night, came back around under water and swam right into the swimming pool wall. It's a wonder I didn't knock myself out and drown. As it was, I carried a dark, circular memento on my forehead for several weeks.

During the course of that summer we saw a lot of America: Washington, D.C., the Grand Canyon, Disneyland and Knott's Berry Farm. Coming back along the California/Oregon coast we did the Drive Under Tree, the Drive Around Tree, the Drive Through Tree and every other commercial version other than the Drive Into Tree, since my dad drove better than I dove.

In Fort Meade I made the usual rounds, renewing acquaintances, comparing lifestyles and circumstances. Even went out one Saturday night to the Lone Oak Inn to try to meet some girls.

The next afternoon we were all hanging around a gas station where one of my friends worked. It was across the street from The Pit, a name long before given to the small alligator-infested lake that served as a public swimming pool. The Fourth of July was approaching, so there were a lot of rockets and firecrackers around in order to celebrate the birth of a nation of free and honorable peoples. The immediate activity centered on rockets that were being arranged in the vicinity of the gas tanks, for what purpose I little realized.

Shortly, an elderly Negro couple, resplendent in their best Sunday finery, and whose arrival had obviously been anticipated by my friends, passed along the sidewalk in front of the gas station on their way home from church. The next thing I knew a half dozen rockets were air-borne in the direction of the couple, accompanied by great howls of laughter. Fortunately there were no direct hits

though it wasn't for lack of trying or due to any evasive action on the part of the elderly couple.

They were in their sixties. They had raised a family. They were, no doubt, grandparents. He held his head high, and she held onto his arm. And as they proudly and deliberately continued on their way, she turned her head and fixed me with a look that has stayed with me the rest of my life. I could have protested to my friends. I could have run to the couple and apologized for the behavior of my friends.

But I just walked away.

I've never gone back to Fort Meade, though the memory of that incident at the gas station still hangs on my conscience like a heavy, self-reflective ornament—to this very day.

Denali

During the troubled winter of 1989, Shelli gave me *her* look—disgusted, dismissive; penetrating eyes, tight lips—and said, "You're just trying to run away from your problems."

I wasn't. I wanted to face those problems my way. I found it hard to explain my need to exorcise the personal demons that blocked my path to becoming the husband, mate and friend she so wanted.

We were separated—living apart. I said, "Shelli, with due deference to self-help books and counseling sessions, I need to do something different, something tangible—something big." Denali certainly was big, and I had made up my mind to climb it.

I added, "I know what I'm doing. Please believe me," trying to sound reassuring for both of us. There was no reply, but I sensed fear, which wasn't all bad because it told me she still cared.

I had met Shelli Shannon all those years ago between Christmas and New Year's Eve of 1978 at a dinner party at Elevation 92. She was accompanying Bill Jacobs, my partner in Chilkoot Charlie's, the bar we had opened eight years earlier. Koot's, as locals referred to it, had become a startling success; it was the hottest club in Anchorage. Bill was a local attorney and the dinner was in honor of his secretary, Winnie, who had held the office together at Koot's while I was on my runaway to Belize, a depression-induced mid-life crisis from which I had recently returned. Winnie was now retiring.

All I knew about Shelli was that she was Bill's girlfriend, and though I certainly found her intelligent and attractive, the thought of any kind of entanglement never even entered my mind. On the other hand, Shelli was looking at me and wondering why I didn't have a date. The next time I saw her was from across the room at the Chilkoot Charlie's annual employee party at the Rabbit Creek Inn. It was November, 1979. She was wearing a black Bedouin dress and sporting a pair of large-rimmed glasses, her waist-length dark hair falling over her shoulders. I thought she was the most exotically beautiful creature I'd ever seen, and I was envious of Bill—but that's where it stopped.

Later at the club she said, "I find you very attractive."

"I find you attractive also," I said.

A month later I was vacationing in Hawaii with my friend Norman Rokeberg. We stayed in the one-bedroom condominium I owned with Bill, on the top floor of the Royal Kahana on Maui. Bill and Shelli were supposed to meet us and stay there longer—after

Norm and I left for more vacation time on Oahu—but Bill, at the very last minute, cancelled his plans. He said to Shelli, "You go by yourself. Mike likes you. You'll have a good time."

Shelli says her mother gave her the only good advice she had ever offered: "You've had this trip planned for a long time and your plane ticket is paid for, so you just go on over there by yourself. Bill will come along if and when he can."

Norm slept on the small hide-a-bed in the living room. Shelli and I took the one bedroom's larger king-size bed. Neither of us got a wink of sleep the first night. We set off tropical magnetic storms each time we accidentally touched. We all dined together the next night, and went to see *Apocalypse Now*, Shelli, fumigated on one side by aftershave and the other by hair spray, felt like she was suffocating in the same Vietnam heat that was being so vividly portrayed across the theater's screen. We spent the next day at Kaanapali Beach sunning and swimming, where Shelli and I spent more time looking at each other underwater than at tropical fish or coral.

Since Norm and I were soon moving to Oahu for a few days I needed to teach Shelli how to drive the manual four-on-the-floor Volkswagen "Thing" we kept at the condo. Our hands together on the gear shift; decorum collapsed. Shelli expressed her feelings for me in no uncertain terms and I yielded, in spite of my misgivings.

That evening, we walked together on the beach talking about art and books. I loved art, had a small collection of paintings, and enjoyed literature. Shelli, I discovered, had a bachelor's degree in art, art history and American literature. The brilliant author, Annie Dillard, had been one of her professors at Western Washington University's Fairhaven College. They were friends. I was smitten.

It took more restraint than I've ever shown just waiting until we got back to the condo to make love to her.

I hadn't known of the problems Shelli and Bill were having, but I got an earful on Maui. Shelli had telephoned Bill immediately after arriving at the condo following her solo flight from Anchorage and told him they were finished. She was fed up with Bill, who might have tended his pot plants with tender loving care, but would let his dogs crap all over the house and wouldn't pay his electric bills until threatened with a cut-off notice. I was having my own problems with Bill, who was now constantly demanding more money from the business to cover the debt from building the triplex they were living in—the one our banker had warned him not to build. Our combined resources were incapable of pulling him out of the financial hole he had dug for himself. Still, he had recently demanded another $40,000 under the threat of corporate dissolution.

Norm and I left Shelli on Maui and moved on to Oahu, where he had an affair with an old high school classmate of ours and I tried to encapsulate my affair with Shelli, foolishly thinking that I might get away with acting like it had never happened. Of course I should have known better, but I was raised on the game of denial. It was a family imperative. Soon after returning to Anchorage, I began receiving cards in the mail from Maui inscribed with romantic poems. When Shelli left Bill and got an apartment of her own we began seeing each other. Finally, on a chilly March morning, my daughter, Michele, helped Shelli move her clothes and few personal belongings from her one room basement apartment into my condominium on Sorbus Way.

I did not steal Shelli from Bill. She had announced her intention to leave him before our affair on Maui, but Bill, understandably, did not see it that way. One afternoon on the old deck in the backyard of Chilkoot Charlie's, where the resurrected Bird House Bar is now, he closed his fist, raised his thumb skyward and pointed his finger at me—his hand now a pistol aimed at my forehead. People—customers and employees alike—took sides in the matter. There might have been some shouting. I left before anyone did anything regrettable.

It didn't help that I had a reputation for being a playboy and most everyone felt the relationship would not last, that I would simply move on to the next conquest. But there was more depth to our relationship than people could see. We had lived together for a year when I proposed. I then dragged my feet for the next two years, reluctant to make that commitment again after the two failed marriages and two property settlements I'd already endured.

Shelli started searching for an apartment and finally said she was moving out if I didn't follow up on my proposal. I acquiesced. We were married in a hot air balloon on September 17, 1983—a beautiful autumn morning of blue skies and golden leaves in Anchorage.

In truth, it wasn't long before I was up to the old habits that would eventually lead to our separation and subsequent marriage counseling less than five years later. I had been unfaithful to both of my previous wives, so falling into the routine was almost natural for me. But this time I had myself convinced that misbehaving in Thailand was somehow different. Shelli was so young, impressionable and in love and I was such a callous bastard. I destroyed something pure and beautiful that can never be entirely repaired, but at least I had the wherewithal, plus the support of a woman stronger than me, to work my way through the issues that continued to put distance between us and damage the marriage I desired, but to which I was unable or unwilling to fully commit.

I had my work cut out for me. Like so many others in Alaska, I started using cocaine during the oil pipeline construction of the 1970s. For years I hardly knew or associated with anyone in any profession or job who didn't use it, and I knew a lot of prominent people. At any house party, half the people would be in the bathrooms. In the Crow's Nest restaurant at the Captain Cook Hotel, when people weren't just blatantly snorting it off their tables with hundred dollar bills, they were locking the elevator on the "thirteenth floor," a nonexistent place, the only floor without its own button. People snorted up their cars, their homes, their jobs and their relationships until there was nothing left but a screwed up, lonely, empty, broke, paranoid shell of a person with messed up nasal passages. I hardly ever had to buy the stuff because people were always turning me on, but that was the hitch: I couldn't go anyplace without running into someone who was "carrying" or wondering if I was.

The real nadirs in our lives are the times when we actually commit the acts that precipitate the inevitable consequences we later mistakenly think of as nadirs, but which are in reality only painful reminders of the need for self-reflection and atonement.

I knew the party was over and feared waking up one day with my kisser plastered on the front page of the *Anchorage Daily* News under the headline "Scandal at Koot's." My priorities were turned upside down. The cocaine was stimulating paranoia, so I wasn't enjoying it anymore—a sure sign of addiction if I hadn't noticed it before—and I dreaded when its usage would inevitably surface during our discussions in therapy. Shelli had no idea of the role coke played in my life, but it was the main demon I needed to exorcise, and I wanted to be able to say, "I don't do that anymore" when it came up in therapy.

At the time I was reading *The Seven Summits*, the story of Dick Bass, owner of Snowbird Ski Resort, and his quest to become the first person in the history of mankind to make it to the top of all seven of the continents. On April 30, 1986—at age fifty-three—he also became the oldest person to summit Mt. Everest. What got my attention was that both Bass and his climbing partner, Frank Wells, were older than me when they began their journey, and neither were climbers at the start. On a clear day I could see Denali, the highest mountain on the North American continent, from my living room window. I knew people who had climbed it, but I had always thought it required special skills and years of experience, so never seriously considered doing it myself. Now it became clear to me that if Bass and Wells could climb that towering magnificence so could I, and I decided it would be a perfect way to avoid all those problem folks, start a new life for myself, and make some new friends. The fact that everyone thought I was nuts and had no interest whatsoever in joining me made it even more appealing. I saw the chance of a great adventure, a new life, and a marriage that would survive—as long as I did.

I was in good physical condition. I had quit smoking after Dad's death from esophageal cancer a dozen years before, back in 1977, and had completed thirteen marathons. So I picked up the phone and called Mike Howerton, head guide for Genet Expeditions, a well-known local Denali guide service started by Ray Genet, who had recently died while guiding on Everest.

Mike and I discussed Denali and I said, "I have a problem I need to confess if you promise not to laugh." Of course he laughed out loud when I told him I was afraid of heights.

He said, "I'll take you ice climbing a few times, get you familiar with the equipment, and when I get through with you you'll think Denali Pass is a cakewalk."

I breathed a sigh of relief. Denali Pass, the focus of a lot of my fears at the time, frequently accompanied the names of dead climbers.

Mike, good to his word, generously spent a number of his weekends during the winter of 1989 teaching me the basics of ice climbing with ice axe and crampons, such as how not to step on the rope or puncture my lower legs with all those sharp, metal pointy-things strapped to my boots.

When I announced my intention to climb Denali to my Anchorage friends, they said I'd kill myself. Deaths and perilous rescues on Denali are annual fodder for the local media. Knowing me better than most, Shelli and my family also feared I'd want to do all of the Seven Summits. I tried to assure them that wasn't my intention. They all knew it was an empty assurance. Who was I trying to fool? It was a foregone conclusion.

Once the full scale of my climbing ambitions were in the open Shelli suggested I make cachets for each summit. These were commemorative postcards of sorts, in the tradition of the Iditarod dog team racers who would postmark their cachets in Anchorage, carry them on their sleds 1,100 miles to Nome, postmark them again and then either sell them to raise money or give them to friends and sponsors as collectibles. I had my cachets designed by Ruben Gaines—a dear friend, Alaskan poet laureate, radio raconteur, talented cartoonist and creator of Chilkoot Charlie, Alaska's legendary titan sourdough reprobate after whom he had permitted me to name the wildly successful Spenard watering hole.

My climbing cachets were adorned with Ruben's caricature of

Chilkoot Charlie in an outfit appropriate to each mountain. On the cachets for Denali and Everest, Chilkoot looked like himself, a sourdough wearing a parka, hat with ear muffs and climbing boots; for Kilimanjaro he was dressed as a French Legionnaire; for Elbrus he wore a big Russian-style fur hat; for Aconcagua he wore a serape and an Argentine gaucho hat; for Vinson he was shaking hands with a penguin on the summit, and for Kosciuszko he wore an Australian Outback hat.

I dedicated each cachet and climb to an important person in my life who was no longer alive. I had them stamped and postmarked at a post office near the base of each mountain, carried them to the summit, had a photo taken with them, and then had them stamped and postmarked at a post office again near the base of the mountain. Getting the stamping and postmarking done on the various continents was often a challenging experience, but the climb was never over—in my mind—until the job was done.

Upon my return to Anchorage, Ruben hand-colored each cachet, a job he dreaded but did with kind-hearted tolerance, and signed each one. I then numbered and signed them myself. People enjoyed collecting them, and I was proud to later see them framed and hanging on walls in homes and offices.

I began by setting my sights on Flattop, the most climbed mountain in Alaska. Located right in Anchorage's backyard, this remains a popular afternoon hike for scores of residents on any warm and sunny day. I, however, had to ask employees at Alaska Mountaineering and Hiking for directions. By the time I got back to my truck after my first climb, wearily post-holing my way through knee-deep freshly-fallen snow, I thought my friends might be right about my decision.

Training for Denali, I ran a regular circuit of the bike trails and climbed Flattop so many times that soon, I could have done it with my eyes closed. I'd fill a big pack with snow at the base and then dump it out on the summit, a 1,280 foot elevation gain from the Glen Alps trailhead. Flattop was the perfect mountain for my purposes: very close to Anchorage and offering authentic snow, ice, winter weather and steepness near the top. One day I climbed Flattop, came home, changed clothes and ran twenty miles.

Denali expedition time finally arrived in May, 1989 and I found myself at the Talkeetna airport waiting to be flown to Base Camp. Reality hit hard when a Lama helicopter landed with two injured climbers. High winds had blown them right off the mountain at 16,400 feet, sending them down a thousand feet, still in their tent and sleeping bags. They were damn lucky to be alive, and they looked frightful, both with frostbitten hands, faces and feet, complaining to the two doctors present of various aches and pains. Both were noticeably relieved when told their appendages would be okay, but one of the doctors cautioned them not to do *anything* with them: "No walking. Don't open any doors—nothing! Any injury right now will be serious, indeed!"

Afterward, we found ourselves paying keen attention to head guide Gordy Kito, a Tlingit-Haida whose lobbyist father I knew, and assistant guide John Evans, a Welshman well trained in paramilitary search and rescue, as they instructed us in self-arrest and crevasse rescue techniques. Some of us were wondering what the hell we were doing there. I sure was. One climber backed out and flew home to San Francisco before we flew to Base Camp. Of the six remaining climbers, I was the oldest at forty-six. Maybe Shelli was right. Another self-help book wouldn't kill me. Denali might.

Some in the group had climbed other mountains. I had climbed only Flattop. I thought of how much I had invested physically, financially and emotionally. I had actually drawn up a new will. I had finalized an agreement with my young manager at Chilkoot Charlie's to acquire stock in my company. I had visited my dad's grave, and I had also collected $10,000 in pledges for the Alaska Mental Health Association in honor of my schizophrenic son from my first marriage, Michael, so I wasn't backing down.

On the lower part of Denali, from the Kahiltna Glacier up to Motorcycle Hill, we roped up in three teams of three or four climbers. We each wore snowshoes and pulled plastic sleds that carried thirty to thirty-five pounds of camp gear, in addition to the thirty to fifty pounds of personal gear in our backpacks. We fell into a pace that would mark the hours and days ahead.

Most climbers in expeditions essentially climb the mountain twice. You carry a load up to the site of the next camp, then you return to the first camp for the night and do it all again in the morning, weather permitting. Or you carry a load partway to the next camp, caching it under a mound of snow to protect it from marauding ravens and marked with wands in case of snowfall. The next day you leapfrog the cache while carrying a fresh load, drop that load off at the next camp, then return to recover the cache.

This is where I learned about false summits. You struggle mightily to get to what you think is the summit of the day's exertions, only to reach it—wrung out, thinking you'll be done for the day—and realize you can't even see the day's final destination from the high point upon which you now stand.

Stashing our cumbersome snowshoes at the 11,000-foot Camp II, we switched to crampons and ascended Motorcycle Hill, making a carry to Windy Corner at 13,500 feet, feeling like we were finally climbing a mountain instead of just trudging through snow. Back at Camp II, we had a dinner of spaghetti and returned to our tents. Someone made a comment about the altitude and Bob John, a salesman for IBM who should have been a stand-up comedian, put things in perspective by saying, "Let's face it. We've got friends that live higher than this."

I decided to wash my hair, and nothing had felt better since we left Base Camp. My face was badly sunburned and my lips were a mess. I would awaken in the night, open my mouth, which had glued itself shut, and pull the flesh as well as the lips apart before I realized what I was doing. Then I'd attempt to staunch the bleeding—mouth full of the ferric taste of blood—before going back to sleep. At least I hadn't sun-burned the roof of my mouth, which is not uncommon.

The second time out of Camp II we leapfrogged the cache at Windy Corner and slogged into Camp III at 14,000 feet. From our tents there, we could see the Headwall, rising another 2,200 feet—a wide, white wall sticking practically straight up into the sky, like a prop from Cirque de Soleil. It was beautiful—and intimidating. After one day of rest we were to make a carry to the top of it, leaving a cache at either 16,200 feet or 16,400 feet, creeping ever closer to the summit.

Anyone in Alaska will tell you with pride that Denali measures 20,320 feet starting directly from sea level, whereas Everest rises to 29,028 feet from the Tibetan Plateau of 12,000 to 14,000 feet. Denali is a taller mountain, in and of itself; it is 1,292 more vertical feet from Denali's 7,500 foot Base Camp to the summit than it is from Everest's 17,500 foot Base Camp to the summit, albeit at a lower altitude.

Choosing Denali as my first climb, I had no idea what to expect. Nothing could possibly have prepared me for the scale of it. You could pile fifty Empire State Buildings in one spot, back up a few miles and they would be completely lost in the ice and snow. Worst of all, with no previous experience, I had no idea of what I was emotionally or physically capable. But I did remember Mike Howerton saying, after I made a braggadocious comment about my marathon experience, "After summiting Denali you'll feel like you've run three marathons."

I had my first experience with acute altitude sickness on the way down from the Headwall. By the time we got back to Camp III, I was stumbling and had a debilitating headache at the base of my skull—the worst headache I'd ever had. Gordy sent me to the medical facility—two canvas Quonset huts packed with gear. The doctors checked my pulse, blood pressure and absorption rate, listened to my lungs and announced that I did not have pulmonary or cerebral edema. I swallowed an Advil with a glass of water, thanked them and left. Less than fifty feet away, I puked my guts out and was whisked immediately back inside.

Coincidentally, the medical staff was conducting a study on the use of Diamox, historically used as a diuretic, to aid people adjusting to altitude and recovering from acute altitude sickness. I agreed to be a guinea pig. They asked me a lot of questions, had me blow into various measuring devices, took a blood sample, monitored my vital signs and gave me half a pill, which might have been Diamox or might have been a placebo.

John Evans brought over my sleeping bag and some clothes and announced, "Mike, tomorrow is a rest day."

That was good news, since I didn't think I'd be ready to tackle the Headwall again the next morning. Lying there in the medical tent, it was hard to believe I had been on the mountain one day short of two weeks already.

Few of us stirred before noon the next day; we cooked and talked for two or three hours, then napped and read. It was such a clear day we could see great distances. We could tell where Anchorage was by picking out the little bump in the terrain that was Mt. Susitna or Sleeping Lady, a picturesque landmark near town. Mt. Foraker, Mt. Hunter and the rest of the Alaska Range stood out brightly in all their blazing glory, especially from the Camp III outhouse.

A few days later, I was snugly wrapped in my sleeping bag at 16,200 feet in a small but beautiful campsite precariously perched at the bottom of the West Buttress Ridge and overlooking the Peters Glacier, with a view of the North Peak of Denali. We had climbed the West Buttress Ridge—where you can see thousands of feet down on either side just by turning your head left or right—all the way to Camp V at 17,200 feet, left a cache and returned to Camp IV. At Camp V it was obvious how windy it was above Denali Pass, though some climbers were attempting the traverse in spite of it. Almost everyone was exhausted when we arrived back at Camp IV.

I was tired, wind-burned and sunburned, but at least I wasn't sick. I had taken my pills the previous two mornings and, whether it was the Diamox or not, I hadn't suffered from either headaches or nausea. We had now lost one climber due to frostbitten fingers, which had apparently occurred climbing the Headwall. We had our second casualty when we got to Camp V, before we had erected our tents and built snow walls to protect us from the wind. This one was due to severe foot injuries in ill-fitting climbing boots. John Evans took him back to Camp III, where they would pick up the other climber and head back to Base Camp and Talkeetna. I felt badly for the two climbers, and I worried that I was going to miss John because I thought he added some balance to the guiding of the group. His was the fate of assistant guides; he had been on the mountain five times and never reached the summit, having to escort injured or sick clients back down every time.

On Wednesday morning, June 14, 1989, we were still at Camp V after several days of confinement in our tents. The wind had howled without letup, crashing into the snow walls around our tents and shaking the bejesus out of the tents themselves. The temperature without the wind chill factor was around zero degrees Fahrenheit. Exiting the tent to go to the outhouse was a hellish affair. We all wished we had brought a book, but had gotten brutally selective about what we were willing to carry the higher we got. I laid on my back for hours imagining faces in the changing ice and snow residue clinging to the tent's outer surface. We entertained ourselves by making up extravagant menus of the food we were going to eat when we got off the mountain.

At 3:00 p.m. on Friday, Gordy came by the tent and hollered, "Saddle up. Let's go!" Having been confined to our tents for a week by the storm, we were scheduled to descend the next day and had been lounging around thinking mostly about heading down, not up. Clambering out into the open, though—lo-and-behold!—the sky was clear, with no lenticular, lens-shaped cloud over Denali Pass or higher up, which would have been an indication of high winds. Off we went, dressed for cold weather, with clothing for even colder weather available in our packs. We spent three hours ascending the thousand feet to Denali Pass, breaking trail through waist-deep snow most of the way, wary of "the Autobahn" to our left, so named because you would tumble—with no speed limit—a couple thousand feet to certain death should you fall there.

We took a break at the top of Denali Pass and headed up toward the sub-peak of Archdeacon's Tower, then around the tower toward the Football Field at 19,200 feet, arriving around 10:30 p.m. The sun covered only half the Football Field and it was a brittle, biting cold, but at least there wasn't much wind—yet. We took another break before ascending the hill up to the base of the summit ridge. It was a long, steep haul; we used fixed lines in a couple of places, our backs to the astounding scenery all the way, totally focused on every labored step.

I was whipped and wallowing in self-doubt by the time we got to the base of the summit ridge around 12:45 a.m. The wind had picked up and the temperature was probably minus thirty-five degrees, not including the wind chill factor. We all began frantically getting into our summit clothing.

Gordy came over to assist me, looked intently at my face and said, "Mike, you've got frostbite on your nose."

I figured he was right, but reaching up with a big, bulky mitten to touch the numbness, I said, "It's just zinc oxide."

He asked, "How are you doing?"

I said, acting pugilistic, "You want to go a few rounds?"

He liked the answer; walked away. I breathed a sigh of relief.

Off we went again toward the summit. I had long since given up on my glasses and goggles, totally fogged up, ice-encrusted, hanging uselessly around my neck. The sun had gone down to the western horizon, lending everything a beautiful alpenglow. The summit ridge is a narrow affair, with cornices of snow hanging over the edges. We stayed well away from them.

As I plodded along I was in an other-worldly dream—step, breathe, breathe, breathe, step—marveling at the beauty and worrying about my nose, my frozen feet and my stamina. Finally, one ridge distant, I saw apprentice guide Wayne Mushrush with his hands up in the air and Bob and Henrik milling around. Not until that very moment did I realize I was actually going to make it. Gordy, Big John and I, the second rope line, were soon standing on the summit.

We hugged. In my exhausted, half-frozen state it was impossible to fully embrace my own emotions. I was elated, but I almost felt as if I wasn't really there. I was outside my body watching me being there. I was stunned—temporarily incapable of fully grasping the significance of the moment.

Who was this person? Was it really me? If so, wow!

It was so cold and dark that we snapped flash photos of each other as quickly as possible and high-tailed it down diagonally across the face of the massif, heading toward the Football Field rather than descending by the longer summit ridge route we had ascended.

It took a long time—forever—to reach the Football Field. When we finally got there, John Schroder aka Big John, not to be confused with Bob John, fell down on his back and said something like, "I'm done. I can't go any further."

Gordy said, "You better get your act together, get on your feet and get moving or you're going to die. No one is going to carry you down, and I don't want a death on my hands. Now get your ass up!"

Meanwhile, yours truly went into a major coughing spasm. Bob John stared at me between coughs. I managed to blurt out, "Don't worry about me. No one's leaving me on this fucking mountain!"

When we started out again Gordy put Big John in the lead. It was a good idea because it forced him to think about what he was doing and where he was going. He could set his own pace. It worked nicely down the fixed line and to the upper reaches of Denali Pass, where Big John started to fade. He began stopping more and moving less. He would stand motionless looking around, as if getting his bearings, but then do nothing. The rest of us were cold and tired, most suffering from frostbite, and desperately wanted to get back to Camp V. Gordy finally walked down to Big John, had a few words with him I couldn't hear, and began marching downhill side-by-side, arm-in-arm with him.

Soon we were all back in Camp V, warming up in our sleeping bags. It was 6:30 a.m. and it had been the most grueling fourteen hours of my life. I had intended the climb to be a spiritual purgatory and it hadn't disappointed me. I'd been through so much physically and emotionally, I could cinch up my belt a couple of notches on both accounts. During my struggles I had thought emotionally about my son, Michael, my love for and commitment to Shelli, my eight-months pregnant daughter, Michele, who had recently left her husband in California and moved back to Alaska with my three-year-old granddaughter, Courtney, and her little brother, Eric, and how much I looked forward to seeing them all again.

It was not until we got back to Camp V that I realized the extent of my frostbite. My left cheek was so swollen my left eye was practically closed shut and my nose was very tender and taut looking, as if it was pegged down on either side like a tarp. I looked like I'd taken a hard, winding left hook to the side of my face. Gordy asked an intern from California to visit my tent. The guy wasn't worried about my cheek saying it was superficial, but he was worried about my nose.

He said, "I don't think you'll lose it, but you'd better be very careful about damaging or refreezing it."

Not being keen on the idea of losing my nose, I fashioned a swank bandage to cover the whole mess for our descent. In addition to my nose and cheek, Henrik had frostbitten toes, Wayne had frostbite on the tips of some of his fingers and even Gordy had a frostbitten toe. Only Bob John and Big John were free of frostbite.

The day after our summit, Sunday, the 18th of June, we awoke at 8:00 a.m. The wind was blowing like nobody's business and breaking camp was like packing to move in the middle of a hurricane. We prepared to leave Camp V via the Rescue Couloir by 10:00 a.m. because Gordy wanted to avoid the knife's edge of the West Buttress Ridge in all that wind. The Rescue Couloir isn't without its own difficulties, however—a narrow chute that drops absolutely straight down the face of the mountain like a wide-open two-thousand-foot elevator shaft, almost to the level of the 14,000 foot Camp III, where the medical facility was located.

I didn't have to use my imagination to understand what Scott Wollems had meant when he said, "I don't do nighttime summits," but I certainly was glad we had gone for it.

Gordy had made the right call, though admittedly, things might have turned out differently. I could actually feel the look in Scott's eyes telling me how precarious my situation had been. It was a chilling reality check.

The sun from the long summer days had been working on the snow, opening up many more crevasses to cross on the way down the mountain. Henrik was on the line in front of Wayne, both in front of me, and it seemed every time he got right over the top of a snow bridge that was particularly scary for him, Wayne would have to stop and adjust his boots, or slow down for some other reason. Henrik got very agitated, and I couldn't blame him, but it was amusing in a perverse way because it always occurred at just the right (wrong) moment.

We spent our last night on the mountain at the 11,000 foot Camp II after descending six thousand feet in one day. I could literally taste the sweet, life-sustaining flavor of oxygen. I slept so soundly I don't think I turned once in the night, until I heard the unwelcome sounds of crampons crunching snow and the gas stove hissing at 7:19 a.m.

The weather was beautiful when we arrived at Base Camp and we waited only an hour for our flight to arrive. In the plane we passed mountain after mountain, glacier after glacier, huge, craggy, barren and cold; mile after mile of stark, rugged, raw beauty, until we saw the first green moss on some lower mountainsides, and then more and more green and less and less white. It was full-blown summer. We passed over lakes and trees and rivers—calm wilderness—then the first remote lake and river cabins, then all-terrain-vehicle tracks in the tundra, then homesteads with air strips, then a road, a highway, a railroad and finally, Talkeetna.

Back home, I felt better about myself than I had since my youth. I had worked hard at earning a new respect for myself, a better ap-preciation of friends and a deeper commitment to loved ones, and I was doing something that fulfilled the sense of adventure I'd had since early childhood—before I ever moved to Alaska in the early '50s. In other words, I was hooked.

Central Junior High

Speaking of the early '50s, what I remember most fondly about the old Central Junior High was the cafeteria ceiling covered with paper straw wrappers. We would bite off one end of the wrappers and dip the other in peanut butter. Then we'd blow hard through the open end of the straw to shoot the wrappers to the ceiling where they would hang like skinny stalactites, waved to-and-fro by the big ceiling fans. Had we been properly represented by modern art agents our work might adorn a ceiling in the New York Museum of Modern Art today. I've seen less inspiring works hanging in modern art museums.

A sadomasochistic master must have engineered the cafeteria seating. The seats were round wooden butt platforms attached to a horizontal bar more than a foot long. The bar was attached to an upright leg of the table, from which it swiveled out to be used or in to be put away. The problem was if the chair was forcefully swung inward, it would impact the knee of the student seated on the other side of the table. The potential for mischief was practically unlimited.

Central Junior High was located where the Performing Arts Center is today. Across the street to the northwest was Anchorage's main department store, Northern Commercial Company. There was Parker's Department Store in Spenard, but it didn't really qualify as a department store since it didn't offer a large or varied enough range of products. And there was Caribou's Department Store, also in Spenard, where REI is today. Advertised by a grizzly old sourdough character named Caribou Pete, it eventually became Caribou/Wards and sported the first escalator in town. Spenard was an official address with zip code for mailing purposes and had its very own Spenard Utility District known as SPUD. Directly across the street to the west of the school was the outsized Jonas Brothers Taxidermy—a log structure with a huge Kodiak brown bear standing on its hind legs inside, peering out at passersby through a big picture window.

There were two paved streets in town: Fourth and Fifth Avenues. Going to Spenard was literally going to another town and going out to the O'Malley Road area, past all the potato farms, was an afternoon adventure. My family used to drive out there in our 1956 black Mercury with red window under-panels, to a little place that made great hamburgers. I think it was called The Hamburger Hut. Northern Lights Blvd., then named KFQD Road, was a two-lane dirt road that ended on the east at Blueberry Lake where C Street is today, and on the west at the KFQD radio station and tower.

My least favorite teacher of all time was at Central. Old Lady Bargen was a harridan English instructor with unruly red hair, who reeked of cheap perfume, kept a pint bottle of booze in her desk and applied her gaudy red lipstick during classes, between bouts of reaching into her blouse to adjust the mammary flesh barely hidden within. Another of my teachers was Dick Persons, a friend of my parents who I remember fondly, though he had a habit of sneaking up behind you with a ruler to smack you hard on the back of your hand when you were goofing off. Most fondly I remember another English instructor, the young and beautiful wife of Coach Bill Wiltrout, who didn't need a ruler to keep my rapt attention. It's too bad I didn't have her for math since I always struggled with it, but mastered verb conjugations in record time.

My mother was also an English teacher at Central and my dad was a social studies instructor as well as one of the coaches. Family lore has it that my dad started the local branch of the National Education Association (NEA) in Anchorage. A female junior high student, who apparently didn't have proper bathing facilities at home, was washing her long black hair in one of the toilets in the girl's locker room. When she flushed the toilet, it forcefully pulled her head into the bowl. She was drowning. Someone alerted my dad, who ran in there with a pair of scissors and cut the hair from her head—saving her life. To show their appreciation, her parents sued the school district, as well as my dad. It appeared he was to be made a scapegoat and left to defend himself, until he joined the national teachers union—Anchorage's first public school instructor to do so—and brought in legal representation from the broader NEA.

It was about this time I heard the first song of what was to become the musical revolution called rock 'n roll. It was "Sixteen Tons," a country crossover song written by either Merle Travis or George S. Davis and recorded by the bass-baritone Ernest Jennings Ford (1919-1991) aka "Tennessee Ernie Ford." The song was number one on the country charts for ten weeks and topped the pop charts for eight weeks. I can still sing the lyrics, "I owe my so' to the company sto'…"

The next hit song I remember was "(We're Gonna) Rock Around the Clock," recorded by London-based Decca, a part of Universal Music Group, in the 12-bar blues format by Bill Haley & His Comets and released in both 1954 and 1955. Pretty soon the rebellious youth of Anchorage were combing their long hair into "duck tails," or "DAs," rolling their Lucky Strike or Camel cigarette packs into the arms of their white T-shirts and wearing their jeans too low beneath their black leather jackets with the collars turned up, James Dean style. I was never rebellious enough to try to adopt these extreme dress styles, and my parents were right there at the school.

Girls were still wearing poodle skirts and bobby socks and, though it was exciting at the time, it all seems terribly naïve and innocent from my present vantage point.

Central Junior High, from an earlier era, wasn't comfortable and it wasn't pretty. Built of concrete and metal like a forerunner of Soviet architecture, it was too hot and dry in the winter and too cold and dank in the summer. It didn't come within earthly orbit of the later Americans with Disabilities Act mandates and I can't say with certainty that my attendance there was during the mostly formative time in my life. But I have more fond memories of it than of Anchorage (West) High School, where I spent twice as much time. I'm not sure why. Perhaps it's because Central Junior High is irretrievably gone—a wistful memory—whereas Anchorage West High is still standing, albeit somewhat rearranged by the 1964 earthquake. Maybe it's due to the lost wonder and innocence of those junior high school years being replaced by the confounding, confusing years of high school adolescence and uncertainty about myself and my future.

Or could it be that in some dark, perverse, nostalgic part of my subconscious I pine for Old Lady Bargen?

Satchmo

For a time, the old Central Junior High location was home to the Sydney Laurence Performing Arts Center, the only building in Anchorage that had my name on a plaque at its entrance, since I was on the Anchorage City Council when we renovated it. When the plaque was installed I felt like Navin Johnson in *The Jerk* when he saw his name in the new phone book: "I'm somebody!" Alaska was wallowing in big oil money, so the building was soon razed to make room for the Project '80s Performing Arts Center that now accommodates the Anchorage Opera, the Anchorage Symphony and the Anchorage Concert Association. The only building in town to have had my name on it is just another wistful memory.

Until Anchorage High School was built on Romig Hill in 1953, Central housed both junior high and high school classes. My parents were the last two teachers married to one another who were allowed to teach in the same Anchorage school. Having my dad for a coach was no problem, but I have been eternally grateful that I, unlike my older sister, somehow missed having my mother for an English teacher. Don't get me wrong. I loved my mother, but it was bad enough just having both parents teaching in the school I was attending. Having my mom for an English instructor would have been too much, *and* I'd have missed having Mrs. Wiltrout.

I played alto saxophone—the one my sister inspired Boid with—in the band at Central. When I moved on to high school, I played in the Anchorage (now West) High School band during all four years. As a freshman, at five feet, one inch tall and one hundred fifteen pounds, I had the distinction of being the smallest person in the band of one hundred twenty kids, with the exception of Elaine Stolt, a dwarf.

My other major extracurricular activity during all four years of high school was playing defense on the Anchorage High School hockey team. I was too small for football or basketball, but the ice was for me a great leveler of the playing field. There were no other high schools in Anchorage at that time and we were so much larger than the schools elsewhere in Alaska that, in order to help the smaller schools around the state stay competitive, our football and basketball teams were divided in two. We had an East and a West team. There were, however, no other high school hockey teams around, at least ones that could be reached within our budget, so we played in the Anchorage City League, the semi-professional hockey league of grown men that included Hohn Plumbing, York Steel, and both Elmendorf Air Force Base and Fort Richardson. When I first started playing there was a shortage of equipment, like shin and elbow pads. I have a couple of especially prominent elbows to prove it.

As a defenseman I got lots of exercise—the other team usually controlled the puck and it was mostly in our territory. I and the other defensemen would frequently give up on trying to go after the puck or play position against our offensive opponents. We would just double-team a wing or center as he came down the ice with the puck and try to take him out of the game. I went on to play first string defense at the University of Alaska Fairbanks during my freshman year of college. They were impressed with how well I played position, but I had played four years under the most difficult circumstances a hockey defenseman could possibly imagine. In high school I had hated a defenseman on the Elmendorf Air Force team named John Nubar because of what I considered dirty tactics. When I later found myself playing alongside him as a University of Alaska Fairbanks Nanook, having a different perspective on the matter, I thought he was pretty amusing.

There were no indoor rinks back then. We used to have to shovel the snow off the ice ourselves before we could play. If it was minus fifteen degrees we played anyway, as the spectators—what few there were—stood around in the cold. High school and college hockey were not spectator sports in 1950s Alaska like they are today.

I still have a photo of that high school hockey team. Some of the players became noteworthy personalities. Gordon Unwin formed USKH, Inc., a successful engineering firm, in 1972, but died tragically in 1983 while piloting a helicopter in Turnagain Pass. Don Simpson, along with partner Jerry Bruckheimer, became a successful movie producer with credits such as *Hunt for Red October*, *Flashdance*, *Beverly Hills Cop*, *Top Gun* and *The Rock*, grossing more than three billion dollars altogether. Simpson died of a drug overdose in 1996. Norman Rokeberg served six consecutive sessions in the Alaska State House of Representatives (1995-2007), and is presently one of Alaska's five utility commissioners.

During my sophomore year at Anchorage High, the band, with the assistance of its boosters and the KFQD and KBYR radio stations, raised $20,000 through cake sales and various other means and flew to Los Angeles to play a thirty-minute concert for the Music Educators National Conference. We were the first band from outside the contiguous United States (Alaska was still a territory) ever to play at the event and received three encores after our performance in the Philharmonic Hall. While in Los Angeles, the band was housed in the Hollywood Knickerbocker Hotel. We were guests on the set of the Lawrence Welk Show, we visited Disneyland and Knott's Berry Farm, and we even stopped by Hugh O'Brien's (Wyatt Earp in the television series) home on the way to the airport to fly back to Anchorage. The real highlight of the trip for me though was when "Satchmo," aka Louis Armstrong, came to the hotel for lunch one afternoon and played his trumpet for us. What a performance! And what a kind-hearted gentleman he was. I still have his autograph somewhere.

Another memorable event occurred on the return flight. The band was flown to Los Angeles and back in two brand new Alaska Airlines fan jets. I was sitting in the right-hand window seat during mid-flight, looking outside, when the engine caught fire. The pilot reacted quickly by feathering it and the fire went out almost immediately, but it was a sight I'll never forget. I was momentarily convinced that it was all over for me and everyone else on the plane. We had departed an hour earlier than the other plane and arrived in Anchorage an hour later—with fire trucks parked next to the landing strip—because of having to finish our flight with only one engine.

Imagine the scale of the disaster that would have faced the small city of Anchorage, with only around forty thousand residents, if a plane full of high school students had crashed. And sadly, there would never have been a plaque with my name on it at the entrance of the Sydney Laurence Performing Arts Center, even briefly, or a Chilkoot Charlie's in the heart of Spenard for the past forty-five years.

Kilimanjaro

Though I was fortunate enough to have moved to Alaska and been raised on hunting and fishing, in my middle years I still had a hankering to go to those far-off places of my youthful fantasies. I would never have guessed when I did get to Africa it would not be to hunt big game, but to photograph them. And climb a mountain.

I had no sooner finished climbing Denali and attended my sister's wedding in Coeur d'Alene, Idaho, when Mike Howerton suggested I accompany him on an expedition to climb Mt. Kilimanjaro, the highest mountain in Africa, and Mt. Elbrus, the highest mountain in continental Europe, in one trip. Shelli and I were still living separately, so what else was I going to do that summer? I felt our relationship had improved but she still wasn't exactly "lovey-dovey." I had, however, walked (climbed?) away from my old lifestyle and was more committed than ever to self-improvement, building my business and saving my marriage.

After meeting up with Aileen Hansen at the Zurich airport, the only other person in our expedition besides Mike and me who was going to both Africa and Russia, we boarded our flight to Nairobi, arriving very tired midmorning of August 14, 1989. Mike's travel agent connection, an East Indian named Aziz, met us at the airport, where our luggage was hauled in a rickety cart to a rickety van and we headed for the Boulevard Hotel. The people, buildings and countryside reminded me a lot of most of the Caribbean countries I had visited, but the temperature, due to the 5,000 foot elevation, was much more temperate—the reason why wild animals thrive in the area.

We had just finished checking into the hotel when Lew Freedman, the sportswriter for the *Anchorage Daily News*, showed up accompanied by another climber, both members of our expedition, and joined us for lunch. During lunch another two expedition members stopped by our table. One mentioned he had taught school with my dad; he seemed to have fond memories of the relationship. I was feeling good about the trip, already enjoying the camaraderie, when one climber informed me that the airline had lost his bags. I readily lent him my plastic Asolo climbing boots, which happened to be his size, because I figured my leather hiking boots would be adequate until I got to Russia.

Our expedition departed from Nairobi in two Land Rovers at 9:00 a.m. on the 16th of August. We reached the Kibo Hotel at the base of Mt. Kilimanjaro after ten hours of Grand Prix-style driving at breakneck speeds, over narrow roads, frequently tailgating buses that emitted previously unimaginable amounts of thick, black, noxious exhaust fumes. Our driver, despite our complaints, maintained a position immediately behind every bus we caught up to for long stretches at a time.

All the way to the border with Tanzania, we had been driving through Masai country—unmistakable with their above-average height, regal bearing and colorful attire—and were given strict instructions by Mike Howerton to never photograph them because they feel you are stealing a part of their soul. There were also very large signs at the border and elsewhere warning against the practice. It didn't seem possible anyone could miss the point and we soon found out just how seriously the matter was taken by the Masai.

I watched with disbelieving fascination as Aileen tried to photograph a group of Masai standing just a few feet away, right next to a warning sign outside the Tanzanian immigration building. She stared back through the windows in wide-eyed blondeness while the Masai screamed at her and made threatening gestures with their spears. Several people inside the building then simultaneously and roundly denounced her—all of which seemed only to baffle her.

Not long after we got our first glimpse of Mt. Kilimanjaro off to our left, standing magnificently above the clouds. At our request, the driver pulled over so we could take a few photographs. Some Masai kids tending cattle on the roadside pasture thought we were trying to photograph them and started running toward us, picking up rocks along the way and hurling them in our direction. We snapped quick photos of the mountain and roared off down the road, setting aside our cameras for the rest of the white-knuckle ride with our driver "Mbuto Andretti," hanging on for dear life while gagging on exhaust fumes.

Before going to sleep that night, I fantasized about the Seven Summits. I had put down a deposit on a Mt. Aconcagua climb that winter as well as an expedition to the north side of Mt. Everest in the spring; I was well on my way to the adventure of my life before even starting my second climb.

The next morning, awakened by a backyard rooster at 4:28 a.m. and later served an excellent breakfast of ham and eggs, we went directly to the park entrance, signed the register and then waited... and waited. After an hour I decided to investigate and discovered the park service people listing in their record books the serial numbers of every Tanzanian bill used to pay our fees. Counting the rocks in the parking lot would have been more productive.

Finally, we started up the jungle trail that took us from approximately 7,000 feet to Maranda Hut at about 9,000 feet. Though my running shoes were soon soaked and muddy, I was pleased to learn I still had plenty of residual fitness left from my Denali climb a couple of months earlier. Upon reaching Maranda Hut, all eight of us moved into two four-person tin-covered huts and laid our sleeping pads on the bunks. Dinner was impressive: beef steaks, liver, vegetables, cucumber and tomato salad, potatoes, noodles, bread, tea and even beer. The food preparation was done in a separate building by all the porters of different groups working together. They served us our meals and did the dishes when we were finished—quite a departure from Denali.

I thought, "I could get used to this!"

We left Maranda Hut the morning of the 18th, arriving mid-afternoon at Horombo Hut. Traveling through jungle and muck for the first hour, we then broke out into rocky alpine terrain. I felt strong with no noticeable effects from the increasing altitude, but I downed a Diamox that afternoon as a precautionary measure. Horombo Hut was a large camp with a community A-frame for tea and snacks. We enjoyed the company of a hundred other people of various nationalities, mostly European. Our entire group slept in one of several A-frames that Mike Howerton informed us had been built by the Norwegian government as a gift to Tanzania.

The next morning, Mike thoughtfully took off early in order to acquire the best accommodations at Kibo Hut, so we could all sleep in the same building again. We even had our own dining table. The climb to Kibo Hut at 15,520 feet was beautiful, warm and gradual, over desert terrain and volcanic scree. We passed in and out of the shadow of Mawenzi's jagged peaks, in sight of the Kilimanjaro ice cap the whole way, with a view of the trail going up to Gillman's Summit and the Headwall, which looked pretty steep.

After a fitful sleep, common at altitude, seven of us and our African guides headed up the mountain at 1:15 a.m. at a demanding pace. The landscape was so illuminated by the moon that we didn't need our headlamps on the way to Hans Meyer Cave at 17,500 feet, our first rest stop.

Hans Meyer, a German geographer, and Ludwig Purtscheller, an Austrian mountaineer, were the first to reach Kibo Summit, more than 40 years after its discovery. It was Hans Meyer's third attempt, one that started in Mombasa and was achieved on Purtscheller's fortieth birthday—October 6, 1889. They were the first to confirm that Kibo had a crater and reported it was filled with ice, though by the time I saw it a hundred years later, the ice had retreated dramatically.

After a short break at Hans Meyer Cave we took off again at a brisk pace in near-darkness. My feet were cold most of the way and I missed my plastic Asolo climbing boots. Arriving at Gillman's

Point, on the edge of the crater at 18,500 feet, most of the group decided they'd come far enough. Only Aileen, Tom (the guy who had taught with my dad) and I elected to continue with one guide, Steven, around the crater for an hour and a half to Uhuru, the actual summit at 19,341 feet.

At a certain point I started pulling away from Tom and Aileen. I was the first of our group to arrive at the summit, at 8:20 a.m. I stood in awe of the huge ice fields, walls of ice and icicles many stories high. There had been no recent snowfall and the sun had created beautiful "snow cups," as Aileen later referred to them, on the surface of the crater's rim. It was a gorgeous day. Snow-peaked Mt. Kenya, the highest mountain in the country next door, poked through the low-lying clouds that stretched as far as the eye could see. I waved hello to three other climbers on the summit: two Frenchmen and an Englishman. We took photos for each other and I placed a Chilkoot Charlie sticker amidst numerous others, on the plaque commemorating Julius Nyerere, the first president of Tanzania.

Standing there on the rooftop of Africa following in the footsteps of climbing pioneers such as Meyer and Purtscheller was a grand feeling. I had been reading *Uhuru*, which means freedom, by Robert Ruark. In the bright sunlight above the clouds, the pages unfolded before my eyes—brutal, bloody Mau Mau Rebellion (1951-1954) in the British Kenya Colony and all.

Tom, Aileen and Steven arrived twenty minutes later. We soaked up the stunning vistas, took more photos then began our descent. I initially felt nauseated, but it vanished as I proceeded to lower altitudes. We made incredible time, literally running down the precipitous grade of loose scree, digging our heels in for purchase. As it turned out, Aileen, Tom and I—the three oldest in our group of seven—were the only ones who made the summit. The others had either reached their climbing endurance level or suffered from altitude sickness. Mt. Kilimanjaro was a straight-forward climb but its summit also required a significant altitude gain in just a few days, with a blistering pace set by the guides on summit morning. I couldn't have been more pleased with my performance.

Our African head guide, David, allowed us only a half-hour rest at Kibo Hut, insisting that we begin the descent to Horombo Hut. I had left my moleskin in a pack the guides were already carrying down and limped painfully into our destination in filthy, chafing socks. We settled into our A-frame by mid-afternoon. I was whipped. I stretched out on my pad for a while, trying to sort through my gear until dinner. Others preferred sleep, easy to understand, but I was too hungry to pass up a chance at food.

By the time I ate and got back to my sleeping bag that evening, I was so tired and so sore that I had a tough time going to sleep. I wasn't aware I had drifted off until I woke up in the middle of the night to relieve myself. Standing on the porch watering the lawn, I would have sworn there was fresh snow on the ground. I stepped down lower so I could move my foot through it, just to be sure, then stepped even lower and tried it again. Nothing! It turned out to be the most incredible moon glow I had ever seen, and in my exhausted state it had me wondering if my trip to Africa was real or a fantasy—like when I was a boy in the citrus groves with my BB gun, hunting imagined lions, rhinos and flying snakes.

The next day our group essentially flew down the mountain, racing through sage and prairie terrain into temperate rain forest, tropical rain forest and muddy trails. We stopped only at Mandara Hut for lunch then marched through mud and jungle all the way back to the park entrance.

There were no showers at Kibo Hotel, but I have never had a more satisfying bath. I was filthy—caked with mud. After cleaning up and doing some laundry in our tubs we all met in the bar to discuss tips for the guides, then joined them out behind the hotel, where Mike told them they were the best group of guides he'd ever had. The guides sang a beautiful song about Kilimanjaro and handed us certificates to commemorate the climb. Several rounds of beer were purchased, one too many it turned out, as the natives did not handle their liquor well and began unceremoniously pestering us for more tips.

After a wonderful dinner of salad, bean soup, steak and potatoes and a couple of Coca-Colas, we called it a day. I relaxed for a while on our veranda, listening to a group of locals singing a song close by in a school or church as the birds chimed in. A heavy mist concealed everything beyond the garden around the hotel. It was so beautiful and peaceful that I promised myself I would return. Africa was the only place in the world—other than Alaska—that had gripped me so emotionally. It was the wildness of it all. It seemed like a land of endless possibilities. It filled me with wonder and certainty. Though I didn't feel the exhilaration I had felt after summiting Denali, I had been the strongest member of the expedition. My confidence was growing and I looked forward to the challenge ahead in Russia.

The rest of the trip went by in a contented blur. Flying to Mombasa and the beaches for two nights, we returned to Nairobi by first-class train in private sleeping berths with nice, clean white sheets, pillows and blankets for a few shillings. The rail cars were well-maintained 1950s vintage. Swanky. After a wonderful night's slumber, we awoke to the African savanna streaming by and a man walking down the corridor, striking tom-toms to the melody of a Kalimba Thumb Piano, an exotic handheld instrument that resembled a miniature harp crossed with a piano. We received a full-service breakfast with linens and silverware, waited on by smartly dressed servers in black-and-white attire as the wildlife of Africa passed by our windows. I was a long way from rummaging through Dumpsters in Richardson Vista. I felt like I was in one of those old 16mm newsreels that had captured my imagination as a child. It was moments like this that had me thinking about Shelli and how much she might enjoy sipping tea and watching giraffes feed off the tops of trees as we rhythmically clacked and swayed along the rails.

Arriving once again in Nairobi, we departed our hotel for a trip to the Masai Mara animal refuge. We stayed in the luxurious Aga Khan's resorts, where the food was so wonderful I made a comment to Mike Howerton about gaining weight.

He said, "Oh, don't worry about it. You'll lose it in Russia."

We visited a Masai village, where for $10 each we were allowed to take photos. It felt like criminal behavior after all the warnings I'd seen and heard, not to mention the thumping spears and hurled rocks. The Masai lived in small huts built along the interior edge of a large circular enclosure made of intertwined branches with sharp, dagger-size thorns, into which they herded their cattle, sheep, goats and families at night. The thorny fence protected everybody from large predators. The entire central area was covered with cow, sheep and goat dung, with the kids playing "Leap over the Dung Heap." It was quite the training regimen—like drilling with live rounds. I didn't see even one of those future Olympians fall short of his mark.

The enclosure itself was a pretty unpleasant environment. Flies constantly crawled all over people's faces though they didn't seem to be bothered by them. I ventured into one of the huts at a woman's invitation to find low ceilings and several small rooms with interlocking corridors. In the kitchen was a smoky fire, so smoky that I had to leave after a few seconds, but at least there were no flies. In spite of the conditions, everyone, adults and children alike, appeared happy. It was a matter of simplicity and integrity and I was in a relaxed enough state of mind to be able to recognize and appreciate it. Happiness and contentment: two things I might have had in Alaska had I made different choices.

A fourteen-year-old named Daniel, who was as tall as me, asked if I would be his friend and write to him. I was delighted, gave him my card and wrote down his name and address in care of his secondary school. Daniel spoke excellent English and was well-mannered. He said he had four brothers and three sisters and told me proudly that his family owned seventy-eight cattle, eighty-two sheep and thirty goats. I wrote Daniel once when I got home, but sadly never received a reply.

The next few days, photographing the animals, I thought constantly about Shelli, and after I left Africa we enjoyed a romantic one-night interlude in Wales during a visit with John Evans, my assistant guide on Denali. It was the first since our separation. Though still traveling in different directions it finally felt like we were falling in love again, and I agonized over leaving her to go to Russia the next day.

The *Wild Duck*

As a boy I dreamed of adventures. As a young man growing up in Alaska, I actually experienced them.

We were sitting at anchor in a small cove on the west coast of Kalgin Island, waiting for the storm to break and listening to the radio. Somehow, Terry—the captain of our two-man vessel—had managed to get his hands on one of the Daubenspeck Cannery secret maps of Lower Cook Inlet. We were independent fishermen, beholden to no cannery and could sell to whomever we pleased. But as a consequence, we weren't entitled to one of those maps.

The map broke Lower Cook Inlet into numbered sections. Fishermen who worked exclusively for Daubenspeck Cannery of Kenai could use those numbers to communicate with one another concerning location, weather conditions, and the presence or absence of fish without giving away their location. How Terry had acquired that map I'll never know, but we were listening intently to the radio jabber and closely scrutinizing the map.

I had never commercial fished before, though Terry had a couple years of experience. I was between my junior and senior years at Anchorage High School. Terry Klingel was a teacher in the Anchorage School District, as was his wife at that time, Dean Anne. They rented the other side of our duplex in Susitna View Park from my mom and dad. It wasn't uncommon for teachers to venture into fishing back then. You didn't have to deal with the present permit system, it was cheaper to get equipped and, of course, teachers had the summers off. Terry had approached me in the spring about being his deckhand and I was excited at the prospect. My parents agreed it would be a good experience for me. Pay was to be $500 per month, plus room and board and a percentage of the catch if we made money.

Presently, the radio clattered and some guy in a numbered section of the map on the Kenai side of the inlet said it was flattening out over there and he was in the middle of a school of "jumpers." Fishermen kept an eye out for "jumpers" because it generally indicates a school of salmon. Back then we didn't have much in the way of sophisticated electronic equipment. By comparison, today the fish don't have a chance.

If you were a seiner and had located a school of salmon you'd try to encircle the school with your net and scoop them in with your power winch. If you were a gillnetter you'd simply try to stretch your three shackles of net out in front of their path. A shackle was 300 feet in length made of webbed 5 1/8" mesh diamonds hanging 45 meshes deep, held together by a cork line on top and a lead line on the bottom. The *Wild Duck* was a gillnetter, and the "winch" was one man and one boy. The only assistance provided was a roller on the stern that was, in reality, no help at all. The three shackles of gear acted as a sea anchor, so you didn't really pull the net to the boat; you pulled the boat to the net, then hauled the net over the stern and into the hold.

The *Wild Duck* was a thirty-two footer and as fast as any sleek-lined bow picker. It had, so the story went, been one of two of its type used by a preacher in Southeast Alaska as a rum runner during Prohibition. It was a substantial boat and pulling in the gear by hand, fish flopping or not, was damned hard work, especially in rough seas.

Clatter, clatter on the radio and more talk of "jumpers" on the other side of the inlet. Terry couldn't stand it. If there were fish to be caught, he wanted to be in on the action. It wasn't turning out to be a very good season and he probably had a bank payment to make. So, we (I) hauled anchor and we headed off into the inlet towing what I swear was the world's heaviest skiff.

We got out to the first rip tide and it was rougher than a cob. In shallow Cook Inlet, rip tides are a confusion of water—a magnet dragging in all manner of debris. Add bad weather and you've got a very unpleasant and unhealthy set of circumstances. Of the three rip tides in Cook Inlet, the middle one is the strongest. Terry didn't want to try to turn around because he was afraid of losing the skiff and of taking a hold full of water on the maneuver, which could have swamped us. So he secured the steering wheel and came aft through shrieking winds and bashing waves to help me pull the world's heaviest skiff over the stern. When on board, it covered most of the deck. By now the *Wild Duck* was getting close to the tempest in the middle rip tide and I was frantic to get the skiff secured. I fell once during the effort, having nothing to hang onto but the as-yet-unsecured skiff itself.

The waves, suddenly upwards of twenty feet and more between trough and crest, pummeled us from every direction. We would become airborne, the water beneath us simply disappearing. Then, the boat would free-fall, crashing to the dark bottom of the trough. Logs as large as telephone poles flew through the air. Had I understood just how perilous our situation was, I'd probably have been paralyzed with fear.

Terry screamed over the roar for me to go down into the cabin and try to get things under control. One moment I'd be up against the ceiling with every pot, dish, bottle and miscellaneous utensil in the cabin, the next moment, I'd be groveling on my hands and knees on the floor as everything crashed down around me. It was a miracle we made it across the inlet. Other boats—and lives—were lost.

When we had anchored again in the Kenai River, not being much in the mood for fishing after our high-adventure crossing, Terry broke out a couple of beers that erupted as he opened them. We just looked at each other and laughed through the beer spray that covered us both. The rest of the summer wasn't as exciting, but it was wonderful. Fishing for a living and being on a boat for weeks-at-a-time has a touch, smell and texture, of its very own. And you get used to finding fish scales in the oddest places, stuck to your skin like round, silvery talismans.

The hard work filled me out physically, speeding my development into manhood, and I learned a lot from the many discussions with Terry. He didn't talk much about WWII, but he had a limp in one leg from an injury he received in Italy. His war experience had certainly shaped his outlook on life. He wasn't cynical; he was simply very realistic. He had his own world view and not much escaped his observation. I remember once we were in some philosophical discussion and I used a quote from the Bible to prove my point. He said: "You mean to tell me you believe that shit!?"

My face turned red and I didn't know what to say. The carpet had been pulled from beneath my feet. I was more astonished that I had, all that time, accepted something on pure faith without questioning it than I was shocked about what Terry had said.

The rest of that season we set nets, hauled in fish, delivered them to tenders, mended nets (at which I got pretty good) dug clams (we ate so many razor clams I never wanted to set eyes on one again), and poked around Cook Inlet. Seldovia before the earthquake was the most beautiful and interesting place I had ever seen, built entirely on a boardwalk inside a gorgeous cove. We occasionally visited the city of Kenai, which wasn't a big deal for me because I was too young to go to the bars or brothels and that's about all the city had to offer.

At the end of the season we motored back to Anchorage, took the *Wild Duck* out of the water and completely went over her from bow to stern. We re-caulked her, repainted her inside and out, put new fiberglass on her bow, scraped the bilge and prepared her for sale, which did not take long. She was a beautiful boat.

I don't know whether it was the experience of the storm or the poor fishing season that pushed Terry to sell the boat, but it certainly wasn't that he hadn't enjoyed the experience. Years later, whenever I'd run into Terry at a cocktail party or anywhere else the conversation eventually turned to the *Wild Duck* and our summer together on Lower Cook Inlet . . . and that damn secret map that nearly got us killed.

Johnny Tegstrom

"Friendship is unnecessary, like philosophy, like art... It has no survival value; rather it is one of those things which give value to survival."

C.S. Lewis, *The Four Loves*

Some people leave a mark on your life. Terry Klingel was certainly one of these, but there have been others. One was from my childhood and adolescent years, and his early death punctuates his importance to me.

I remember more friction than anything else between Johnny and me during junior and senior high school. Never mind that we were raised in the same neighborhood, earned our Eagle Scout awards at the same time, played in the Anchorage High School band all four years, got drunk for the first time together, and were in many of the same school classes year after year, all the way from seventh grade through high school graduation.

Once, in our Central Junior High English class, we both got into trouble and had to stay after class. Old Lady Bargen, the floozy, was sitting at the head of the class adjusting her bra straps by reaching into her blouse, applying rouge and gaudy red lipstick while pandemonium ruled the classroom. I, among others, was shooting spit wads at other kids and having the favor returned in multiplicity. Johnny was not actively involved in the melee, but at the end of the class Old Lady Bargen looked out over the unruly mob of students and announced that Johnny and I—just the two of us and only one guilty of disruptive activity—would be staying after class to clean up the mess on the floor.

Johnny and I spent the better part of an hour on our hands and knees cleaning up, while Old Lady Bargen sat at her desk making obscene adjustments to her attire and nipping from the bottle stashed in her desk drawer.

We had the floor spotless by now, but our tormentor gazed around the room and said, "I see more spit wads."

Sounding more like John Wayne than Johnny Tegstrom, he said, "You spot 'em lady, and we'll pick 'em up."

I thought I would die laughing. Of course we were sentenced to another half-hour of hard labor, but it was worth every minute.

Johnny was the big kid and I was the little kid, though we were the same age. I was slow to mature physically. Johnny had a schlong; I had a wee-wee. We nicknamed him Lash LaRue after the popular 1940 and '50s cowboy star who carried a long whip.

Johnny was in the school play our senior year and was featured in the senior yearbook as "Best Actor." I wasn't featured. But my size and state of physical maturity were no indication of any lesser social placement in my mind. Johnny was aggressive. He liked getting his own way and he usually got it. Not always with me, though. I could be a real thorn in his side. When he'd try to dismiss me and I wouldn't be dismissed, or try to force his way and I wouldn't budge, he'd get mad, threaten violence and storm off. He and I never did get into a fight though I got into plenty of them, perhaps because he thought I was too little to worry about or that I might possibly embarrass him.

High school graduation came around and Johnny went to college in Oregon. I went to college in Fairbanks and, the following year, to the University of San Francisco. Johnny visited during my junior year at USF. I was flattered that he went to the trouble. I was married with a pregnant wife, doing well in school and working part-time, all of which seemed to impress Johnny. Surprisingly, he had dropped out of college and returned to Anchorage. Johnny was very intelligent and had done extremely well on his college entrance exams. I surmise he thought school was a waste of his time.

I ended up back in Anchorage a few years later, broke and trying to re-establish myself. By then Johnny already had a real estate broker's license, his own four-plex, his own airplane and a brand new Camaro. I had a wife who was pregnant again, a small daughter, and was struggling financially. Johnny helped me out between paychecks a time or two when I was getting started as a salesman for New York Life. The nature of our relationship was changing—I had earned his respect.

It was about this time that Johnny discovered he had leukemia at twenty-four years of age, an unwelcome gift from the U.S. government. His dad was an electrical foreman and had gotten him a summer job at the one-mile-deep Cannikin atomic test site on Amchitka Island. The test was the largest in U.S. history at the time. Three hundred eighty-five times larger than the bomb dropped on Hiroshima; it spawned the creation of Greenpeace. Johnny's dad died of cancer also—in the same year. Shamefully, the U.S. government refused to admit culpability until the immediate families of the afflicted were all dead. They were collateral victims of the Cold War.

Johnny's leukemia didn't change things much at first. We had recently been on a successful moose hunting trip and decided to go goat hunting. Johnny had spotted some from his plane on the mountain top behind Kenai Lake.

We took a little aluminum boat along the far side of the lake, towing a small raft, and pitched a base camp. The next day we climbed to the top of the mountain from around the back side so as to have the goats between us and the sheer drop-off into the lake. We pitched a tent for the night in the tundra among stunted evergreens, got up early the next morning and headed with our rifles toward the ridge. As we approached the ridge a large billy goat spotted us at the same instant we spotted him, and raced off across the near-vertical lakeside face of the mountain. In the few seconds it took us to reach the ridge, the goat was already on the other side of the face but still barely in range.

I fired and hit him in the hind quarter, which stopped him long enough for Johnny to squeeze one off with his scope-equipped rifle. The billy goat just pushed himself right off the mountain and tumbled clear out of sight. We were fortunate it was early in the day because by the time we climbed halfway down the face of the mountain, found the goat, cleaned and deboned it and packed it back up the steep rock, it was so dark we had difficulty finding our tent.

Near the end of our climb back to camp, I came close to falling several thousand feet off the rock face. It was very steep, the rocks were crumbly, and I had a heavy load on my back. I was hugging the mountain and making sure that I had solid footing with my left foot before I moved my right to another location. As I took the weight off my right foot, my left foot slipped. I could feel the weight of my pack pulling me backwards into the void and, balanced right there between life and death, I literally embraced the mountain, digging in my fingernails, focusing with laser-like intensity on every tiny detail—the earthy smell, the tiny plants, the seams in the rock—and willed myself to hang on. When I got to solid ground Johnny said my eyes were like saucers; I was sweating and ghostly white. I came so close to falling off that mountain that I can feel the queasiness in my chest as I type this, over five decades later.

The next morning we carried our gear and the goat back down to base camp and hung the meat to dry. It was windy and the lake was too rough for our little armada so we spent the night. That evening in the tent—the goat hanging outside and the wind howling—we had our only real heart-to-heart conversation. Johnny confided in me how he felt about being twenty-four years old and knowing he was going to die within a year or two. We talked about our families, our friends and our relationship over the years. That night we became friends for the first time, because a friend is not just someone with whom you spend a lot of years. A friend is someone you can open up to and who can open up to you. A friend is someone with whom you can share and share alike your deepest thoughts and emotions—your dreams and your fears.

It had taken over ten years, a lifetime at that age, and a huge personal crisis for Johnny to open up to me enough to become my friend. I'm sure glad we had that one good talk before he died. It didn't necessarily have to have happened, even considering Johnny's circumstances. It never happened with my own father under similar circumstances. But when I think of Johnny, I can't help but think about that night in the tent and how close we were.

Early in the morning, Johnny went out to relieve himself and said, "Bear. Hand me my rifle." Boom! The bear—attracted to our goat—had been looking for breakfast, on us.

Johnny laughed and said, "Gordon, you came out of that tent like you had a coil spring in your ass!"

Our skiff and raft were packed to the limit with gear and meat, but we managed to get back to the highway safely. We soon became partners in the Bird House Bar forty miles out the Seward Highway along with another school chum—Norman Rokeberg, recently returned from Outside, though Johnny was sick and receiving treatment in New York most of that year. He married his New York City nurse and I participated in the wedding ceremony. It was a short-lived but loving marriage.

Johnny died before his twenty-seventh birthday, with his whole life before him. I was one of his pallbearers, and he was one of my few good friends.

John Edward Tegstrom,
born June 2, 1942,
died May 7, 1969,
buried June 11, 1969
Angelus Memorial Park Cemetery
Anchorage, Alaska.

First Love

After graduating from Anchorage High School in 1960 and spending my freshman year at the University of Alaska Fairbanks—but before the goat hunting trip with Johnny Tegstrom—I had told my dad I'd rather dig ditches the rest of my life than return to school in Fairbanks. UAF in the early '60s did not in any way, shape or form represent what I had in mind for my college experience. I yearned for something more cosmopolitan—like perhaps a dorm room without huge icicles inside the windows or a geographic location where it wasn't so cold you had to run between class buildings.

My sister had broken away and gone to Stetson University in DeLand, Florida—my parents' alma mater. I wanted to go to a party college in California, like San Jose State. I had taken nineteen units in one semester of my freshman year and eighteen-and-a-half units in the other and worked damn hard to earn the average I had, after having barely cracked a book in high school. But I couldn't get into one of California's state-run universities as a non-resident with lower than a B average, which I didn't quite have. So, Dad and I visited the superintendent of schools in South San Francisco, an acquaintance of his who suggested we apply at the Jesuit-run University of San Francisco because they were a private institution and didn't have to operate within the state-imposed rules.

The Jesuit priest who interviewed me said, "You've proven you can carry a full load at a four-year institution, so we'd be happy to have you." It was as easy as that.

At USF, we'd host "mixers"—an evening of dancing with the Catholic girls schools. These social events gave us an opportunity to meet girls other than the handful of nurses we had on our own campus. On one of these evenings during my sophomore year, I spotted the most beautiful creature across the room. The other girls, dressed in bobby socks, pleated skirts, sweaters and other typical college attire of the day, couldn't hold a candle to this city girl, who was dressed in a form-fitting black dress, and wore long black gloves, her hair in a beehive.

Born in Bergen, Norway, Lilla and her family had converted to Mormonism and moved to Salt Lake City. Lilla left home and, with her parents' approval, worked as a nanny for a year before moving to San Francisco with two of her friends, both German girls, who were with her at the dance that night.

My stomach muscles tied in a knot, uncertain of my footing on the perfectly level floor, I mustered the courage to ask her to dance. On our first date, a basketball game against rival Santa Clara University in the War Memorial Gymnasium at USF, Lilla strolled along in another stylish black dress, hand on my arm. As we searched for seating in the bleachers of our all-boys university, my classmates delivered me a standing ovation.

We had a pretty torrid affair during the rest of my sophomore year, though we did not have sex, unless one would label very heavy petting as such. I returned to Anchorage, working through the summer for Continental Van Lines, which had the contract for moving military families for Elmendorf Air Force Base and Fort Richardson, whether the family lived on or off base. Many of the lower ranking families we moved lived on Government Hill, which always brought back a flood of childhood memories. The apartments were in two-story buildings with narrow staircases and there were days when we, a crew of three—one driver and two swampers—would move three families.

We could predict with ninety-percent certainty that if we were sent to move a full colonel it was going to be a good day. In such cases we were instructed to take our time, be polite, and to not break anything. Moving high-ranking officers' belongings as a twenty-year-old college student gave me an insight into upscale living. They had very nice furnishings and art collected from all over the world. They lived in the nicest part of the base or post in quality housing and they were generally gracious and hospitable, offering snacks and soft drinks during the day's work. I was impressed by their exotic, worldly collections and wanted to visit those distant places myself someday.

With most of the high-ranking officers' belongings, not only was everything packed as carefully as possible, but the boxes were then frequently taken to our warehouse where they were crated in wood for additional protection. Moving down the ranks, the conditions generally deteriorated from something like a picnic at one extreme to a literal pig sty on the other. One move in Richardson Vista was so filthy that our driver called our manager, Eldon Paulson, to say we just couldn't do it. The sinks were overflowing with dirty dishes and pots and pans. There were piles of dirty diapers in the corners. I've never seen—or smelled—anything like it before or since, except for maybe a Third World outhouse, and the couple we were moving, comforting their screaming baby, acted like it was just another day. Eldon came over, looked around disgustedly and said, "Just throw it in boxes," which we did, though we should have been wearing biohazard suits.

The drivers and other swampers used to tease me about graduating from college and returning to Anchorage as a fancy, uppity lawyer. Content with my circumstances, I made great money as a twenty-year-old Teamster and I liked the hard physical labor. Still, as I busted my butt and sparred with my co-workers, I yearned for Lilla. I had never had a girlfriend in junior high or high school and I was seriously in over my head.

Though I had no communication with Lilla over summer break, I looked her up when I returned to San Francisco in the fall. The torrid affair began anew. We were both young, inexperienced and in lust as much as in love. I hardly knew the difference. Between fall and spring semesters I proposed, sitting unceremoniously on the clothes dryer in her apartment while asking for her hand. Lilla consented to be married in the Presbyterian Church near campus; one of my roommates in our bachelor apartment on Grove Street, Jim Braun, was my best man.

My dad said, "Well son, you're on your own now," and that was that. I was pretty let down by his abruptness and remember thinking, "Well Dad, now you've got more money for drinking." By the time I'd gotten to junior high my dad had become a full-fledged alcoholic, consuming a fifth of whiskey a day. He eventually ended up at Providence Hospital in a straightjacket suffering from delirium tremens.

Lilla and I found a basement apartment on Frederick Street above the Haight-Ashbury district. She worked as a clerk in an auto underwriter's office for Transamerica in the financial district, while I worked part-time as a clerk typist for a construction firm and pounded away at my typewriter and my studies. I was taking a full load of classes and allowed myself to watch only one television program once a week—*Combat*, with Vic Morrow. Being a "war baby," born in 1942, it's only natural I'd have an interest in WW II. One of my courses included the history of the war, which I had completely committed to memory—names, places and dates—and regurgitated in its entirety to Lilla the night before my final exam.

Lilla and I made love for the first time on our wedding night, after I read aloud in bed a book about the subject that had been given to us by the preacher who had counseled and married us: "Be considerate. Don't pursue any activity your husband or wife is uncomfortable with."

Believe me; we made up for lost time. By the end of the first week I could barely walk. Lilla must have been walking around the insurance office with an embarrassing glow on her beautiful face and became pregnant sometime in those first few days. Our daughter Michele was born in the old Anchorage Providence Hospital on L Street during the trip to Alaska for summer break. When it was time to return to San Francisco for my senior year we couldn't afford the move, so I continued working for Continental Van Lines until they laid me off right before the Christmas holidays.

The Teamsters Union Local 959 got me another job driving a delivery truck for K&L Distributors, the local Budweiser distributor. I was not yet twenty-one years old and when I made deliveries to bars there was always some loud-mouth who'd holler, "Hey, kid, you don't look old enough to be in here!"

I resented the unwanted attention, but at least I had a job. This was one of my early experiments of jumping in with both feet, something I'd do time and again in various situations, for better or worse—and this time I found myself as a twenty-year-old, married with a child, and no college degree.

K&L had hired me to fill in during the Christmas season. Once the holidays were over, they announced their intention to lay me off. When I protested, insisting I could work in the office typing invoices and purchase orders, they kindly accommodated me. I handled the secretarial work and inventoried the split-stock room until Artie, the guy who arranged the display windows in liquor stores, decided to leave. Soon I was driving a van around town, decorating liquor store windows. It was fun and I enjoyed the independence my duties afforded me.

In the midst of my second Christmas season at K&L, two days after President Kennedy's November 22, 1963 assassination and one day after my twenty-first birthday, I had a falling out with Ziggy, the Anchorage manager for the company, and quit. I honestly don't recall the dispute, but I do remember him chewing me out in front of other employees, which I didn't appreciate. So I quit. I sent Lilla and Michele back to San Francisco by plane and followed them in March with the intention of re-enrolling at the University of San Francisco.

It's a miracle I made it back to the Bay Area, driving through blizzards and whiteouts in the Canadian Rockies in our red-and-white, two-wheel drive, 1959 Volvo sedan on summer tires. I once spun out on black ice, whirling 360 degrees on the edge of a precipice with no guard railing. I wound up not only back on the proper side of the road, but also headed in the right direction. It was the sort of experience that makes one believe in protective angels or fairy godmothers.

I'd wander into a lodge in the middle of the night, have a cup of coffee, and head back out into a blizzard as people wondered out loud if I was crazy. I needed every penny I had, so I couldn't afford overnight lodging, but I did manage to make it to San Francisco. In the process I also managed to miss the magnitude 9.2 Good Friday Earthquake when it struck Alaska on March 27, 1964.

I seem to have a knack, about which I am somewhat ambivalent, for narrowly missing momentous events in Alaska—arriving the day after Mt. Spurr's Crater Peak vent erupted on July 9, 1953, covering Anchorage with ash; driving around the Lower 48 with my parents as the Alaska Statehood Act was signed on July 7, 1958, when Anchorage residents celebrated with a bonfire on the Delaney Park Strip; and now leaving the state two weeks before the devastating Great Alaskan Earthquake, the second worst quake ever recorded.

My parents were still in Anchorage in a home on McKenzie Drive at the time, only a block or so from the duplex where we had lived during my junior high and high school years. Civilian communications were down in Alaska, so there was no way to contact them. The only relief I had for several days, until my dad was able to call me from Elmendorf Air Force Base, was an aerial photograph on the front page of the *San Francisco Chronicle*. It clearly showed the duplex in a hole in the ground and a large crack in the earth that approached the McKenzie Drive house, which still stood intact.

In San Francisco, my intention was to complete the seventeen credits I needed for my degree in political science, having quit my job at K&L on an emotional impulse, and naively assuming there would be some financial assistance available for me. When it turned out there was none, I found work to support my young family. I loved San Francisco, so it wasn't too bitter a pill to swallow at the beginning. My first job was as a "Hooper Snooper" for the Hooper-Holmes Bureau, Retail Credit's only national competitor, conducting background checks on people who were applying for jobs, insurance or credit. While doing a face-to-face investigation of a New York Life Insurance Company salesman buying a policy on himself, which seemed a little redundant, I was recruited to work as a salesman for "Ma Nylic," as New York Life was referred to by its employees. At the age of twenty-one, I became their youngest salesman in the entire country.

Initially we lived in a multi-story apartment building managed by college friends, Pat and Karen Lonergan, under the freeway on Octavia Street. The building had an interior staircase with a metal chute into which tenants dropped their garbage. Directly below us lived "Old Lady" Fogel with her beautiful young daughter.

When we would party above her on weekends she'd bang loudly on the garbage chute with her broom handle, shouting, "Go home, you stupid from Alaska!"

I was doing pretty well selling insurance and bought a spanking new poppy red Mustang convertible with wire wheels. It was the coolest car on the road in 1964. Lilla and Michele and I moved into a nice second-story, two-bedroom apartment on Stanyan Street between Haight and Page Streets, overlooking Golden Gate Park. The Haight-Ashbury District was just becoming a hip scene, with art galleries, coffee shops, book stores, restaurants and the like. It's where my first brother-in-law introduced us to marijuana. You could buy a "lid"—a tin Prince Albert tobacco can filled with pot—anywhere in the neighborhood, no problem. Haight-Ashbury was hip all right—too hip—and eventually overrun by vermin. By the time I went to work for Hallmark Cards and moved across the bay to Orinda they were running bus tours through the neighborhood, and it was soon a burnt-out, dismal-looking district that took years to rejuvenate.

I had escaped the district at the right time, but eventually found myself stuck in California, not living the life I had intended. I felt trapped. I had been unable to continue my education and instead gotten completely wrapped up in corporate and family life with the all-too-attendant credit obligations. I didn't see myself going much of anywhere, and what I did see I didn't like. After several years of working as a salesman, I wound up at Gillette Safety Razor Company, Toiletries Division. Working for a year at the privately-owned Hallmark Cards had been a nightmare. It was hard to tell who they treated with less respect—their employees or their accounts. Though Gillette was a much better company to work for—like night and day—it seemed that management there had less security than I had.

You had to sell your soul to the company, move whenever and wherever they wanted and be able to joyfully participate in a group orgasm over a price-off promotion on Right Guard spray deodorant. My parents had so wanted me to become an attorney, and it stung me to think that I would not be mired in this situation had I continued my education. In the end, I realized I also had a tap root in Alaska and that I didn't mind working for a corporation, as long as I owned it.

By now Lilla was pregnant with our son, Michael, and we were living in Sacramento. I was one of the top twenty salesmen in the country, so when I told my district manager I was quitting Gillette and moving back to Alaska, he and the regional manager flew in to try to dissuade me. When I wouldn't change my mind they generously told me to take whatever product samples I had in my garage to use for trade at my accounts. I was thus able to outfit us for the trip. We bought a VW bus and sold everything we couldn't fit into it or the 4 x 6 trailer we towed behind us.

We went from a three-bedroom house with a double garage and large backyard in Sacramento for $135 a month to a crowded Quonset hut in East Anchorage for $175 a month, the best deal we could find. I went back to work selling life insurance for New York Life and spent a very cold winter driving that VW bus with its notoriously inadequate engine air heater. But it was nice to be home, and there were good friends to help us through the difficulties.

Aconcagua

Three decades and two marriages later, tossing and turning in my hotel bed in Miami on my way to Argentina to climb Mt. Aconcagua, the highest mountain in South America, I sat up and called Shelli. We had a nice long talk that included a comment that would remain with me throughout the climb.

"I love you too, Michael," she said with more feeling than I had heard in a long time. No five words could have meant more to me.

Shelli had been traveling back and forth to England doing genealogy research on her family while I was climbing. Planning ahead to September of 1993, she said, "I've worked out the arrangements for our trip to Wales and our renewal of vows. We're going to have the ceremony in a very old church where one of my relatives was vicar!" It was the second chance I'd been hoping for.

I was still trying to learn how to pronounce Aconcagua when I plopped down in the airplane seat next to Bob John, my pal from Denali, for the long flight to Buenos Aires. Upon arrival we met up with Vern Tejas, one of our guides, passed customs and immigration, then boarded an Aerolineas Argentinas plane for the two-and-a-half hour flight to Mendoza.

Our group rode in a brand new, air-conditioned bus from Mendoza at about 2,000 feet—a lovely city of parks, tree-lined avenues and European-style architecture—to Punta del Inca at about 10,000 feet, the starting point for the trek into base camp. On the way up we passed an eighteen-wheel semi and trailer that had, on its way down, overturned and spilled its load of Chiquita bananas all over the highway. Was it an omen?

That night in Punta del Inca, I contemplated my status as the late-starting, inexperienced climber in the group. But with two summits and three climbs under my belt in seven months—having failed on Elbrus in the USSR only due to extraordinarily bad weather—I was feeling mostly confident about my climbing ability. Still, I was a little intimidated by Aconcagua, considering it was twenty-five hundred feet higher than anything I had yet attempted.

After spending one night at Camp I, 11,300 feet, we hiked for seven hours up a wide riverbed that steepened gradually as we approached the glacier at the base of the mountain. We arrived at the main camp, known as Camp II, or Plaza de Mulas, around mid-afternoon. Walking into the persistent dusty wind off the glacier, we wore surgical masks or kerchiefs over our faces. At a certain point along the way, we spotted the massif of Aconcagua. I was stunned. The peak appeared to reach into the deep blue of the ionosphere. I thought, "Holy Cow!" It was difficult to imagine myself standing on top of it.

At 22,831 feet, Mt. Aconcagua's summit was first reached in 1897 by Matthias Zurbriggen. Though its peak is in the Mendoza Province of Northern Argentina, famous for wines, its western flank rises from the coastal lowlands of Chile. A long-dormant, eroded volcano on the sere side of the Andes, it is not particularly icy or snowy despite its great height—so great, in fact—that you would have to travel to the Hindu Kush of Pakistan to find a higher mountain.

We went about setting up camp, leveling tent sites and building rock walls for wind protection. The mules arrived within an hour, bringing the large mess tent, tables and chairs. We could actually stand up in the mess tent and walk around comfortably. While erecting our sleeping tents, I started experiencing a headache and nausea due to the altitude change and strenuous effort. I couldn't eat my spaghetti dinner, so I took a Motrin and stretched out for a while. I had been through it all before; it didn't worry me as it had on Denali. All I needed was lots of water and a good night's sleep.

We left Camp II the next morning with heavy loads of food and camp gear for the carry to Camp III, Cambio de Pendiente, meaning "Change of Angles," at 17,500 feet. Todd Burleson, the expedition leader, kept a reasonable pace. It was a beautiful day and we all performed well, arriving at Camp III around 2:30 p.m. As we descended, I started getting another headache. By the time we reached Camp II again I could barely move, so I swallowed two Motrin with a lot of water, stretched out again for about an hour and a half, and was finally able to make it to the mess tent for dinner. I had also acquired an ominous cough—always a reason for concern—which created a nagging doubt in the back of my mind.

Saturday, a rest day, I stayed in camp, while others decided to make another carry to Camp III. I didn't want to push my luck because of my cough. On Sunday we all left for Camp III again and, because I had not carried the previous day, I now had the heaviest pack of the group. It probably weighed seventy pounds—a bitch just getting it on my back, much less carrying it 4,300 vertical feet at altitude.

The next camp, at 18,050 feet, was Nido de Condores, or "The Condor's Nest," to which we made two carries on Monday, and where we now had everything but what we had left down low at Plaza de Mulas.

We passed two climbers returning from a failed summit attempt. "No one has made the summit yet because of high winds," they said, disgruntled.

The view from Nido de Condores was spectacular, the snow-capped peaks of the Andes stretching to the horizon. It was a lazy day that ended with the most awful crap imaginable for dinner, a sort of Dark Ages gruel prepared by Vern. I wasn't the only one who couldn't eat it, and when Vern heard us grumbling about it he came around trying to persuade us to eat it. I put mine in a plastic bag and hid it in my sleeping bag planning to throw it away in the morning.

Vern Tejas possesses a cast iron stomach and will eat almost anything. He could mix his spaghetti from the night before with his oatmeal in the morning. I am certain he could mix his hot chocolate in his pee bottle and think nothing of it. I pride myself on being somewhat of a gourmet. What would my fellow members of the Chaine des Rotisseurs say? "Sacre bleu!" The next morning, we had rice pudding with dried apples for breakfast, which was a big improvement, but then so would have dog food.

It wasn't only the food, or the dirt and wind that made Aconcagua such an unpleasant climb. Finding clean snow or ice to melt for water was difficult all the way from Base Camp to Berlin Camp. Because of its location on the sere side of the Andes, Aconcagua does not get a lot of precipitation; what it does get is blown away by the strong winds. When we were fortunate enough to find a pool of frozen or iced-over water, it was likely that someone had taken a crap in it.

A more pressing problem at the moment was the weather. It had been ideal at lower altitudes, but was deteriorating the higher we got. I was charmed by the country and its people and wanted to summit without delay so I could spend some more time in Mendoza and Buenos Aires. I figured I might never get another chance.

The carry from Nido de Condores to Berlin Camp at 19,500 feet took a little under three hours and went without mishap. On Friday, December 16, we made an attempt at the summit. In spite of strong winds some of us reached the base of the Canaletta, a huge gully that descends from the summit ridge and poses the last real obstacle to the summit: large rocks and boulders that make for precarious footing.

We milled around the foot of the Canaletta for fifteen minutes, debating whether to continue since the wind was blowing so hard it was difficult to keep your balance. A solo Latino climber passed us by, heading toward the summit as if it were a balmy day at the beach. Todd decided we should head down a little lower to a snow-filled A-frame, which was more of a reference point than a shelter, and wait for the weather to improve. It did not, so we returned to Berlin Camp. As we descended, and encountered a couple other groups moving up, oblivious to the weather, I thought of the large cemetery at the base of the mountain. Back at Berlin Camp the solo Latino came through around 5:00 p.m., reporting that he had made the summit. It turned out a few others had made the summit also, but I was satisfied we had done the right thing by turning back.

Some in our group wanted to attempt the summit again the next day, while others wanted to rest. The weather resolved our differences. The wind blew all night and until the sun was well up, around 10:30 a.m. Cowering in our tents that night, unable to sleep, we could hear the wind coming like a colossal locomotive, roaring through canyon after canyon until it finally and abruptly slammed into us with tremendous force. It was so bad that at times I thought we would be blown off the mountain or have our tents torn to pieces. On Saturday the weather got even worse, bringing both snow and stronger winds that battered us all night. Sleep was impossible, but at least we now had a fresh source of clean water.

Two Argentine climbers who had imprudently attempted the summit in the middle of the storm staggered into our camp in the dark. One was in terrible shape, hypothermic and disoriented, his hands almost completely black with frostbite. They had no campsite. We warmed them up, got some liquids in them, and gave them medications. They headed down the mountain to lower altitude and a doctor as quickly as they could; a graphic reminder of the dangers inherent in what I was doing. The visuals were hard to erase from my mind, just like the two climbers I'd seen at the Talkeetna airport after they were blown off the mountain in their tents and sleeping bags. It was disturbing, to say the least. Given the altitude they needed to descend and the distance they needed to travel, it was tough to visualize a happy ending.

Monday morning, we all waited in our sleeping bags for Todd to make a decision about a summit attempt. It was still cold and windy. At 10:30 a.m., Todd decided we should wait until the next day, but two climbers were determined to go so Vern went with them.

The three returned at 8:00 p.m., having reached the summit. Albie said in his thick Boston accent and with great emphasis, "It was the hardest thing I've ever done!" He was probably the toughest guy in our group, so that didn't do a lot to bolster my confidence.

Dan added, "There was no wind and it was clear of clouds. We could have lit a match on the summit and held it aloft."

I walked a short distance from camp and returned with some snow to melt for water and the effort wore me out. My energy would only deteriorate the longer I stayed on the mountain and I wished I had gone with them, now worried I wouldn't get another chance.

On the morning of the 19th, at about 8:30 a.m., after forcing down a few tiny spoonfuls of oatmeal and some tea, I started up the mountain with Bob John, two other climbers, Todd, and Vern, who was climbing the route for the second day in a row. It was cold and my hands and feet suffered until the sun came up at around 20,000 feet.

At 12:30 p.m. I reached the rocky outcrop at the bottom of the Canaletta called "The Thumb," where we had turned around on our first attempt. After a short rest, Vern and I stepped up to the actual base of the Canaletta within an hour, about 1,200 vertical feet from the summit ridge. I was trying to pace myself with two Japanese climbers ahead of me. It seemed we were all moving in slow motion. I'd stop, sit, have a drink of water, eat a bite of candy, and get up again to find that the Japanese apparently hadn't moved at all. We worked our way up the right side of the Canaletta, eventually reaching the summit ridge, then continued left toward the summit itself. In clear weather a climber can look all the way down the south face from the summit ridge, but it began clouding over as soon as we started up the Canaletta and was now completely fogged in and snowing lightly. I could still sense that big void out there on my right. It made me uneasy, though by now I knew I was going to summit.

Todd took photos of me with my Chilkoot Charlie's, American and Alaskan flags, and a makeshift cardboard sign that read, "Shelli, Will You Remarry Me?" Though still living apart, we had made a lot of progress on our relationship between Denali and Aconcagua, so I felt confident enough to make my proposal public, especially after hearing her parting words over the phone in Miami.

I had written on a postcard from Punta del Inca to Shelli, "You are on my mind constantly. I brought the most recent photos of you with me and look at them several times a day. I miss you and can't wait to see you at the airport X-mas eve."

I wasn't particularly tired or feeling any affects from the altitude, though we were higher than anyone else in the western or southern hemispheres, unless they were in flight. Aside from the rocky real estate we stood upon, with its iconic metal cross protruding askance from the summit and the other climbers in our small group, I could see absolutely nothing. I felt, however, like I had overcome a lot of fear and uncertainty with this climb. Maybe Everest was really within my reach.

My cachet for Aconcagua was dedicated to Johnny Tegstrom, who had at that point been dead for over twenty years. I thought about him and how, ironically, I almost preceded him in death by falling off that mountain on our goat hunt. I gave thanks for my survival—then and now.

The Canaletta was covered with freshly fallen snow; it was hard to see our footing, and it was slippery. We took an eternity reaching the bottom, slipping, falling and swearing. Once out of the Canaletta, Vern sped down ahead of us on solid footing to put things in order at Berlin Camp. I felt great when we got back to camp at 8:00 p.m., eleven and a half hours after our departure and damned proud of my achievement. But there was to be no rousing welcome for us, since the other climbers had departed for Plaza de Mulas, having either thrown in the towel or summited already.

Next morning we got up around 10:00 a.m. as the sun hit the tents, had some breakfast, broke camp and started down the mountain with very heavy packs. Albie came up to meet us as we arrived hours later, exhausted, at the overlook of Plaza de Mulas. He offered to assist with some of our gear as he told us of a cantina below selling hamburgers and beer, news that revived our spirits.

Plaza de Mulas was now a tent city. We hastily unloaded our gear and headed for the cantina like a pack of hungry wolves. I gobbled up five hamburgers and drank eight beers, so dehydrated that I didn't pee once. Preparations for dinner were cancelled and Vern brought over his harmonica. We were joined by three German climbers and a group of three Americans who had come down the day before. Everyone was in a celebratory mood—the Berlin Wall was being torn down. We drank beer and sang for hours; I woke up with the lyrics of *God Bless America* ringing in my ears, hungover, but proud.

Just before noon we began the roughly twenty-five mile journey back to Punta del Inca. It was a clear, warm day except when the wind blew, which was often, and mostly downhill on feet already sore and covered with moleskin. Those ahead of us had just finished fording the river, considerably higher than when we had crossed it on the way in, and which Todd had told us not to attempt without him. When Bob and I arrived, they indicated the best place to cross and we took off our shoes and packs, threw them across, and waded with our arms locked together into the raging, waist-high, glacial water.

Bob, upstream from me, lost his balance and knocked me over. We struggled mightily to keep from being swept downstream and to reach the outstretched hands of our friends on the other side. We emerged wet, cold, battered and more than a little shaken. I had lost my hat and while wringing out my clothing I discovered a rock embedded in the flesh below my right knee. I dug it out with my pocketknife, got back into my clothes, and tried to get started again, but could barely walk. A hundred yards down the trail, I stopped to apply more moleskin and discovered the problem: a rock the size of a pin head embedded in the bottom of my right big toe. Unable to remove it with tweezers, I squeezed on it hard with both thumbs and it popped out like a shot. Fortunately, we were only three miles from Punta del Inca.

I called Shelli, who told me excitedly that she had made plans to go ice skating at Westchester Lagoon and that we were going to host a Christmas gathering at our home on Sorbus Way. I was more than ready for some sea level holiday festivities. The next day, after my second long, hot shower, we were off to Mendoza. We did a little Christmas shopping, which was pretty disappointing, the shelves as bare as when I was in the Soviet Union the previous September. Argentina was on hard times, people standing in lines at the banks because of the hyper-inflation, but soon I was back in the States, my mind on Shelli—and Mount Everest.

Early Bar Years

That first winter back in Anchorage, 1966-1967, our fuel oil heater blew soot all over everything in the Quonset hut, including us—twice. It was that kind of winter for Lilla and me, but our son Michael was born. As I peddled life insurance, I looked around for another way to support my family. I wanted to be on the buying end, not the selling end. I always felt awkward thinking of friends and acquaintances as prospects, and though I made cold calls by phone, went door-to-door and followed up by phone on marriage, birth and professional leads in the newspapers, I hated it. I've never been very good at handling rejection. If I got a rude response to my first cold call of the day, I was done.

Serendipity played a major role in my first business venture. Johnny Tegstrom had dropped out of college for reasons of his own. Norman Rokeberg, later with me on Maui when I became intimate with Shelli, had lost his student deferment, been drafted into the Army and was now discharged—none of this making me feel any better about not having finished school myself. As previously indicated, Johnny was already well established. Norman was working as a "ramp rat," handling baggage for Alaska Airlines. With the money Norm's father, Mel, loaned us to get started in business we were thinking mostly of purchasing an apartment building.

It so happened that the estranged wife of Cliff Brandt, the creator of the Bird House Bar, also worked at the airport, where Norm got wind that she wanted to sell. The Bird House Bar, located forty miles south of Anchorage, seemed to fit our needs perfectly. We were all excited about being the owners of what was already a small but landmark operation.

Norm said, "I understand she's asking $20,000 for the business, liquor license and some land."

"I wonder how much land is included," Johnny said.

I said, "Well, we'd better not waste any time. We need to make an offer before word gets out."

Johnny said, "We can get a boiler-plate earnest money agreement at Adam's Stationers on Fourth Avenue and make her an offer."

"Let's go out there this weekend," Norm suggested.

We agreed that Norm would be the managing partner, taking care of banking, ordering and other business matters, and work the bar five days a week. Since I had a family and a job with New York Life, I'd work weekends. Johnny would fill in where he could, ill as he was with leukemia and soon to travel to New York City for treatment with interferon, a new drug we hoped would cure him.

We drove down the Seward Highway that Saturday night in December of 1967, made an offer that was accepted, and suddenly we were bar owners. The three of us operated the Bird House Bar for approximately a year, building up the volume of the business dramatically. Norm worked his five nights a week and took care of managing the business. I worked my two nights, Fridays and Saturdays, and sold insurance during the week. I'd drive from town each Friday afternoon, take over the bartending, work the place until 5:00 a.m., stagger to the little shack we owned behind the bar and pass out. At noon the next day I'd reopen the place and run it straight through until 5:00 a.m. again, stumble back to the shed, pass out and reopen Sunday at noon. Norm relieved me around 6:00 p.m., when I'd drive back to Anchorage and present myself bright-eyed and bushy-tailed in suit and tie for an 8:00 a.m. Monday sales meeting at New York Life.

But as busy as I was, I'd had a taste of success and eagerly sought out other opportunities. I proposed to a friend who worked at Barter Island, made a lot of money, and wasn't doing much with it, that if he put up $20,000, we could buy an apartment complex and I'd be the managing partner. We purchased a half block of property on East Sixth Avenue with three duplexes, a garage with a rental attached to the rear, a two story six-plex and a very nice, large log cabin with a full basement—all of which I was certain we could one day sell to Alaska Sales and Service, the Chevy dealer right next door to the east. I was right. The log cabin—the only building left standing—remains a sales office for the car dealership today. That log cabin was my family's first home but, sadly, during the last days of my first marriage.

Johnny spent most of that year in New York City undergoing treatment. By late 1968, it was apparent he was not going to live much longer. Norm wanted to return to university, so we put the Bird House Bar up for sale and sold it immediately for twice what we'd paid for it. The buyer was ex-school teacher Dick Delak, who had made some money in oil field services on the North Slope.

While bartending at the Bird House during my year of weekends, I met my future partner in Chilkoot Charlie's, Bill Jacobs. Bill owned a condominium at the base of Mount Alyeska and travelled back and forth from Anchorage to ski on weekends, regularly stopping to imbibe at our establishment. Norm and Johnny and I had frequently discussed the tongue-in-cheek idea of loading the Bird House Bar onto a flatbed truck and hauling it to Anchorage, where all the people lived. At that time, though Fairbanks had the Malemute Saloon, Juneau had the Red Dog Saloon and even little Homer had the Salty Dawg Saloon, Anchorage had no bar with an authentic Alaskan theme. All the bars were either trying to mimic Outside operations, or they were neighborhood bars, night clubs or strip joints. I saw an opening.

Bill and I became friends and I convinced him of the idea of creating an Alaska-themed bar in Anchorage. Bill soon made an arrangement to borrow $20,000 from his mother, who lived in Chicago, and the hunt was on for a location. We were involved in probably ten different potential deals over the course of a year. First we looked at the Alibi Club on Spenard Road, but I felt the owners, Skip Fuller and Jack Griffin, were asking too much. Then we looked at Swiftie's Club 25, the bar that eventually became the Cabin Tavern on Muldoon Road, but the owners jerked us around.

Meanwhile, I was tired of selling insurance and looking for a change. A lot of people had suggested to me that I should be in radio or television, mostly because of my voice, a baritone I've been accused of affecting, though it's the same voice shared by my father and my son.

In those days, broadcasters had to take a simple FCC test for a license before they could go on the air, so I went to the old federal building on Fourth Avenue and got licensed. Next, I applied for a job as a disc jockey with local radio station KHAR. Station manager Ken Flynn ushered me into a little booth to read an ad for Volkswagen.

When I was finished, he said, "I hate it when some kid walks in straight off the street and sounds better than I do!" Then he hired me.

As I was trying to put another bar deal together, crawling around under prospective building purchases through the reeking fumes of space heaters placed to prevent the plumbing from freezing, I went to KHAR every morning to learn how to work "the board." My instructor was Ruben Gaines. This chance meeting was one of the most important in either of our lives, though neither of us could have possibly guessed it at the time.

Ruben was the consummate raconteur, a truly gifted and professional writer and entertainer in every sense of the word. I marveled at his abilities. He had a program called *Conversations Unlimited*, in which he entertained Alaskans every weekday for an hour during prime drive-home time with his storytelling, wit and social commentary, mixed with easy-listening music. His theme song, I nostalgically recall, was Claude Debussy's "Clair de Lune." Ruben had different established characters in his stories, including Doc, Mrs. Malone, Six-Toed Mordecai and Chilkoot Charlie, a character Ruben concocted during a long, rainy winter in Ketchikan in the late 1940s. Ruben would bring these characters to life for his audience, virtually becoming each one. The character I remember most avidly watching him produce was Doc, the crusty sourdough, for whom Ruben would pooch out his lower lip to produce the appropriate vocal personality.

Before settling in Anchorage, Ruben had also worked a spell in Fairbanks, where he and another talented radio guy, sportscaster Ed Stevens, would brilliantly broadcast "live" major league baseball games. Of course, there were no satellites back then, so Alaskans had to wait several days for tape recordings to arrive, and calling the States was expensive, if not impossible for most people. Ruben and Ed would receive the play-by-play information about a game from a buddy in the Lower 48 by telephone, on the station's dime, and would then "broadcast" the game as if it were live, including the excitement one would expect from the announcer, the sound effects of the ball being hit, the crowd roaring and all. Many people in the Bush never knew the difference between Ruben and Ed's broadcasts and the real thing.

Not long after my introduction to "the board," oil was discovered on the North Slope and a state auction raised $900 million from the sale of leases at Prudhoe Bay. That was a colossal amount of money in 1969, though today the state's annual budget is well over ten times that amount. Given the changing circumstances, I figured I would visit Skip Fuller again to see if the Alibi Club was still for sale. It was, but the price had gone up. The price of everything had gone up.

Not wanting to miss the potential bonanza of owning a bar during a boom period, Bill and I bit the bullet, borrowed the pre-arranged $20,000 from his mother for the down payment and closed the deal. Now I had to decide on a name and specific Alaskan theme for the place. I kept a note pad by my bed and woke up throughout the night to write down ideas. One had to do with a much-maligned local variety of salmon—the pink, or humpy. I had schools of ideas about Mr. and Mrs. Humpy. You don't have to think long to realize the possibilities and, of course, many years later someone did employ that name. The other idea was Chilkoot Charlie's, after Ruben's titan, sourdough reprobate, arguably the best known literary character in the state at the time. But I was torn.

I had a school teacher for a tenant in the six-plex who had been a customer at the Bird House Bar and was one of my New York Life policyholders. When I went around monthly to collect rents, he and his wife would sometimes invite me in for dinner.

One night over dinner I presented my dilemma and Mel didn't hesitate, saying, "What, are you crazy? You've got to call it Chilkoot Charlie's!"

I took Ruben to lunch at the Black Angus restaurant on Fireweed

Lane, where he agreed to give me permission to use the name in the bar and restaurant business, saying, "Chilkoot Charlie's! That's a great name for a bar!"

We opened Chilkoot Charlie's on January 1, 1970, New Year's Day—the worst night of the year for any bar. But in the tradition of old Alaska, Skip threw a welcome party for us, inviting all of his loyal patrons and friends.

He said, "When you sell a place you want to make sure the new guy can make it, and you've got to allow for him to do it in the way you treat him and structure the deal." We grossed an incredible $464.50.

After the party he said, "Hang onto your money. You won't have another night like that for a long time."

The original bar was in a 100-foot-by-25-foot building. To the north sat Spenard Bingo, to the south was America Rents, later occupied by Barry's Motorcycle Shop. Eventually, I would expand Koot's by buying those adjacent properties and others, adding themed bars throughout the establishment and a big parking lot across the street to replace the original four parking spaces out front. When I bought the place from Skip, I boldly stated I was going to triple his business.

He replied, "You may double it, but you'll never triple it."

When he saw me replacing the cocktail tables with wire reels, the chairs with stumps and beer kegs, nailing spruce slabs to the nice paneled walls and fishnet to the ceilings he was noticeably worried that I would ruin the place and it would be a mess when he'd have to take it back. At the end of that first year, I had quadrupled his business.

Skip then said, "This place is going to pay for a lot of mistakes."

Of all the more senior men in my personal life, Skip Fuller is the one who taught me the most. He was my mentor. He believed in me and never faltered in his support of me until the day he died. In fact he made a point of calling me "son" when I drove from Las Vegas to visit him for the last time in 2005, as he was near death, in Mesquite, Nevada.

My first manager at Chilkoot Charlie's was Cliff Martin. He was the original "wild and crazy guy"—years before Steve Martin—hence his nickname, Crazy Cliff, or just Craze. We never contemplated having professional entertainment at the time. We were the entertainment. Cliff would often wear the colorful outfit of a reservation Indian with one of those huge round-topped hats with a big feather in it. My original working outfit was long-handled underwear, "bunny boots," an Australian Outback hat, a fur-lined jock strap worn on the outside and a kazoo in my mouth. Then I came across an intact, original WWI infantry uniform with leg wrappings and all, added a WWI vintage blue fabric flying hat with goggles and a scarf around my neck and presto: Rocky the Flying Mutherfucker, an X-rated takeoff on Rocky—the flying squirrel—from the popular *Rocky and Bullwinkle* cartoon series.

For years at Koot's I made up nicknames for employees and, since I wrote the checks for payroll manually, even put their aliases on their pay envelopes. Rocky Fuller was Rocky Roll. Harlow, because of his large nose, was Hook. We had a small bartender named Bobby Trujillo working the Show Bar for a long time; he had a nose like Harlow's, so he became Little Hook. A bartender with the first name of Wind was known as Breaking Wind. A guy named Bob Link, who worked the South Long Bar for a while, and could touch the tip of his nose with the tip of his tongue—doing so regularly to impress the girls—was also a little ditzy. He became known as Line Drive, the implication being that he had taken one to the head. Then there was Allen, or Teen Angel, who'd come to work as a bartender at a tender young age.

Early on we had a female server named Bobbi, who wore her hair in a beehive. She carried her tray and served her drinks from a unicycle. She was a real character—Bouncing Booby Bobbie. There was the bartender, No Cherry Larry, and the bartender/hockey referee, Jimmy Brett. When Jimmy, aka Hockey Puck, took his false teeth out and started over the bar, a patron knew he'd gone too far. Fred Lamarone, a fabulous day bartender as well as a first class con man, used to pack the day shift during pipeline construction, pushing his homemade soups and chili over the bar. He was aptly known as Fast Freddie. Fred was a tenant in my log cabin on Sixth Avenue when I decided he needed to work elsewhere. He went to work in Edna Cox's Northern Lights Hotel on Northern Lights Boulevard, since condemned and removed, and tried to steal all my managers, entertainment and employees. He didn't succeed in that but he did steal everything from the log house, right down to the drapes and toilet paper hangers. He fancied himself a promoter and, in fact, was a damned good one aside from being unscrupulous. Many of my pipeline-worker patrons invested heavily in a Bachman-Turner Overdrive concert he promoted up in the Mat-Su Valley and lost every cent. I surmise it was an over-subscribed over-expensed scam—Freddie's version of *The Producers*.

As for Chilkoot Charlie's, we ushered in professional entertainment starting with a piano and banjo duo called the Rinky Dinks. We provided our customers with song sheets for singing along and shaker cans for the rhythm section. I bought some cases of empty salmon cans and a hand-crank canner at the old McKay's

Hardware store around the corner on Fireweed Lane, and put a few little rocks in each can with a specially-made Koot's label on the outside. Such were the modest beginnings of the eventual fifteen thousand square foot entertainment juggernaut that has presented musicians, comedians and DJs from all over the world.

When it was time to replace the Rinky Dinks, I placed a blind box advertisement in the Anchorage Times to which I received several replies, only one of which I answered: a guy named Doug Haggar, who billed himself as the pianist "Mr. Whitekeys." He filled out a medical claims form as his job application, listing "None" in the space provided for "Total Cost of this Illness." He didn't have a phone, so he drew a map of where I could locate him near Fish Creek, halfway between Spenard Road and Turnagain by the Sea.

I brought Doug to the club one evening to audition with as many of my regulars on hand as possible to judge his act. The results were mixed; about half my customers liked him a lot and the other half didn't like him at all. I tilted the balance in favor of the choice to hire Mr. Whitekeys because I recognized his talent. The rest is history. Doug worked for me steadily for four and a half years and proved himself to be not only quite the talent, but a self-motivated, professional entertainer. He would take a month or six weeks off and return with a whole new set or two that would have tears running down our cheeks, especially the first night. Like Frank, he did it his way. He refused requests. "Hava Nagila," the traditional Jewish folk song, was a very popular sing-along at the time—but Whitekeys would never play it no matter how many times it was requested. Nor did he like being coerced to play other favorites of the time, such as "Great Balls of Fire," by Jerry Lee Lewis. He would say, "I'm not going to play that song, but I'll play one with some of the same notes in it."

During the time Whitekeys worked for Chilkoot Charlie's, we had two others locations in operation, one referred to by the locals of Girdwood, aka Girdweed, as Chuck's, and the other on First Street in Fairbanks. I sent Doug to Fairbanks Chilkoot's to entertain. One night soon after his arrival, having said something about the American flag—I don't remember what—he took a break, stepped off the stage, and was cold-cocked by a guy who had taken offense at his comment. I could never convince Doug to venture north to that interior city again, though he did write a song about Fairbanks, in which he said, "It's not the end of the world, but you can see it from there!"

Doug was also our "promotions manager" for a time. He created a clever ad campaign titled "So You'll Know Who to Blame," which featured each of our zany employees. I was portrayed as Dagwood Bumstead's boss, Mr. Dithers.

All good things come to an end though, and Doug eventually moved down the street to occupy a portion of the Fancy Moose, a large club where he basically had his own area in which to perform. He called it the Fly by Night Club, with the fuselage and wing of an airplane jutting out of the front of the building. A few years later he moved back toward Chilkoot Charlie's, along with the plane, and opened his very own Fly by Night Club in a free-standing building on the west side of the street, where he performed until his retirement.

Business boomed at Chilkoot Charlie's during our first year of operation. I felt as if I were holding onto the bumper of an accelerating vehicle, trying to move my legs fast enough to keep up. This was shortly before pipeline construction brought the unruly masses through town—all of whom were sure to show up at Koot's looking for a wild night in Spenard. As if I wouldn't soon have enough problems, I started off the decade with a doozy.

Things on the home front weren't going well. One afternoon while I was bartending, a pretty young lady from the *Anchorage Daily News* stopped by to sell me some advertising. I didn't buy any because we were doing just fine with a mailing list. That and our silkscreened sweatshirts, worn around town by our many regulars, were advertising enough. When she got off work she stopped by again and stayed until closing. I wasn't very happy in my marriage, and it only took one night with another woman to realize just how unhappy I'd been.

A couple days later I told Lilla I wanted a divorce. All we did was fight anyway. I was angry that Lilla, a stay-at-home mom, couldn't manage to keep a clean house. In retrospect, I'm sure she was suffering from depression. I had always been disappointed that, though her first language was Norwegian and she had a lovely accent, she was embarrassed by it and refused to teach our children a word of her native tongue. There were other issues, not the least of which was my headstrong arrogance and ambition.

I moved in with the advertising saleslady, and I was in bed with her when her big, tough oil rig hard-hat diver fiancé showed up, bags in hand, at her door from Louisiana. He was as understanding as a guy could be under the circumstances, even helping me move my belongings into the apartment of my bar manager Cliff. That arrangement suited us, so when I got back into my log house on East Sixth Avenue, Cliff moved in as my roommate.

Two bachelors, now living in the beautiful old log house, we brought home a revolving door of different companions. One winter night, I was sound asleep in my bedroom with someone, when Cliff and his someone decided they were hungry. Cliff went to the kitchen, put some shrimp on the stove in a pot of grease, lit the burner and went back to the bedroom, where I guess he got distracted and then passed out.

Waking suddenly, I realized that the house was full of smoke, the kitchen an inferno. The smoke was so thick and the heat emanating from the kitchen so hot, I had only enough time to awaken Cliff and his date, call the fire department, and haul out a few business records and clothes. I've often wondered what it was that woke me up—maybe that angel or fairy godmother that sometimes appears in times of need? We all surely would have died otherwise.

As I sat there on the hood of my new Opel GT in my underwear, holding onto what's-her-name and watching the flames licking out of my attic, I wondered how I was going to replace everything. But the fire department arrived within minutes and tackled the blaze from every angle. To my utter amazement the house suffered only smoke damage and a destroyed kitchen, which was replaced in short order by the insurance company.

If there was a lesson to be learned it was this: "Never put the shrimp on the stove before you put the sausage in the oven." But that wouldn't be my last experience with fires.

Soon after, a girl named Tiffany came to work as a waitress for me at Chilkoot Charlie's, stating that she wanted to get away from go-go dancing. She had been introduced to me by my friend, Tucker Hurn, and somehow I've managed to forgive him over the years. She certainly was a beautiful girl, with long legs and arms and perfect facial features. She would buy a drink and have it sent to me by the bartender.

One night when I was bartending she caught me at the right moment, mentioning that she had to fly to Seattle for a court appearance and was hoping to find someone to join her. "What about you, Mike Gordon?" she said.

A year after my divorce from Lilla, a traumatic experience that involved a bitter child custody battle over my son and daughter, I remarried on the rebound. Tiffany assured me the baby was mine, though in my heart-of-hearts I never believed it. I remember standing in front of the fireplace in the log house right before the ceremony with my best man, Dale Vaughn, also my general manager at Chilkoot Charlie's in the early '70s.

He looked at me hard and asked, "Are you sure you want to do this?"

I honestly don't remember my reply, or if I just looked back at him. But I went through with it, even though it didn't feel right. Old school, you know—she was pregnant; it was the proper thing to do. Seven long years later, I was worn to the nub by a street-hardened female with the mettle of an ice cold razor blade. Exhausted by the responsibilities of managing a manic hub of local activity and dealing with a business partner whose financial needs I could never satisfy, having served a three-year stint in public office to boot, I would bolt from the state, spurred by a mid-life crisis come early.

The Operation

This little tale, though true, is presented simply for entertainment value and as an insight into the lives and times of those of us involved in the bar business in Alaska in the late '60s and early '70s.

It's an unpublished historical fact that in the mid-1960s, there were more characters around Turnagain Arm than anywhere else in the world.

"The name's Planter!" echoed around the small Bird Creek bar known as Diamond Jim's, where Jim Redmond was proprietor. Gus Planter was a part-time gandy dancer (a slang term for railroad workers who laid and maintained tracks before it was all done by machine) on the Alaska Railroad and a full-time inebriate. Fortunately he favored the more modern accommodations of Diamond Jim's to the rustic quaintness of the Bird House Bar a couple of miles further down the road.

Lord only knows what I was doing in Diamond Jim's on this particular occasion. I'd probably closed up early. I remember I was drinking a beer and playing a game of pool with someone.

"The name's Planter!" rang out loud and clear again as if no one had heard the previous dozen or so pronouncements. Leonard and I glanced at Jim to read his reaction from behind the bar.

Leonard was a barber from town who lived in the vicinity. His wife, Hanna, worked as a cook in Girdwood at the old Double Musky Inn. He was a pretty good drinker too and a good customer of ours, for better or worse, at the Bird House Bar. Jim had already muttered something about stitches being in Planter's eyebrow a couple of weeks too long.

"The name's Planter!" rang out for the umpteenth time. That was it. Jim told Planter in no uncertain terms that if he announced his name one more time, he was going to personally remove those eyebrow stitches. Planter had recently, and not for the first time, run his car off the road. It was more "windy" then, but not "windy" enough for Planter.

"The name's Planter!" Have you ever known a drunk that could take a hint, no matter how resourcefully or forcefully presented? Well that was the end of the pool game because Planter was soon lying across the table on his back, arms and legs restrained, staring wildly up at the Budweiser surgical light. Cocktail napkins appeared over the faces of Jim and Leonard. From behind the bar, 190 proof Everclear grain alcohol as an antiseptic. Planter didn't need an anesthesiologist.

There was simply the surgeon, Jim the assistant surgeon, Leonard plus myself and a couple of others holding the struggling Planter to the green felt operating table. Jim and his wife, Mary Lou, lived in the back of the place so it was easy to procure scissors and tweezers. The operation was underway!

Jim, who had the steadier hand, would snip the stitches. Then Leonard's pudgy fingers would gleefully grasp the loose ends with the tweezers and yank them from Planter's head, held in place by yours truly. The operation continued into the long Alaskan night despite Planter's frequent vulgar pronouncements. Though we probably did Planter a favor by removing those stitches before they became infected, I can certainly understand his unhappiness, staring up at that fiendish hospital crew.

"The name's Planter!" was heard no more that night, nor ever again at Diamond Jim's Bar (now defunct), formerly of Portage (now defunct). But it's been resounding off the walls of my brain ever since.

Mt. Everest, First Attempt, North Side, 1990

Half a world and decades away from Diamond Jim's, still in bed at the Yak and Yeti Hotel in Kathmandu, Nepal, Shelli and I were awakened by a very loud explosion early in the morning of March 1, 1990. We soon discovered there was no electricity. There had been a lot of civil unrest in the city and we thought perhaps someone had blown up a power plant or transmission line, but whatever had been the cause of the interruption, the power was restored within the hour. We had already returned to bed, thinking that was probably the prudent way to respond to a violent revolution in which we had no discernible personal stake.

There were still hard feelings between Shelli and me, especially on her side, and we had not as yet renewed our vows, but she had agreed to travel with me to Kathmandu and see me off to Tibet in my attempt to climb Mt. Everest. We stopped in Tokyo on the way and were met by Shelli's friend, Yuko Kuwai, with whom we spent a full day. She took us on the subway to the fish market, a religious shrine, the Ginza district, and later, to a sushi bar tucked into a narrow street one block from the fish market.

Arriving in Bangkok we took a van from the airport to the Oriental Hotel. After three hours of driving around, dropping off other people and looking for their obscure hotels, I had had enough and told the driver to let us out along Thanon Sukhumvit. We unloaded our abundance of baggage onto the sidewalk, had a taxi within minutes, and were at the Oriental Hotel in less than ten.

After cleaning up Shelli and I had a hotel driver take us to the Seafood Market Restaurant, my favorite dining experience in Bangkok. The wait staff remembered me from previous visits and crowded around for Chilkoot Charlie cloisonné pins. Soon the entire staff of dozens was proudly sporting my logo. One fellow proudly showed me that he was still wearing the one I had given him two years before.

The Seafood Market Restaurant operates like a grocery store and a restaurant. Moving along the back wall with your grocery cart from left to right, you select first from mostly French wines, then every imaginable kind of seafood, much of it still alive and including some varieties you've probably never seen or heard of. Then, moving farther to the left, you select fresh vegetables and finally fresh fruits. Someone will help you choose, slipping your selections into little plastic bags and onto your cart, making suggestions about what item might go well with another. You roll your cart to the central checkout station, where everything is tallied and you pay your bill. Then someone else guides you to your table. I like to sit out in the open-air patio, surrounded by tropical plants, where the big, stone grill is located. Once seated, you discuss how you want things prepared and in what order you want them served. Then you just sit back and wait for it to come. It is always way too much, but there are plenty of stray cats wandering around the premises to assist with that problem.

The next morning we got up early and took a taxi to the airport. The others in our expedition had stayed overnight at the Amari Airport Hotel, and were already at the counter checking in. The Amari Airport Hotel has a very convenient arrangement, being attached to the terminal from across the street by an elevated, air-conditioned overpass.

Right after being informed I owed $200 in overweight charges, I was told Shelli didn't have a Bangkok-Kathmandu-Bangkok ticket. We had an exciting last-minute adventure running to another counter through the throngs of people to buy her missing ticket, paying overweight charges, then running back through more throngs of people to the original counter, nearly missing our flight. Our travel agent had been one of my ex-girlfriends and Shelli was inclined to think the incident wasn't a mistake. It probably wasn't.

Our group had a lot of gear and customs officials at the Kathmandu Airport looked into every bag and every box. It took hours. They also took five members of the group into private rooms and searched them physically.

One of our guides was Peter Habeler, a wiry, energetic-looking man who, along with Reinhold Messner, had been the first to climb Mt. Everest without oxygen. Martin Zabaleta—another guide, a Basque, and the first Spaniard to climb Mt. Everest—was more heavily built. Still another was Vern Tejas, who I already knew from my Aconcagua expedition. The expedition leader was Todd Burleson of Alpine Ascents International, with whom I had also summited Mt. Aconcagua. The first night in Kathmandu, we all went out for a spaghetti dinner in the Tamil district. I brought along some Chilkoot Charlie's Sourdough Ale and had it chilled down before serving; it was a big hit. Peter Habeler, an Austrian, said, "I love it and I know my beers. It reminds me of a Czechoslovakian beer."

After changing currency and shopping the next day we attended a surprise birthday party for Todd in the Potala Guest House and had a Thai dinner at the Yak and Yeti before retiring. The following day Shelli and I were fortunate to be able to purchase some Thanka paintings in the morning because all the shops closed midday in support of a national strike. Nepalese soldiers were everywhere in riot gear, carrying bamboo sticks, rifles and unfriendly dispositions. We had a stressful moment when our rickshaw driver turned into a square where a mob was on one side and military police were closing on them from the other. The driver got us out of there in a hurry. There was a demonstration planned for someplace, but we never saw it. Nor did we see any actual physical violence between soldiers and populace, but the circumstances were certainly ripe for it. The strike itself was successful, with virtually all the shops being closed except for the food purveyors.

I had a lengthy conversation with a well-spoken Nepalese merchant while we waited for authorization of my American Express purchase.

He explained, "The people want to retain the king because they love him and feel that he adds legitimacy to the nation, making it less likely that India will 'absorb' us."

India is the very large, wealthy and powerful neighbor with whom they conduct ninety percent of their commerce.

"The people," he continued, "want a British-style monarchy, where the king is a figurehead and the country is run democratically. As it is, the king still has the final word around here." The merchant went on to say, "I think the king is a good man and I am optimistic he will do the right thing. The problem is the people surrounding him."

I said, "Well, you will soon know whether the king is a good man or not by whether he listens to the people or to the people surrounding him."

Later, we caught a taxi to the Swayambhunath Temple, or "Monkey Temple," which is virtually overrun with the little critters. The temple is on a prominent hill with a good overview of the city, but there were lots of little Nepalese kids playing in the area who were better photographic subjects. Prior to leaving Alaska, Shelli and I had made up one hundred two-inch diameter lapel pins with a photo of a smiling, gesticulating Dalai Lama on them. We figured they would be well-received, but we had no idea. The kids went absolutely crazy over them, surging around us and shouting in a frenzy, "Dalai Lama! Dalai Lama!"

The expedition was scheduled to leave Kathmandu for the Chinese border on Saturday, March 3, and Shelli was scheduled to depart late in the day on Sunday, but the organizers of the expedition couldn't get all the shopping, dealing with the notoriously corrupt and inept Nepalese bureaucracy, and all the gear loaded in time to meet the schedule, so Shelli and I had an extra day together. She had been consistently bratty and snotty with me on the trip and I found myself wondering how long I was going to be able to tolerate it, contrite or not. In Anchorage, we were still living apart, and I was obviously not forgiven for my infidelities. However, we had a very warm and intimate experience before breakfast. She had gotten out of bed right away and was showered and half-way dressed before I got up and moving—an uncommon occurrence—so I was prepared for an arm's length separation that would have left me despondent. I felt forgiven and whole again.

Breakfast was with Norm, a fellow climber, and Bob John, my buddy from Denali and Aconcagua. Then Shelli and I went to the Tibetan Refuge Center, purchased a couple of beautiful Tibetan rugs, one with the Tibetan name for Everest, Qomolangma, (goddess of mountain) worked into the design, and almost started a riot with Dalai Lama pins. There was quite a frenzy of grasping and wailing when I ran out, so I started handing out Chilkoot Charlie's cloisonné pins, which were just as eagerly snatched from my hands by the throng. Finally I resorted to handing out little orange pins with the outline of Chilkoot Charlie in white.

The next day, Shelli and I arrived at the airport a couple of hours early and experienced the usual problems, including an $111 overweight charge just to Tokyo, where Shelli would spend more time with her friend Yuko. I later discovered that a bronze and copper statue of the elephant-headed Hindu god Ganesha, son of Shiva and lord of success, caused intense scrutiny in Tokyo's Narita Airport, leaving Shelli the only traveler in a gigantic customs and immigration room. Before her departure from Kathmandu we had some time for a couple of beers and a serious conversation in the lounge.

Shelli said, "It's been hard for me to be nice to you on this trip and now, as I'm leaving, I feel terrible about it."

I said, "It's too bad it has to be that way because I've tried to make amends for over two years. You remaining mad at me all this time reminds me of my being mad at my dad all those years. It's damaging to yourself and your relations with everyone else, especially me. One day you love me; the next day you hate me. I'm trying my best, but I must tell you, it's pretty discouraging."

In Anchorage, Shelli and I had reached a comfortable arrangement living separately, though it confused our friends, who would sometimes say they didn't understand our relationship. We both knew we didn't want to be with anyone else, but we weren't going to rush into living together again either. We both liked our space.

I figured she'd have three months to think things over and hoped the Everest expedition would usher in a watershed in our lives, the statistical chance of us never seeing each other again being one in ten.

From Zhang Mu, Tibet, I wrote her a postcard that said, "I'm having mixed feelings about our trip, but I'm very glad you said what you did at the airport. I think of you often and wish so much that we could turn back the clock. Please try to forgive me and think well of me. I do love you dearly and wish for the best for us. I'll write as often as possible. So far, so good. I love you, Michael."

I spent my last night in Kathmandu with the rest of the expedition at the Potala Guest House, and had breakfast with everyone the next morning at 6:00 a.m., after which we climbed into a bus and headed for the Chinese border, followed by two heavily loaded trucks. We stopped for lunch at a small town named Bharabase, finding ourselves in the middle of a festive wedding ceremony. Lunch itself was pretty basic, consisting of *dahl bhat*, or rice with little lentil beans in it. The road to the border was crude and downright precarious in places. We saw people fishing from the riverbank with long wooden poles; others made gravel from larger stones by hand, sitting on the ground cross-legged and pounding the stones with hammers, stacking the final hard-won product, in long concentric rows around them.

We arrived at the border with Tibet around noon, processed through Nepalese immigration and customs with no problems, then pulled up to the "Friendship Bridge," aptly named since it is just wide enough for a Chinese tank to cross over if reassurance of the sincere mutual friendliness of the relationship is ever required.

Tibet, itself, is in such a friendly embrace as I write. I recently witnessed the sincerest expression of it: smartly dressed young Chinese soldiers attending machine guns set in sand bag emplacements on rooftops overlooking Barkhor Square in central Lhasa. That's where you'll find the Jokhang Temple—the first Buddhist temple in Tibet and part of the Potala Palace, centuries-old home of the Dalai Lama—itself with a Communist Chinese flag fluttering menacingly from its rooftop.

We unloaded our personal gear on the Nepalese side while the truck with the camp gear backed across the bridge and unloaded on the Tibetan side. We enjoyed the sunny weather for an hour while our gear was carried over the bridge by porters. I imagined the worst about Chinese immigration and customs, and was particularly worried about them discovering my Dalai Lama buttons, which I had buried deep inside my sleeping bag before compressing it. To my relief, Chinese immigration was a breeze, with Vern playing his fiddle for them while they nosed around. They were teenagers for the most part, officious and courteous, dressed in part-civilian clothes and part-Chinese military uniforms. Vern and Todd knew a couple of the officials at customs and that went smoothly as well. The officials checked our passports, accepted our declaration forms, inspected our watches and jewelry, and looked into the expedition's walkie-talkie boxes.

By the time we got checked into the hotel, just across the street from customs, it was dark. After placing our gear in our rooms we all met downstairs for an excellent Chinese dinner. The hotel was distinctly and drably Communist in appearance, but better than anything I had experienced in Russia, and the food was vastly superior.

I shared a room with Norm. Around 3:00 a.m., we were both awakened in the pitch dark by a loud scurrying across the concrete floor between our beds, headed in the direction of the bathroom. The sound had obviously been made by a large, four-legged creature.

I said, "Did you hear that?"

Norm said, "I sure did!"

I said, "That was no cockroach!"

We jumped out of bed, turned the lights on, armed ourselves with ice axes and approached the bathroom with extreme caution. We never saw the rat. We had expected to find him cornered and ready for a fight, so the adrenalin was up, but he had made his escape through a good-sized opening in the wall just above the lip of the tub. Needless to say, neither of us could get back to sleep right away and, in spite of my best efforts, I kept trying to visualize that rat and how big it must have been.

In the morning we had fun trying to use the shower, which had an in-line heater that didn't work and leaked all over the place. There was an old hand lever switch on the device and the electrical wires were bare. We tinkered with it, all the while afraid of electrocuting ourselves, finally settling for cold showers—so cold that washing my hair gave me a headache.

After breakfast, Bob and I went to the bank with Kelsun, a multilingual Nepalese member of the expedition. The bank was about two hundred fifty vertical feet above us, and climbing up through the narrow passageways at seven thousand feet of altitude made me acutely aware of my couple of months of inactivity. After exchanging some U.S. currency for Chinese, we ascended another two hundred fifty feet to the post office and spent the next hour and a half on my cachets. We would never have been able to get the job done without Kelsun. The postal clerks were cooperative, but it was a large, complicated transaction for them and they didn't understand what I was trying to accomplish. Relieved that the ritual was complete we walked back down the hill taking photos of the locals coming and going. One memorable shot was of a barefoot middle-aged man carrying on his shoulders a couple of huge squared logs—each about eight inches by eight inches by eight feet—up a steep hill toward us, using only a strap.

The next day we reached Shegar, the closest settlement to the road leading to Mt. Everest Base Camp, after a twelve hour drive. We were welcomed by members of Jim Whittaker's Earth Day 20 International Peace Climb expedition and invited to join them for dinner. The purpose of Whittaker's internationally recognized expedition was to put a Russian, a Chinese and an American on the summit simultaneously.

The road out of Zhang Mu had featured steep inclines, heart-stopping declines, and bottomless chasms on the downhill side with no safety barriers. I felt fortunate to be in a nimble Isuzu four-wheel-drive vehicle instead of in one of the big old Chinese army trucks some people were riding in. Vern, Willy (another guide who worked for Todd) and all the Sherpas stayed behind to sort and load gear. When our Chinese driver discovered there were to be two passengers in the front seat, Peter Arndt, a friend of Todd's and supposedly base camp manager, had to get out and remain behind also. Our driver looked like a stereotypical Chinese Communist Party functionary in his khaki suit and hat with a red star emblazoned on the front of it. He was also a jerk, and loved leering at the girls off on the side of the road doing their business, there being nowhere else for them to do it because the edges on either side were either straight up or straight down.

On the Tibetan plateau the weather improved, as did the roads, but I had never seen a more barren landscape and couldn't imagine how people might eke out an existence there. It was surreal. At midafternoon we were presented with our first view of Mt. Everest. Stopping on the outskirts of a small village to take some photographs I took what I believe to be the best photograph of my years of climbing. An obviously poor, dirty, but rustically handsome and happy Tibetan family stands in the road with the Himalayas in the background. The portly grandmother on the left and two younger children in the foreground are looking at the camera. In the background, the mother of the family looks with unbridled pride at her eldest son, a young man who is himself smiling at the camera. I was to witness more simple lives, simple pleasures, and genuine familial happiness in Nepal. After taking the photo I gave the family a couple of Dalai Lama buttons and sprinted for the bus.

We saw four other eight-thousand-meter peaks on the drive to Shegar. When we first entered the plateau country we got a glimpse of Sisha Pangma (26,397 feet), the fourteenth highest of the eight-thousand-meter peaks. Later, when we first spotted Mt. Everest, we could also see fifth-highest Makalu (27,766 feet), on the left, fourth-highest Lhotse (27,940 feet), in the middle, and sixth-highest Cho Oyu (26,906 feet), on the right.

The plateau is huge. As you drive across it you see one village after another roll into view, usually quite a distance apart and juxtaposed with the remains of ancient cities, temples or fortresses along the river valleys and surrounding slopes. The landscape, though barren, has an almost fairyland, storybook appearance.

In Shegar we were housed in an austere, two-story block building of the same unmistakable communist-era "people's architecture." The toilets were the stand-while-using variety, but the place was clean and there were two heavy comforters on each bed, a night stand with two basins, and a hot water canister in each room, as well as an extra-large canister at the end of the hallway from which we could refill the one in our room. Norm and I shared one room. Bob and Brad shared another. We found the thermoses and heavy comforters to be essential since water left in the sinks overnight froze solid.

After Todd, Vern, Peter and the Sherpas arrived with our camp gear the next morning, we all had breakfast together around 9:30 a.m., and I had the opportunity to visit with Jim Whittaker, a very nice fellow. Jim had been a member of the 1963 American Mount Everest Expedition, led by Norman Dyhrenfurth. On May 1 of that year, along with Sherpa Nawang Gombu, the nephew of Tenzing Norgay (who had summited with Edmund Hillary), Whittaker became the first American to stand on the summit of Mt. Everest, despite having run out of oxygen. Jim's peace climb expedition, in which he was not a participating climber, was well-financed and publicized. They were also well-equipped. They had, among other things, one hundred fifty titanium oxygen tanks and two satellite hookups with which they planned to communicate with President Bush, President Gorbachev and Chinese "Paramount Leader," Jiang Zemin from the summit of Mt. Everest on Earth Day. By comparison, our expedition's outfitting was paltry.

I was not happy about being left in Shegar with Brad, Norm, Vern and Ellie while Bob and everyone else went ahead to Base Camp. Nor was Norm, though Brad had planned to stay anyway because of a head cold. Norm and I felt the expedition's purpose should be to get paying climbers to the summit and keep us all together. We were worried that Todd had us along to pay for the experience while he summited, perhaps bringing along one paying client, such as Bob. These were the sort of thoughts and feelings that are rife on big mountain expeditions, though in this case no one was to get anywhere near the summit anyway.

Shegar was an armpit, the food was terrible, and the lights were turned out by 9:00 p.m., so you couldn't do anything but go to bed and attempt to sleep for twelve hours every night, which is hard to do. With plenty of daylight time on my hands I had been busily decorating the building we were in, as well as others, with Chilkoot Charlie decals. I also placed them on our trucks and jeeps. One of our Chinese truck drivers who had a sticker on only one side of his truck's hood refused to perform his job until he got a sticker on the other side as well. I had no more on me, but since another driver had one on each side of his hood, this guy would not budge until his truck was equally adorned. I managed to find a lapel pin that satisfied him and later, after replenishing my supply, I put a decal on the other side of his truck's hood. He lit up like a light bulb.

Whittaker's expedition left Shegar on Saturday morning to much fanfare, including a Tibetan television crew that arrived after the expedition had already departed. Meanwhile, we waited around for another hour and a half processing papers and obtaining gas for our vehicles. During the wait, I had what I felt was a close call with Chinese authorities.

I was aware of a recent international incident in which a Chinese soldier tried to rip a T-shirt with the likeness of "Sergeant Bilko" off of a young British female tourist named Kris Tait, mistaking the actor Phil Silvers for the Dalai Lama. A group of Tibetans gathered around shouting, "Dalai Lama!" as she wrenched herself free to replace her clothing. That incident was one of the reasons I had been so cautious about how I brought my Dalai Lama pins into the country and at least tried to be discrete about how I doled them out. I suppose it's appropriate to ask why I did it at all. My best explanation is that it was a personal act of civil disobedience in sympathy with the Tibetan people, though it might as easily be described as just plain stupid.

It started with me giving a couple of buttons to a little girl and her younger sister outside the compound in front of where we had been lodged. The girls pinned them on the outside of their clothes and then told the first people they encountered where they had gotten them. These people now wanted some, so I acted like I didn't understand what they wanted in order to avoid starting a riot. The little girls began playing around in the middle of the compound, perhaps a hundred yards distant, when a couple of Chinese ladies approached them and I could tell the girls were showing off their buttons. Then the girls pointed at me. The Chinese ladies looked at me and the next thing I knew, there was an armed Chinese soldier in the group and he was looking at me, too.

To my enormous relief, the soldier continued on his way across the compound. The ladies also went on their way and the little girls continued to play. As soon as I felt it was safe, I dumped the four remaining buttons I had on me in the brush behind the compound. I imagined myself sitting in a Chinese prison, beaten up, telling my captors through broken teeth that I wanted to talk to my friend, U.S. Senator Frank Murkowski, when our ride arrived. I was still worried about passing the checkpoint through which we had previously passed on our way to the road to Everest Base Camp. Vern was worried, too, because he didn't have his passport with him. It had been sent ahead to Base Camp with his personal gear. As it turned out, our concerns were totally unfounded because we passed through the checkpoint without even being stopped.

We caught up with Whittaker's group when they stopped at the top of a pass to take in the panorama of Mt. Everest, Cho Oyu and Makalu. They had spent an hour at the checkpoint that we had driven straight through. It was a crystal-clear day and everyone was visiting and photographing the spectacular array of eight thousand meter peaks.

Jim Whittaker was standing next to Vern, so I walked over and asked, "Mr. Whittaker, would you do me the honor of having your picture taken with me?"

"Sure," he said. "Let's walk over here where there are no other people in the way."

We had two photos taken by their group's physician, Kurt Papenfus. A year before I wouldn't have been able to tell you who Jim Whittaker was. Six months earlier I would have been happy just to have seen or met him. He hadn't been back to Mt. Everest in twenty-seven years and now I found myself having my photo taken with him, the mountain in the background.

The rest of the drive to Base Camp was scenic, though mostly barren hills and valleys and occasional small Tibetan settlements. We stopped at the Rongbuk Monastery, a perfect place from which to photograph the north face of Mt. Everest, though the monastery itself had been mostly destroyed by the Chinese. Arriving at Base Camp around 4:00 p.m. on Friday, March 11, I put my gear into a four-man tent with Vern and Bob. I was dealing with some altitude adjustment issues, but next morning I woke up feeling fine with a pulse of seventy-two. We had breakfast of scrambled eggs, bacon and potatoes. I helped myself to two large servings.

The next day a group of us hiked a couple of hours up a frozen river that ran out of the Rongbuk Glacier. The scenery reminded me a lot of the Horcones Valley on the way into Base Camp on Aconcagua. The mountains on our left were almost identical to the Andes, the main difference being seven to ten thousand feet of altitude and a looming Mt. Everest. On our return we walked into Whittaker's camp and visited with Dr. Papenfus, who accompanied us up a small hill that overlooked their camp. On the top of the hill were a number of rock cairns with slate nameplates and carved messages—memorials to climbers who had perished on the north side of the mountain. I got emotional when I looked down and saw the one dedicated to Marty Hoey, a climber on the one expedition attempted by Dick Bass on the north side of Everest. The two had been close friends. Dick looked down to see Marty below him. A moment later he looked again and saw nothing but an empty harness. Having read The Seven Summits twice, I almost felt like I had known her.

The one and only item missing from our group's gear upon arrival at Base Camp was a box filled with trail mix that Shelli and I had spent a lot of time and money on, not to mention excess baggage charges. We had scrounged around Anchorage stores, buying a combination of nuts, candy and dried fruits in bulk and then measuring out the appropriate amounts into single Ziploc bags. Having the bags of mix was important to me because I don't have an appetite for a lot of camp food and I was planning on having something to eat as an alternative. One staple on the mountains, for instance, is oatmeal. Though I don't mind eating oatmeal at sea level, I cannot stand to even smell the stuff at altitude. I would rather starve than eat it. The culprit in my mind was one of Todd's employees, Peter, the person supposedly in charge of logistics, who had also been on the Aconcagua expedition. I hadn't been impressed with him in Argentina and I wasn't impressed with him in Tibet. He was lazy and incompetent, and he had a bad attitude. Fortunately, it wasn't until I had returned to Kathmandu that I learned Shelli had secretly slipped photos, poems, love notes and mementos into each trail mix bag inside that box.

On Tuesday, an elderly lama and his protégé arrived and put on an impressive ceremony atop a knoll between our camp and Whittaker's. They sat cross-legged on mats, chanting and ringing bells while the rest of the Sherpas erected a twelve-foot bamboo pole, anchoring it by pulling long ropes covered with prayer flags in five different directions. We all presented gifts of various kinds to the lama, in my case pictures and buttons of the Dalai Lama, all done out of view of the Chinese liaison officer we were required to have with us and who was basically a spy.

After the monks departed, we held a group meeting in the mess tent to familiarize ourselves with the Gamow bag, a sturdy, rubber bag with a plastic window on top at one end. You can slip a person with severe altitude sickness into the bag and still see their face through the plastic window. The atmospheric pressure inside the bag is increased with a foot pump; it's a simple but effective device. One of our guides, Willy, climbed in with his altimeter for a demonstration of how well it worked. We took him from 17,300 feet down to 11,300 feet in ten minutes.

Bob and I went for a climb that turned into quite an excursion. We climbed about two thousand vertical feet up a mountain to the west of Base Camp, turning back at the base of some chimney rocks that formed the summit. I was feeling frisky, leading us higher and higher until Base Camp was a little speck and Bob said, "If you screw up your health on this climb you won't have anyone to blame but yourself."

Dinner of spinach soup, beans, corn bread and boiled potatoes was excellent. After a game of hearts with Bob, Brad and Willy, I related a story from my childhood about a moose hunting trip I went on with my dad's friend, Bill Peters. Bill owned the Portage Garage, south of Anchorage, before the 1964 earthquake lowered the ground level six feet and Portage became a saltwater slough. Everyone was entertained by the tale and it occurred to me that it would make a good short story, so I wrote it down and read it to the whole expedition at Advance Base Camp later. They loved it, and those that followed. Thus began my writing career, such as it is.

Our expedition employed a few Tibetan yak drivers to haul our gear as far as Advance Base Camp. They were real Eastern-style hombres, living right next to us in their rustic yak hide tents. They looked like Hollywood adventure-movie types with their clothing of heavy, coarse material and fur ruffles, their long black hair sometimes in braids. Their weathered, dark faces, were neither Oriental nor Indian, but something ruggedly and handsomely in between, and they wore rings and earrings of silver, coral and turquoise. The yaks themselves were interesting critters, very well adapted to cold and altitude, each with a distinctive appearance and personality. They move at the same steady pace regardless of whether they're going uphill or down. The morning we left for Advance Base Camp, the drivers called the yaks by name and they all came into camp, some more readily than others. They also understood commands on the trail and the drivers whistled a constant soothing refrain to them, escalating to louder, sharper whistles to get their attention when necessary. They all wore bells around their necks and tassels on their ears. Between all the whistling and the bells clanging, I had plenty of audible entertainment while walking along.

The climb to Advance Base Camp was tougher than I had anticipated. My legs were sore and I had started taking tetracycline to break up my head and chest congestion, which had worsened due to the activities of the previous two days—just as Bob had warned. At Advance Base Camp we each got private tents. I got a brand new three-man tent that Lapca Rita Sherpa helped me erect. Suddenly I had lots of room and privacy, and lots of time, so I applied myself to more story writing. I would lie in my sleeping bag, think the whole story through and just write it down in a spiral notebook. Then I'd recite it to the group in the mess tent at dinner time.

The paying climbers had broken into two groups: Bob and me and Brad and Norm. Norm, a single, twenty-six-year-old research engineer from Massachusetts, was having intestinal problems and was still in Base Camp. He had climbed Mt. Rainier and a couple of nineteen-thousand-foot volcanoes in Mexico. Brad was a real estate agent from Denver, a few months older than me, who had quit his job before joining the expedition. He had been climbing for fifteen years and had summited Denali, Vinson Massif, Aconcagua, Kilimanjaro and some others.

On Friday, March 17, all the guides and climbers walked over to a ridge above camp with a good view of the mountain. It was apparent that Todd and the guides had already discussed the route for which Todd had a permit, the Super Couloir, a very steep, tiny gully running straight up the north face of the mountain. We would be exposed to falling snow, ice and rocks the whole way. The Super Couloir had been successfully climbed only once, by a couple of experienced Swiss climbers, and it was not, to say the least, a suitable route for our group. I assume that's why Todd promoted having Peter and Martin as guides, so the focus was on the guides instead of the route.

The discussion led to a plan of attack that involved traversing the West Ridge from the western end of the massif, then crossing to the bottom of the Hornbein by way of the "Ditch." The new plan was a relief to me because I didn't want to have anything to do with the Super Couloir. However, a German climber named Misha, camped near our Camp I, held the only permit for the West Ridge. We were assured that Todd, Peter and Martin would work things out with him.

I was taking tetracycline for my cough. Todd suggested that if the tetracycline didn't rid me of my cough, I might cure it with erythromycin—but any kind of cure is a tall order at over eighteen thousand feet. I had begun to cough all night long, not getting much rest, because if I stayed on my back I couldn't sleep and if I turned on either side I couldn't control the coughing. Over the next few days I made several forays toward Camp I, but I felt so badly that on one trip with Bob I was ready to just gather my gear and return to Base Camp. Finally, I went to visit Anne, our homeopathic nurse, who said I had a pulse of sixty-four and clear lungs. She gave me some of the erythromycin that Todd had suggested, saying that it had an eighty-five percent success rate for the type of symptoms I was experiencing. She also gave me a long back massage to loosen the phlegm in my chest, which was above and beyond the call of duty. I started feeling better almost immediately and my spirits improved, so I planned on making a full carry of my gear to Camp I soon.

Both Advance Base Camp and Base Camp were hammered by fierce winds for three days. Sadly, I learned that Norm was going home via Lhasa. He was one of the guys in the expedition that I liked most and it upset me that he would spend so much money and leave so soon. The "Crazy German," as the climber with the West Ridge permit was known by now, had fired all his Sherpas. He claimed they were stealing. They claimed he was crazy. I thought it highly unlikely the Sherpas were stealing, but not at all unlikely that Misha was crazy from what I had seen of him. He spent an entire day in our camp, during which time Todd and he negotiated on the use of his permit. Misha, having summarily fired all his Sherpas, didn't have the strongest hand to play. During the storm it was too cold in the tent to either read or write, so I spent a lot of time in the mess tent, eating and playing hearts, or just lying around in my sleeping bag thinking. I thought a lot about my business, my life, and my relationship with Shelli, and spent a lot of time wondering what the hell I was doing on the north side of Mt. Everest. Was I trying to avoid my problems, as Shelli had declared before my Denali climb? Funny thing about that, though. Wherever you go, there they are.

In a letter to Shelli the next day I said, "I think about you constantly and hope so much that we can start out anew when I return, not being afraid to be in love again. I'd like just one more chance to show you how much I love you and how good I can be for you. I've never had such an enduring love for anyone. There are so many ways that we're right for each other, so many good times we've had and so many things we enjoy together. Please don't be mad at me anymore and try to love me as you once did. There's so much potential happiness to be found by the two of us and it all seems so senseless otherwise. Give yourself and me another chance, please. I love you, Michael."

On Monday, March 26, I made a carry to Camp I—almost. I was the last to arrive and only five minutes from the actual site when Vern came running down, gave me his pack in exchange for mine, and told me to head back immediately. I didn't argue. The weather was terrible and Camp I was a mess. Tents were torn and broken, with equipment and supplies scattered about. That evening in Advance Base Camp my coughing fits progressed to a new level. I coughed so hard and long that I injured my torso. I wasn't sure whether I had pulled something or cracked a rib. From then on I had to grasp myself around my rib cage with both arms and hold on tightly during my constant coughing fits in an effort to contain the pain.

By the 28th everyone who was still on the mountain was at Advance Base Camp, but Peter had arrived in such bad shape that he was put in the Gamow bag. That night, my cough was so persistent and my side so sore that I got no sleep at all. I was a mess in the morning. I refused Sherpa tea and Vern came over to visit when I didn't show for breakfast. When he saw my condition, he sent Anne over. She gave me an eight-hundred-gram Ibuprofen pill and rubbed some homeopathic cream on my injured rib area, which was bruised and swollen. I stayed in my sleeping bag all day, Anne visiting at intervals to massage my ribs. She brought me breakfast and lunch while I read, napped, coughed. It wasn't all bad, having a beautiful, affectionate nurse-attendant looking after me.

I thought my trip was over but, with Anne's attentions and a better night of sleep on the Ibuprofen, I felt well again the next day. Though my rib still hurt, my cough was almost gone and I prepared to make another carry. According to Anne, there was absolutely no congestion in my lungs and my pulse was sixty while sitting up in the tent. However, on midmorning of the 29th I had an exceedingly painful coughing fit, with a sensation of an actual dislocation in my rib cage. Afterwards, if I moved the wrong way I would feel a painful pop at the lower left anterior edge of my rib cage. I later learned I had torn my intercostal muscles, which run between the ribs and help expand and contract the rib cage with every breath.

I screamed across camp for Anne. She came right away and said, "I think it's time for Kurt Papenfus to take a look at you. He may be coming up in a day or two." Kurt was the doctor with the Whittaker expedition with whom I had visited at their Base Camp.

As caring as she was, she was not a physician, and I had had enough homeopathy, however pleasantly administered. So I told her, "I think the game is over for me. I need to go down—now."

I was in so much pain I could hardly move. We summoned Todd, who agreed I should go down and started making immediate preparations. I left all the Dalai Lama pins with him and the cachets and Chilkoot Charlie's flag with Vern, who assured me he would get them as high as possible. I left for Base Camp around 2:00 p.m., with Peter Habeler and Martin Zabaleta as escorts. Anne came along and Ang Tsering carried the bulk of my gear. I carried only my large pack with a smaller one inside it.

It was an awkward and emotional departure from the dismal setting of Advance Base Camp. Various people assured me I would be returning though I knew in my heart I would not. The descent to Base Camp took about three hours and, upon arriving, we went directly to the first aid tent of the Whittaker Camp. I was laid out under a large down blanket, given some tea, and soon Kurt Papenfus appeared with a Russian doctor in tow. It didn't take them long to misdiagnose me.

The Russian doctor placed a stethoscope on my chest, loudly and forcefully proclaiming, "Pnumonee!"

Kurt said, after listening himself, "I don't hear the pneumonia, but maybe I just can't hear as well." The Russian kept repeating, "Pnumonee!" over and over.

Perhaps Dr. Papenfus was trying to avoid an international incident when he capitulated so readily. I was told I also had pleurisy, but no broken ribs. I asked if I would be able to recuperate at Base Camp and return to the expedition and was told, in no uncertain terms, that my trip was over and I might as well go home. I was simultaneously relieved and disappointed. It was nice to have a professional diagnosis—even though it turned out to be entirely wrong—and to feel like I knew what I had to do. It took a little while for the depression to set in.

I had dinner that night in the Whittaker mess tent, consisting of wonderfully real food, and retired early. I drifted into a restful sleep listening to Kurt, Peter, Anne and others next door socializing and enjoying that nasal country magnificence known as Willie Nelson on someone's radio. I also learned there were a couple of Swedes in camp who worked for a college newspaper in Stockholm. They had brought tuxedos with them for campy photos and an interview with Habeler, Zabaleta and Whittaker in front of Mt. Everest. After the photo session and interviews they would be returning to Kathmandu. Aside from theirs, the next known departure from Base Camp was in ten days. I felt I would be extremely lucky to hitch a ride with the Swedes rather than wait around desolate base camp, sick and depressed, for those ten days.

Next morning I asked the Swedes, Mattias and Jesper, if I could join them. They immediately said, "No problem." We took the photos of them in their formal wear among the climbing celebrities and when the liaison officer finally got out of bed, Kelsun got him to write me a letter for the immigration officials in Zhang Mu.

When they could manage it during the unnecessarily crashing, jarring descent in the Toyota SUV, Mattias and Jesper interviewed Jampa, our interpreter, for their college newspaper. He was surprisingly candid about his political views, saying that he lived in Lhasa and had been educated in Beijing. He loved all things American except the violence in our movies, an observation I found noteworthy. When we got to the main road everyone applauded, with the exception of our chain-smoking Chinese driver.

We stopped at a small, rustic, Tibetan roadhouse where we had some tea, a can of sliced pineapple and some meat that looked like Spam. Jampa and the driver ate some yak meat cut from a side of yak standing in one of the corners, no doubt a healthier choice. The proprietor and his family were camera-shy, but after our bill had been tabulated on an abacus, Mattias gave the weathered old fellow a little hand-held calculator. He grinned widely and agreed to pose for photos with us.

Our gourmet lunch over, we continued over the high pass and into the long valley running down to Zhang Mu, forever after known to me as the "White Knuckle Highway." Snow was piled high on the sides of the narrow roadway, which was littered with huge boulders, recently fallen from the mountain side. Between the boulders were snow and rock slides. We beeped and roared around the eroded, narrow corners gaping into the vast nothingness below. At least my ribs didn't hurt because I was so numb with fear. As it got darker, our driver began switching on his headlights instead of beeping as he approached blind corners. He didn't turn them on and leave them on until it was practically pitch black and we were on the outskirts of Zhang Mu, where a small leopard flew through the beams of light and across the roadway in front of us.

Zhang Mu was a sight for sore eyes. We had dinner at 11:00 p.m., drank three beers each and shared a room with three beds for twenty-one dollars, including breakfast. Fortunately, the night passed without any four-legged visitors. Going through customs in the morning one of the officials showed me a photo of Todd and asked if I knew him.

I replied, "Yes. He's the leader of our expedition."

He then showed me two traveler's checks from Todd missing the second signature. I shrugged, hoping he wasn't going to expect me to cover them and said, "He'll be back through in May," which seemed to satisfy the guy. He let me proceed.

We paid four teenagers 150 rupees each, or about five dollars, to carry our bags down to the Friendship Bridge, walking with them through the woods instead of following the road with its numerous switchbacks. At the Nepalese border I had to buy another visa for ten dollars. The immigration official wanted a photo of me for his form, so I told him I had one in my pack back at customs and when I got my bags I would bring it to him. He gave me the stamp I needed in my passport and that was the last he ever saw of me. We hired an Indian taxi driver to drive us to Kathmandu for forty dollars, for which I volunteered to pay, and we were off to the big city. It was a long drive, stopping many times at road toll stations and once for the driver to eat. When you arrive in Nepal from the west it seems primitive, but when arriving from Tibet it is absolutely cosmopolitan. Nepal is rich and glamorous by comparison to the part of Tibet I saw, which was still practically in the Bronze Age.

I spent a couple of evenings with Jesper and Mattias in Kathmandu. Norm, who was having an affair with an English girl he had ridden out of Base Camp with, looked me up and joined the Swedes and me for dinner one night. I spent a couple hundred dollars on phone calls, talking with my business manager, my mom and Shelli. From Shelli I learned about the photos, poems, love notes and mementos in the missing trail mix bags. I was almost ready to return to Advance Base Camp to use an ice axe on Peter. Half my time around Shelli over the past couple of years it was hard to tell whether she still loved me or not, so it would have meant a great deal to me to have had those items when I was alone in my tent coughing.

A visit to a local physician established that I had not the slightest sign of pneumonia. Things were going well at the club and the strikes in Nepal were becoming more frequent and more violent, so I decided to fly to Thailand and spend a couple weeks on the beach in Phuket or Pattaya.

In spite of my depression about my poor performance on Everest, I was determined to continue pursuing the Seven Summits. My plan was to climb Elbrus in September, Vinson in December, then Kosciuszko and Everest in 1992.

The preceding chapter is what the Chinese Communist government demanded to be removed from this book in its entirety. I refused to comply and spent an additional $8,186.00 to have the book printed in the U.S. All but a handful of the original books printed in China, which had been "FedExed" out of the country to be used for promotional purposes, were banned by the Chinese authorities before they could be containerized and shipped to the U.S.

This is a perfect example of how the tyrannical Chinese Communist government operates, not to mention, their bullying of U.S. companies that operate inside the Communist regime, their theft of American technology, their widespread cheating on agreed-upon behavior of World Trade Organization members, their defying of the Monroe Doctrine in South America, their expanding hegemony in Asia and their increasing military aggressiveness toward their neighbors, as well as the West.

Thank goodness the U.S. finally has a president who is willing to stand up to what is clearly a "bad actor" on the world stage.

The Hired Gun

My mountaineering challenges still two decades into the future, a more sinister sort of challenge hit the streets of Spenard in the early '70s, starting with a motorcycle gang in Anchorage named The Brothers. Rumor had it that when one of them died, the rest would cremate him, roll some of his remains into a marijuana joint and smoke him, taking brotherly love to an all new high.

Someone in the gang got the bright idea of teaming up with the Hell's Angels, so then we had The Brothers roaring around town in Hell's Angels colors. If they decided to visit a bar, they would typically hang in a group and intimidate everyone else in the place, so at Chilkoot Charlie's we banned the wearing of colors. In fact, in the end we banned all manner of motorcycle clothing, right down to the Harley Davidson logo.

The gang then decided to sell "insurance" or "protection" to local bars. They began, logically enough, with the topless clubs, where they also had plans to control the flow of female dancers into the state. Jimmy Sumpter, an elderly gentleman who had already been to a rodeo or two, owned a couple such clubs, including a large operation a few miles out on the Old Seward Highway named the Kit Kat Club. Jimmy wasn't in the market for "insurance" or "protection." He also didn't harbor any desire for a gang of bikers to control the recruiting of his dancers. I am unaware of anyone who actually paid the protection fee, and the gang never acquired control over the comings and goings of dancers, but there was no doubt they took the proposition seriously.

Someone broke into Jimmy Sumpter's house, reportedly stole $20,000 and some jewelry, murdered his forty-year-old wife Marguerite and his stepson Richard Merck, then set fire to the place. Richard's half-sister miraculously escaped, returning through a window after the attack to try to save Richard, only to discover he had been shot to death. Had she not been sleeping in a bedroom with the door locked, she would no doubt have suffered the same fate.

I visited Jimmy at the Captain Cook Hotel, where he was living after the incident, and I can tell you firsthand that the desire for revenge was palpable. There wasn't any doubt in Jimmy's mind about who was responsible, either. His neighbor across the street had seen someone getting into a truck, careening away from the scene after the fire started, and she had the presence of mind to write down the license plate number. Police later matched it to that of Gary Zieger.

Zieger was a pledge for The Brothers/Hell's Angels, a vicious and unpredictable menace responsible for perhaps a dozen murders, including the kidnapping and murder of small-time gangster Johnny Rich, and the rape and murder of several young women—though he had avoided being convicted, mostly because of the rudimentary state of DNA testing at the time. No one will ever know exactly why Zieger broke into the Sumpter house and committed the murders. Did he do it on his own to impress the rest of the gang, simply for the money or because he'd been ordered to? The talk around town, though, was that Richard Merck's father had arrived from Fairbanks, and he and Jimmy were going to take care of the twenty-year-old Zieger once and for all. Jimmy put a reward of $10,000 cash out on the street for information about the murderer of his family, but rumor had it that it was really for killing a member of the gang, so the gang had motivation enough to get rid of Zieger themselves in order to pacify Jimmy Sumpter.

There was more to come. In 1973, Johnny Rich was murdered over a disagreement about the ownership of Cindy's massage parlor. Kim Rich writes sympathetically of her father in her book *Johnny's Girl*. It's a good read and the movie starring Treat Williams is worth seeing, but I knew Johnny and I can tell you he was nothing but a two-bit punk with an over-sized opinion of himself and fast-tracked ambitions that sent him stepping over an honest dollar every day in favor of a dishonest dime. My manager at Chilkoot Charlie's at the time, Dale Vaughn, and I were in PJ's the night Johnny was celebrating his new ownership of Cindy's, buying drinks and playing the big shot. In the midst of the celebration I turned to Dale and said, "Somebody's going to kill that stupid mutherfucker." Within a few days he disappeared. His body was eventually recovered from coal mine tailings north of Palmer.

My recollection is that Zieger was in jail for something else, as Jimmy Sumpter roamed around town demanding justice, and Zieger was not at all excited about being let out—especially since it was Sumpter who had paid the bail to get him released. Within a matter of hours after his release Zieger was found along the Seward Highway near Potter Marsh, a shotgun blast to his chest. Jimmy had a perfect alibi for his whereabouts at the time and the investigation was brief. After all, why try to find out who had killed Zieger? Few people cared.

Zieger's brother Rod asserts that Zieger's murder had nothing to do with the fire and murders at the Sumpter house or with Johnny Rich. He believes it was Vern Rollins. According to Rod, after The Brothers broke into a construction site in Valdez to steal explosives, Zieger was caught hauling them back to Anchorage and the gang was afraid he might turn on them. Rod says Rollins killed his brother to collect the $10,000 in reward money, but to the best of my knowledge Vern was never a member of the gang, nor did he do their bidding. I suppose it is possible Vern took an opportunity when the gang distanced themselves from Gary. We'll never know.

Next the gang tried to blow up PJ's, a strip club that shared a building with a garage on Spenard Road. Hallie McGinnis, the owner, was working the bar one night when he smelled gasoline and started sniffing around. Outside, he spotted a couple guys ducking behind his Dumpster in the parking lot and glimpsed a plunger and wires leading into the garage next door. He ran back inside to get his pistol, but by the time he returned, two members of the gang, Indian and Gypsy, were jumping into a fleeing car on Spenard Road. Hallie popped off a couple of rounds and called the cops.

It wasn't hard to connect the dots. One of the Hell's Angels who had come to Alaska from California had done a tour of duty in Vietnam and gained experience with explosives. The plunger was hooked up to some dynamite stacked beside Jerry cans of gasoline right outside of a room full of late-night partiers. The explosion would have blown through the concrete wall and created a vacuum inside the crowded club, sucking in the blazing gas and torching everything and everyone inside. Indian and Gypsy were arrested at the Canadian border.

Back then Chilkoot Charlie's was a much smaller operation than it became later, but a very successful one nonetheless, so I wasn't surprised when I received a delegation from the motorcycle gang. Gang member Bobby Baer tried to threaten me by asking, "Do you know how close you are to the other side?" I knew that if I backed up one inch I was in deep doo-doo, so I looked Bobby straight in the eye and said, "If you're threatening me, I've got enough money set aside to bury every one of you."

I sent Tiffany, my wife at the time, to Seattle and stationed a guy on my rooftop with a sawed-off shotgun. For weeks, I didn't go anywhere without my stainless steel .38 revolver holstered in the small of my back. The gang decided to leave me alone, though we had issues with the wearing of colors at the club and some minor skirmishes for a while. One night, pushed too far, I stood out in front of the bar menacingly waving my .38 around with the hammer back. One gang member, Happy Jack, shouted, "He's fucking crazy!" and the lot of them left in a hurry.

The east end of the South Long Bar was in those days referred to as "Loser's Corner." The patrons inhabiting that corner knew about the guy on the roof with the sawed-off shotgun and, to make his lonely vigil less of an ordeal, started sending up shots of tequila. He got so drunk he walked off the east end of the building and fell into the Dumpster, sawed-off shotgun and all. Good help was hard to find.

Just ask Jimmy Sumpter. Not long after the ordeal with Zieger, I got word from Dale Vaughn, who was now working as Jimmy's manager at the Kit Kat Club, that Jimmy had imported a hired gun from the East Coast to intervene on his behalf with the motorcycle gang. One evening Dale told me the guy was out there in the bar holding court with the gang. This, I wanted to see.

Dale said, "Bring your friend," referring to my pistol.

"No problem," I said, knowing there were several 20-gauge shotguns at intervals behind the Kit Kat Club bar.

Sure enough, upon arrival, the guy from the East Coast—big, stout, younger than I had anticipated, wearing a plaid sports coat and playing it up as a tough guy—was sparring verbally with several members of the gang. That night was my one and only face-to-face meeting with the hired gun. It was brief, more like an introduction, and I don't remember his name, but it might have been Tommy, which is close enough.

Six months to a year later Tommy left a message on my phone for me to call him. When I did he said, "I need a security job at Chilkoot Charlie's." I cautiously told him I had a full staff of security personnel already.

"I guess you didn't hear me," he said. "I said I need a fucking job."

I hung up on him. He called back, leaving me a nasty message, adding that the next time he saw me I'd better be carrying. I called Jimmy Sumpter, since he had already had dealings with Tommy, to ask if he had any suggestions about how to handle him.

Jimmy thought for a moment and said, "I'd call Vern Rollins," which is exactly what I did, Vern being one of the sort of outlaws that it didn't hurt to know. All outlaws are not bad guys and some of them could come in pretty handy when the chips were down since the cops would, more times than not, show up only to establish a crime scene. But in order to thoroughly cover my ass I also called Anchorage Chief of Police Brian Porter, a personal acquaintance. Tommy soon received a phone call from both sides of the street. One suggested that if anything happened to me, the police, who happened to like me, knew who he was, where he was and that he had threatened me. The other suggested that if anything happened to me, something was going to happen to him. I never saw or heard from Tommy again.

Vinson Massif

The biggest ever grossing day inside Chilkoot Charlie's was the day MTV VJ Pauly Shore came to Anchorage in 1989 to film an episode of the network's popular music video showcase *Street Party.* Pauly was the teen idol of the day—totally, dude! The mayor presented him with the key to the city, if you can believe it. He showed up early wearing his signature headband and stayed all day and night, playing host to the line of customers shuffling in from around the block—opening to closing.

The night before the big event, while I was driving Pauly to Romano's for dinner, I explained that I was about to leave for Antarctica to climb the highest mountain on the continent.

"Where's Antarctica?" he asked.

My head spun around like an owl's as he said to others in the car, "Look! He's shocked that I don't know where Antarctica is. Where is it?"

Was he joking? "It's one of the seven continents," I said finally, "the one at the bottom of the earth."

In November, I found myself in residence at the Cabo de Hornos Hotel in Punta Arenas, Chile on the very southern tip of South America, still scratching my head over Pauly Shore's popularity and still a nine-hour DC-6 flight from Patriot Hills, Antarctica—our first stop on the continent.

The DC-6 was well equipped for the journey. It carried fifty-five gallon drums of aviation fuel strapped to the inside walls of the fuselage for the refueling stop at Patriot Hills before it returned to Chile. Patriot Hills wasn't much more than a landing strip—a big ice field marked by a few fuel drums painted bright red. If we flew down there and couldn't land we'd be "screwed, blued and tattooed," as they say, so the weather had to be pristine. For the time being, we were stuck in Chile, waiting for clear weather over the ocean, our large backpacks and group gear already loaded onto the plane.

We had met two Japanese members of our expedition in Santiago. One, Kazama San, planned to ride a motorcycle to the North Pole and had brought one along to try it out in Antarctica. Also flying to Antarctica with us in the DC-6 were two other groups and one individual. One group was four Young Presidents Organization members (YPOs,) a global organization of young chief executives. The other was a Spanish duo, and the individual was a neurosurgeon from New York named Michael Schuman. Michael was the only non-climber. He was interested in the Antarctic and its history of exploration, so he planned to stay in Patriot Hills while the rest of us climbed.

The Spaniards joined us regularly for dinner and even accompanied me to the post office to help explain to the postal clerk what I needed done to my cachets since my Spanish was limited to ordering food and drinks, or asking for the location of the men's room.

Martin, the guide for Adventure Network, was to guide the YPOs. He lived in Whitehorse, Yukon Territory when he wasn't working in Punta Arenas and Antarctica. Ann Kershaw, in charge of the DC-6, was the widow of Giles Kershaw, who had pioneered flying to, from and around Antarctica, and whose claim to fame was getting Dick Bass and Frank Wells to Mt. Vinson, significantly assisting Bass to become the first person to complete the "Seven Summits." Ann, an attractive blonde with a good business head and an equally good sense of humor, took over the operation after Giles died in a helicopter crash the previous March.

Ann tried her best to keep everyone upbeat as the weather between the tip of South America and Antarctica showed no signs of improving. We'd check a posted notice in the hotel lobby for news of the weather at 8:00 a.m., 10:00 a.m. and 1:00 p.m. If the weather had not cleared sufficiently by 1:00 p.m., we'd check again the next morning. One day we went for a one-hour drive out of town followed by a two-hour walk to view the penguins. They were a small variety and looked like any other water bird while sitting in the surf. On land they lived in holes carved out from under the sod, like puffins. They'd back into their holes, so you could bend over and look them right in the eye. It's pretty amusing—once. I usually went for a one-hour run in the mornings and spent the rest of the day reading or wandering around town. In the evenings we would meet at the hotel bar, go out to dinner and then to a nightclub or two.

On Sunday, our fourth day in Punta Arenas, a very Catholic community locked up tighter than a drum, there wasn't a lot to do. I did, however, spend some time in the hotel lobby talking to a couple of elderly ladies on an extended train trip. One had been accompanied by her husband, until they were overcome by leaking gas fumes from a faulty heater in their hotel room in another town a couple days earlier. Her friend had discovered the couple and was able to revive the wife, but not the husband. They wanted badly to return to the States, but the authorities wouldn't allow them to leave because they were material witnesses. After hearing their story, I resolved not to fret too much about our problem getting to Antarctica.

Back in my room, weighted down by the tragedy I'd just heard about, I opened the front cover of my journal and stared at the photo I had pasted on the inside of it—Shelli's accommodation to my request for a more "provocative" photo to take with me to Antarctica. There she was in the professional print taken at Boyer's Photo Studio combing her long, brunette hair, with a diaphanous scarf over her shoulders and bosom. I was transported to another place.

The weather in Antarctica remained stubbornly uncooperative. I comforted myself by thinking of the people in Patriot Hills who were just as stuck as we were, but in a desolate place without restaurants or nightclubs. I was doing a lot of reading and was feeling fit from running an hour each day. I came close to tripping a number of times on the uneven concrete sidewalks until I finally managed it, tearing a chunk of flesh out of my right hand and scraping my right knee as I fell into a puddle of mud. After cleaning up and doctoring my wounds at the hotel I walked up the street to a supermarket and bought some beer, Coke, ice cream, toothpaste and laundry soap. I considered opening an account since it appeared I was going to be in Punta Arenas for the rest of my life. We had now been in town for six days and joked about going to see the penguins again.

I took a break from reading *Out of Africa* to read a book borrowed from Michael Schuman—*Endurance*. It was about Sir Ernest Shackleton's attempt at a pedestrian crossing of Antarctica at the outset of WWI that he figured was the last great terrestrial adventure to be had. It turned out to be more of an adventure than Shackleton and his men had bargained for when their ship, the *Endurance*, got stuck in pack ice, was crushed, and sank. The subsequent journey of survival back to civilization took more than two years, without their ever having set foot on Antarctica. Miraculously, no one perished in the ordeal. When they got back to civilization they were astounded to learn the war was not yet over. Sadly, some who had survived the two years of incredible hardship in the Antarctic did not survive the slaughter in Europe.

I got a kick out of asking Michael obscure questions to test how much he knew. What kind of wood covered the outer surface of the *Endurance*? What was the ship's name before she was purchased by Shackleton, refitted and re-commissioned? Mostly, he knew the answers. He wrote down for me the names of a few adventurers' first-edition accounts of their expeditions—where the best and most authentic history is found. At the time I didn't know anything about first editions. Not long after the trip to Antarctica, Shelli and I were in London, where I spent considerable time looking for those titles and couldn't find them in any of the used book stores. I was beginning to despair, purchasing a few other books about Antarctic exploration, but not the titles Michael had given me. One day I happened into an *antiquarian* book store. Eureka!

I have been collecting first editions of the polar explorers, mostly Antarctic, ever since. Reading of the adventures in first editions—in the words of the explorers themselves—is more exciting for me. These rare, expensive, tangible memoirs speak to me in a way that reconstructed stories don't. Many of the books are moldy. They have foxing and they may make you sneeze. You must be careful opening and closing them so as not to damage their bindings. They are authentic pages from history, like rare postage stamps. Shelli once told me I wasn't allowed to buy any more until she got a new bathroom, which should have been finished before she moved back in with me. I don't know why I stalled on that remodel. It wasn't the money. Shelli finally tore out the carpeting to force the issue, and it was done. As for the first editions—I don't know whether to thank or curse Michael for his guidance, but Shelli suffers from no such ambivalence.

My birthday came and went in Punta Arenas. As a present to myself, I climbed up and down the hotel staircase for two and a half hours with a small pack on my back. It was one hundred sixty steps, two minutes up and one and a half down—a good workout and thoroughly entertaining to the maids. Up and down those stairs, it began to occur to me that there was something fundamentally wrong with a business model that relied upon good weather in Antarctica. Sadly, Doctor Mike ran out of time and returned to New York on day ten, the day before we departed for Patriot Hills.

We left Punta Arenas at 10:00 p.m. on November 25, 1990. The unpressurized DC-6 flew between 10,000 and 12,500 feet of altitude, acclimatizing us in route. Every time the plane changed altitude we were treated to an operatic chorus of pinging, panging and ponging from the fifty-five gallon fuel drums strapped to the fuselage walls.

As we approached Antarctica the next morning the scenery was like something in a dream: the pristine landscape; the contrasting deep blue of the sea and the sparkling white of the intermittent ice floes; the absolute clarity, brilliant in the morning sun; and the Ellsworth Range emerging inland, dotted with little cumulus clouds here and there. I had never seen scenery more beautiful.

Arriving at Patriot Hills, we spent a few hours sorting gear and eating breakfast before boarding a fully loaded Twin Otter for the one hour flight to Base Camp. The two Spaniards and Perry Solmonson, the only other member of Todd Burleson's small group besides me, were waiting for us upon arrival. They had flown in earlier in a Cessna 185 that remains in Patriot Hills all year, cleverly driven wing-deep into a trench carved out of the ice and then covered with a canvas lashed to stakes pounded into the surface of the ice.

We immediately set about improving arrangements at Base

Camp and then made a one hour carry of supplies roughly halfway to Camp I. The next day, we had breakfast and hiked into Camp I. YPO's Dave and Don and I went back for the stash at the halfway point while the remainder of the group scouted the route up the face rising before us. It was quite steep, reminiscent of the Headwall on Denali. Meanwhile, the Spaniards were off climbing a dark-colored, almost perfect pyramid of a peak we had passed on the way to Camp I. It might have been a first ascent.

During breakfast Todd, who was jointly guiding the group with Martin, told me of a disagreement he was having with Martin regarding the pace of the climb. Martin wanted to do two carries up the headwall the next day. Todd felt that very few of us could manage it. Martin was feeling the pressure of the late start and the company's schedule of groups behind us. I, however, didn't feel like risking the success of a $20,000 trip because of some arbitrary commercial schedule. The lateness wasn't our fault. We had waited eleven days in P. A., so the next group could wait just the same.

On Friday, we carried a heavy load of personal and camp gear to Camp II. We left Camp I in the morning and returned in the evening. It was a laborious day, climbing a long, steep slope on a recently fixed line, then practically straight up the headwall for two thousand feet, dropping over the other side for three hundred feet then out into a broad, open valley for perhaps a mile. Walking across the valley toward Camp II, I was struck for the first time by the significance of what I was doing, taking in the pristine landscape, literally pinching myself to make sure I wasn't dreaming. Never in my wildest dreams, only a year before, had I ever imagined I would be in Antarctica, much less attempting to climb its highest peak. My dad, I'm sure, would have been impressed that I had now simply stood on each of the seven continents.

Mt. Vinson, 16,864 feet in elevation, is situated in West Antarctica's Ellsworth Mountains, which rise from the Ronne Ice Shelf as part of the Sentinel Range. It is about 1,243 miles from the northern tip of the Antarctic Peninsula and 621 miles from the South Pole. It is named after U.S. Congressman Carl Vinson from Georgia, who supported Antarctic research programs during the 1957 International Geophysical year, when the mountain was discovered and mapped. Nicholas Clinch, leading an American Alpine team, first reached the summit on December 17, 1966. In 1990, fewer than a hundred climbers had reached the summit of Mt. Vinson.

Determined to be among the first one hundred, we were frustrated when on Wednesday morning we heard Martin on the radio telling someone he wanted the DC-6 sent in on the second of December. Virtually every climber on the continent was opposed to the idea. It was obvious we should call for the plane from Camp III or Camp II—after we summited. We had planned for a two-week expedition; Martin was expecting us to complete it in six days. We decided to talk with him before we left Camp II, where we would be leaving the radio.

One of the YPOs came by my tent near noon on Saturday to say, "Martin has agreed to take the radio to Camp III and call for the DC-6 when we return from the summit. As soon as everyone is up we'll have a meeting and decide whether to have a rest day or go for the summit." When Martin came by a little later, I thanked him for his decision.

We left Camp II in good spirits around 4:00 p.m. We ascended in beautiful weather and after a couple of hours traversed over a steep snowfield under huge glacial cornices—overhanging, frequently unstable accumulations of snow and ice. The hill was "loaded," in climbing lingo, and if it had "gone," that would have been all she wrote. The remains of previous collapses littered the broad valley below. In fact, Camp II was built behind two huge seracs (blocks of ice) the size of houses. The second line of climbers carefully followed the first, stepping in their exact footprints, moving very slowly and quietly. Then, right under the cornice, in the most dangerous spot on the hillside, Perry Solmonson let out a loud holler and one of the YPOs, Jonathan Lee, followed suit. Todd assured us that noises didn't start avalanches, but I was not amused. There's a superstitious side of me that has never been comfortable tempting fate.

We rested briefly, waiting for the Japanese, then continued to Camp III, jumping over a couple of crevasses and crawling around another on our hands and knees, balancing on a small ledge. When we arrived at Camp III we learned that one YPO had fallen into two crevasses. He had fallen into the first up to his head and was able to crawl out with the help of his line partners and his ice axes. He disappeared into the second, dangling over an abyss between his climbing partners on either side. Martin, an experienced and capable alpinist, had taken charge and had him removed in about fifteen minutes.

We tended to lose track of time because of the almost perpetual daylight, like on Denali. Lower altitudes were bathed in dawn or twilight when the sun, moving in a circle above us, passed behind the mountains but we were above them all now. The view from Camp III was stunning. We could see Base Camp out in the distance, a tiny black speck in a vast field of white broken here and there by mountain peaks. The ground out in the distance looked more like cloud cover. It was hard to differentiate from the sky.

We set up camp in the wind after donning face masks, goggles, heavy mittens and Gore-Tex coats. I hadn't found that clothing necessary since the nighttime summit of Denali, and we were still a long way from the summit of Mt. Vinson.

Another YPO, Don Casto, had a close call after unwisely removing his crampons and walking around the edge of camp wearing only the inner liners of his climbing boots—a major no-no. He slipped and fell about thirty feet over the edge of the camp area coming to a halt in a small horizontal gully beyond which absolutely nothing would have halted his further slide. I heard him scream, as did several others. Racing to the edge, we found Martin was already with him. Martin and I lent Don our ice axes so he could crawl back up to camp on his hands and knees, one axe in each hand. He was shaken, but not injured—a very lucky guy. By the time we had eaten our dinner of crackers, smoked oysters, cheese, salami, jerky and ramen it was 3:00 a.m. I went to sleep stewing on the number of close calls we'd had.

We left Camp III for the summit at 4:30 p.m. on December 1, 1990. First, we crossed over the back side of a glacial calving area under which we had climbed the previous day and which would someday litter the floor of the valley where Camp II was situated. The climbing became steeper and steeper until we reached the summit ridge. On the massif face, one of the YPOs showed severe signs of acute altitude sickness. Mike Sharp, who had been guiding the Japanese, was designated to take him back to Camp III.

When we began to cross over the ridge, we were hit by the full force of the winds and backtracked to a slightly sheltered place among some rocks to dig out our heavy clothing. I wore crampons, over-boots, plastic climbing boots, inner boots, heavy synthetic socks, vapor barriers and light synthetic socks—and my feet were still numb.

Once on the summit, we hugged and took lots of photos. Of course, there was nothing to be seen in any direction but ice, snow and mountains. Still, I felt like I had done something truly remarkable. I held up a sign that read "Hi Mom!"—a photo she kept on her mantle for years.

It was as cold as it gets in my experience. If I'd pinched myself to do another reality check I would have been too cold to feel it, especially through the big mittens I wore. Standing on top of Denali, Kilimanjaro and Aconcagua had been exhilarating—no question— but standing on top of Mt. Vinson, the highest mountain in Antarctica was somewhere beyond exhilarating. It was unbelievable. I felt like an astronaut.

On the descent, I fell into a crevasse. My right foot went in first and my whole body followed, up to my waist. I quickly rolled over my left shoulder and pack and righted myself on the other side by pulling on the rope I was clipped into. Though I had been roped in, generally a pretty secure feeling, I was still a little shaken up. I had also broken my glasses.

We lost an hour getting back to Camp III because one of Don Casto's crampons kept coming apart. He stopped at least a dozen times to fiddle with it for fifteen minutes or more. One of the guides had broken it making adjustments at Camp II and had jury-rigged it with twine. It was frustrating because I was cold, dehydrated and exhausted, suffering coughing spells so bad they would cramp my stomach muscles, making me nearly throw up and faint. Back at Camp III Todd gave me some codeine cough medicine that solved the problem almost immediately. After drinking as much water as I could and some miso soup I crawled into my sleeping bag for some well-deserved rest.

We collected more gear at Camp I and I headed for Base Camp first, on my own and un-roped, advised of a trail free of crevasses. I kept my eye on Mike Sharp returning from Base Camp in the distance. Then I fell into another crevasse. My right leg went in again and I was able to roll out by the time I got in up to my waist, catapulting myself out of the hole with sheer will. The crampon on my left foot caught on my right pant leg and tore into my calf, slicing the flesh and drawing blood. When Mike reached me I was so pissed off about the incident and lack of safety procedures, having come close to spending an eternity in Antarctica, that I said, "Mike, I'm not fucking moving from this spot until I'm roped up with someone!"

Others began showing up. I had strayed off the trail maybe twenty or thirty feet, not hard to do in a flat landscape with only variations of white and black, no shadows—and no wands!

Mike said, "Mike, I promise you'll be okay if you just stay on the trail. There are no crevasses on the trail."

I reluctantly continued on and encountered two more crevasses right on the trail. Or was I on the trail? It was frequently hard to tell. Jonathan Lee had joined me at the crevasse where I had fallen and we kept walking toward Base Camp, the wind howling across the flats. Occasionally I would stop, bending over and leaning on my ski poles to take the weight of the heavy pack from my shoulders. Jonathan would pull up next to me and do the same. We would chat, bent over like that, and move on.

Perry Solmonson passed us about halfway to Base Camp and I tried to keep him in sight. The wind was whipping up, erasing the reassuring crampon prints in the snow. Not a single wand had been placed between Camp I and Base Camp for orientation. Having climbed Denali and Elbrus, I knew such methods were generally employed for delineating the trails that are so easy to lose sight of in bad weather. At one point, looking everywhere, I couldn't find Perry in front of us. Snow was piling up over the trail and I worried it might get worse. Suddenly I saw him—up in the sky. I had lost the horizon and had been looking down at the ground. At that moment I couldn't believe the expedition company had turned us loose, vulnerable—unguided—on the Antarctic landscape.

When the tail of the Twin Otter came up over the horizon it was literally larger than life, totally out of context with the surroundings. Jonathan and I hugged each other emotionally. Don arrived in short order. Sue, the base camp manager, met us and took some photos. People trickled in one by one, but I worried about one of the other YPOs, who had seemed a little disoriented earlier. He had almost stumbled right into the crevasse I had just fallen into even though Mike and I hollered at him at the top of our lungs. But everyone finally arrived, including the Japanese. Don passed around his plastic water bottle filled with Glenlivet Scotch. A couple of tugs on that warmed us up and instantly brightened our outlook.

We had arrived at Base Camp at 3:00 a.m. Two hours later we flew toward Patriot Hills in the Twin Otter, leaving Sue there by herself in a tent with a bunk, a Coleman stove, a radio and some miscellaneous supplies.

During the flight I leaned toward Martin and said, "On future expeditions everyone should be roped together unless they're in their cots and they'll not only understand, but appreciate it. And if you don't put some wands on the trail from Base Camp to Camp I, you're going to lose someone and your own asses to boot. It's a fun, freewheeling atmosphere here in Antarctica, but you're dealing in the real world, with an international clientele, and need to heed basic safety measures."

He nodded agreement, but I have no idea whether they ever followed up on my suggestion.

At Patriot Hills, we were delighted to see two pots of real—not freeze-dried—stew and a Chilean salad of fresh mixed vegetables waiting for us in the dining tent. We chowed down like we hadn't eaten in a month, but there was no place to lie down, so I put my head on the table. I awoke some time later and pulled my face from the pool of slobber on the red and white checked plastic tablecloth, certain that I had been trying to noisily suck and blow the red checks from the surface with all my strength.

Waiting for the DC-6, I stamped all my cachets with a Patriot Hills rubber stamp I discovered sitting on a desk. The weather was pristine, with very little wind, and the plane arrived around 3:30 p.m. as scheduled. The old work horse was huge compared to the

Twin Otter and the Cessna 185, resplendent and reminiscent of its heydays. In any other setting it would have appeared anachronistic, like a functioning museum piece, but landing on the barren ice at Patriot Hills, adorned with its Antarctic Airways sign, it seemed entirely appropriate.

The new group unloading looked fresh and clean. I met two Kiwis, Rob Hall and Gary Ball, astounded to discover they were completing the Seven Summits in seven months, capping off their adventure with Mt. Vinson; I couldn't have known I'd become close friends with them on Mt. Everest. I also met an octogenarian Japanese couple, married for forty-five years, who were going to the South Pole. They knew of Kazama San, who was a national figure in Japan; they talked excitedly with him and exchanged addresses. Meanwhile, a middle-aged woman from San Rafael who proudly claimed she'd be the third-oldest woman to summit Mt. Vinson, introduced herself to me. Her name was Marge Chippen, and I was to get to know her all too well on later expeditions.

While Kazama San roared around the landing strip on his motorcycle with its newly placed Chilkoot Charlie sticker on the gas tank—the only time he'd been on the bike since we arrived—we strapped into our seats in preparation for takeoff, the doors of the plane still wide open on either side of the fuselage. One of the flight crew came by with a large-diameter refueling hose—apparently to go from filling the tank on the right side of the plane to filling the tank on the left side through opposing open doors—and spewed aviation fuel all over the floor. Thank God, Bruce, our chain-smoking pilot, didn't open the cockpit door. I flew out the nearest side door and as far away from that plane as I could get, as if I had wings of my own.

Eventually, our beautiful, antique flying machine, run by its wonderful but comic and eccentric crew, propelled us from the ice field toward the tip of civilization. We were all chilled. I was still wearing my climbing boots and over boots, my socks soaking wet from the hike to Base Camp, so it was a relief when the heat from the engines started gushing through the floor vents. After warming up and getting some rest I spent some time in the cockpit taking photos of the incredible scenery of offshore islands and ice floes, and talking to flight engineer Connie and one of the pilots, Don King. Both, I discovered, lived in Anchorage most of the year and flew DC-6s all over the world. Don would become a regular in the Bird House Bar inside Koot's until he retired and moved to Cambodia. Turning from him to watch Connie jot notations on a pad, I asked her what she was doing.

"Oh, I'm just making notes of the things that aren't properly functioning on the plane. It's amazing how many things can be wrong and this thing just keeps on flying!" she said.

A couple of hours into the flight I had something to eat and drink, found an empty row of seats, and proceeded to fall into a deep sleep. I woke up from a nightmare where we were going down in a terrible storm, speeding vertically through the clouds in an earthward trajectory. The plane was bucking and shuddering. We were falling to our deaths. I saw ice on the wings. I felt—I knew—I was going to die.

Just then, someone walked by and said, "Strap in. We'll be landing in about thirty minutes."

We had been descending for our final approach to Punta Arenas. When I became more fully awake I realized the reflection of the city's lights on the wings gave the appearance of ice.

The YPOs left early the next morning. Perry left that afternoon to climb Mt. Aconcagua, and the remainder of us went out to dinner. Todd and I relaxed in the hotel bar listening to Martin's tale of the history of their company. He was immensely entertaining, relating a story that would make a good book.

He said, "Can you imagine the quizzical look on the banker's face when he pondered how he might repossess collateral sitting in Antarctica?"

I repeated my concerns about potential liability. Being in the nightclub business, I had become an expert on limiting liability. If nothing else, my experiences in Antarctica made me even more conscious of it. But despite my anger over the lack of safety precautions and the resulting near-death crevasse plunges, I'd had a remarkable experience. Asked about my climbs, I always reply that Mt. Vinson was the hands-down adventure.

Todd and I continued talking and drinking all night, entirely emptying my mini-bar and nearly missing our flight in the morning. Still hungover, we said goodbye to the last of the YPOs in Santiago and parted ways in Miami. I stopped in San Francisco for a couple days of shopping and visiting old friends and was soon back in Anchorage sitting at my desk, shuffling papers, writing checks and going to meetings—with another summit and another continent under my belt. Already I was looking forward to the next summit, Kosciuszko, by far the least difficult of the seven. Shelli and I planned to go to Australia together.

Gordo's

Having told many that the big adventure in climbing was Antarctica's Mt. Vinson, I would be remiss not to mention my big adventure living in the gay world for over a year.

Skip Fuller had a brother named Red, who claimed to have owned all the "B-Girl" joints in Alaska at one time. Red now had only one liquor license left, the High Hat Bar on Fourth Avenue, which had recently burned down, leaving him in search of a new location. Red was going through a divorce and wanted to keep the license out of the reach of his estranged wife, so Skip suggested that he put fifty-one percent ownership of the license in my name and that I find a location and put it to use. We'd have to act quickly. The Alcoholic Beverage Control Board does not allow "warehousing" of liquor licenses. You must operate for at least thirty days a year. In 1971, the thirty-days-per-year operational requirement was strictly enforced. There were no extensions allowed by the ABC Board like there are today, albeit for a price. I'd have six months to pull it off, at a time when there were few good locations available. But being young, ambitious and confident, as well as flattered that I had been given the opportunity, I agreed.

The result was Gordo's, located in leased space on the east side of Gambell Street, just north of Fifteenth Avenue. Like the original Chilkoot Charlie's, there were only four parking spaces out front. I received the certificate of occupancy in the last hour of the last day to open in compliance with the thirty day operating requirement. A health inspector, not surprisingly, had been my bane. Our architect had designed wall tiles in the bathrooms up to a lower level than the inspector deemed appropriate. That last afternoon, the tile installer and I removed the bullnose row along the top and substituted plain white tiles up to the required level, since we didn't have enough of the beautiful blue designer tile left on hand. It looked horrible, but it got us open. The whole experience pissed me off so much that I vowed to do something about power-wielding bureaucrats and run for the Anchorage City Council.

Gordo's was the first disco in Anchorage. I borrowed the theme from a successful operation I had visited with Lilla in San Francisco called The Library; we installed a telephone switchboard and continental phones on all the tables so people could communicate between them. The club was beautiful, the walls decorated with original modern art painted by local artists like Joan Kimura. Opening night, I was behind the bar in a tuxedo when the sewer backed up—badly. Apparently, some building materials had found their way into the sewage lines. The place, full of people, was flooding. I could visualize the badly needed opening night money evaporating into a river of sewage.

Fortunately, the landlord, who owned OK Plumbing and Heating located next door to Gordo's, was in the crowd and hollered over the bar, "Mike, I'll go get a snake!"

After a year of overseeing Chilkoot Charlie's, bartending at Gordo's, meeting myself coming and going, losing money all the while, I was desperate for an idea that would kick-start the new club.

One afternoon, Dennis Powell, a high school acquaintance who owned The Embers, a successful strip club on East Fifth Avenue, came by Gordo's for a few drinks and suggested, "This place would make a great gay bar. You've got the phones on the tables, fine art on the walls and parking in the rear! Ha! Ha!"

I had to admit, it made sense, but I was mortified by the idea and had never been in a gay bar myself. I was unsure whether there would be a sufficiently large clientele in Anchorage to support the business, and I had to be sure since I wasn't likely to be able to change it back to a place for heterosexual patrons because of the stigma. The only gay bar in town was the Bonfire, which sat right next to The Embers. A small, one-room joint that did not require the support of many customers, it was owned and operated by Ed Fletcher, whom I would come to recognize as one of the few truly evil people I have ever met—a bad guy right out of the pages of a Charles Dickens novel.

So I paid a visit to the Bonfire. Luckily, I ran into another high school acquaintance, Toby, known as "The Pekinese" in the gay community because of his facial features and bisexual orientation.

His favorite saying? "I'm a better woman than you'll ever have and a better man than you'll ever be." He assured me we'd get plenty of business. After all, we'd already had an experience with the gay crowd coming into the place and taking over the dance floor until my night manager turned up the lights and closed the place early.

The appointed evening arrived. A regular customer of mine who used to stop by for a few beers after playing handball, noticed guys on the dance floor dancing with one another.

When he brought it to my attention, I said, "I've been wondering how I was going to tell you I've decided to turn the place into a gay bar." Justin jumped off his barstool and disappeared quicker than a moose into an alder patch.

Approaching the end of that first year as a gay bar, Gordo's was firmly established, making money to cover debts from the previous year's operation, and scheduled to host all the major gay parties and celebrations. Tiffany and I treated our gay clientele with respect, she even participating by dancing in some of their events. Ed Fletcher, who used the Bonfire as his personal trap line for young males, and no longer had a monopoly on the clientele, was desperate.

My manager at the time was a very obese queen named Wayne, aka Auntie Wayne, who drank a case of Schlitz a day. He was comical-looking in a dress and sneakers, with his full, bushy, red beard. He got along with everyone and was a draw in the gay community. Both he and Tommy T-Bird, an infamous in-your-face openly gay character around Anchorage all the way back to my high school days, used to delight in running into me in the check-out line at my neighborhood Carrs grocery store, embarrassing me by acting out in front of everyone. Our best waiter at Gordo's was a young man named Jeff Wood, aka Myrna, who now owns the most popular gay bar in Anchorage, Mad Myrna's. Myrna's hosted Chilkoot Charlie's forty-third annual company party.

At the time of the Gordo's operation, I was a trustee on the Bartender's Health Welfare and Pension Trust Funds, and took Tiffany to Miami for the annual convention. One night, when we were out visiting gay bars to see if we could discover interesting trends or novel ideas, Ed Fletcher struck. We returned to our hotel room late and I had just gone to bed when the phone rang. It was Bill Jacobs.

"Are you sitting down?" he asked.

"No. I'm lying down," I said.

"Good. Gordo's burned down."

Fletcher had hired a couple of his young boyfriends to torch the place. Shortly after closing, the two men forced open the back door of the club, sloshed in a couple five gallon cans of gas and threw a match to it. Gordo's was a total loss. The poor lady who owned the beauty salon next door was ruined. There wasn't nearly enough insurance to pay all our bills and it broke my heart, but I was forced to sell Red's last liquor license to clean up the financial mess. I paid off all the artists, whose works had been hung in Gordo's on consignment, out of my own pocket.

Unsurprisingly, plenty of people surmised I had burned the place down myself for the insurance money, as it was well known that we had been struggling. The truth is we were actually beginning to prosper. It was Ed Fletcher who was struggling and could read the handwriting on the wall. Fortunately, the Anchorage Fire Department had a very able young fire investigator named John Fullenwider, later to become the chief, who tracked down the arsonists and convinced them to turn state's evidence against Ed, who was convicted and sent to prison.

Before Ed's sentencing, his cook at the Bonfire, a guy named Cooksey, walked out of the kitchen one night, said, "Hey Ed, I need to talk to you," and stabbed him three times in the torso with a big butcher knife. Miraculously, Ed survived. When Ed got out of prison he was hired as a cook at the Beef and Brew Restaurant, which preceded Elevation 92 on Third Avenue overlooking the Anchorage harbor. I called them and told them that they had hired a convicted arsonist.

They said they needed a cook and I said, "Good luck. You'll never get any of my business."

Ed Fletcher got his in the end. What Cooksey couldn't do with a butcher knife, Ed succeeded in doing all by himself. One night after closing up the Porpoise Room restaurant and bar he operated on the Homer Spit, he drove home to Anchor Point, went to bed with a cigarette in his mouth and burned to death.

*Mike in First Grade, 1948-49
Ft. Meade, Florida*

*Mike and his Dad, Harry (Whitey)
Gordon, Richardson Vista, 1953*

*Mike wears his Eagle Scout award
with his mother, Ruth Gordon, 1956.*

*1959 Anchorage High School hockey team
Back row: Coach "Reggie" Lord, Richard Enberg, Michael Moore, Dennis Hedberg, Gordon Unwin, David Fielding
Middle row: Douglas Weiss, Ernest Webb, Vernon Christianson, the author, Donald Simpson, Timothy Armstrong,
Front row: Norman Rokeberg, Robert Dalkey*

Mike and first wife, Reidun (Lilla), 1962

Original greeter; Chilkoot Charlie's, 1970

Mike with second wife, Tiffany, in front of original Chilkoot Charlie's, circa 1980

Mike hosting a mayoral Koot's fundraiser with George and Margaret Sullivan

Mike finishes his first of fifteen marathons, Honolulu, 1979.

Ruben Gaines celebrates his 70th birthday at the Captain Cook Hotel with Mike's sister, Pat, Mike and Shelli.

Mike and Shelli's wedding photo, September 1983

1985, Koot's crew in the new "Fern Bar"

Ready to tackle Denali, May 1989

Mike ascending Heartbreak Hill near Base Camp, Denali, June 1989

After summiting Denali, 20,037', with frostbitten face, June 1989

Aileen, Tom, Mike and Steven, summit Kilimanjaro, 19,341', August 1989.

Mike, after a bad day on Mt. Elbrus, 18,481', September 1989

Mike on the summit of Mt. Aconcagua with Vern Tejas and Todd Burleson, December 1989

Mike standing in front of summit of Mt. Aconcagua, 22,831', December 1989

Mike makes a proposal from the summit of Mt. Aconcagua, December 1989

Tibetan family on drive from Kathmandu, Nepal to Shegar, Tibet, spring 1990

Mike and Jim Whittaker pose together in front of Mt. Everest, spring 1990.

Beautiful ice formation on climb to Advanced Base Camp, Mt. Everest, north side, spring 1990

Base Camp photo with Peter Habeler and Martin Zabaleta; Mike's first Everest attempt was over, 1990

Mike on his way to the summit of Mt. Vinson, 16,864', Antarctica, November 1990

On the summit of Mt. Vinson, Todd Burleson and Mike, December 1990

The Douglas DC-6 on the ice field at Patriot Hills, Antarctica prepares to return us to Punta Arenas, Chile.

Shelli bags one! She stands with Mike and Vern Tejas on the summit of Mt. Kosciuszko, 7,310', 1991

Mike with a kangaroo at Pebbly Beach, Australia on a magical day in 1991

Mike sending a postcard to Mom from the highest point in Antarctica

Finally, summit of Mt. Elbrus with Sergei Arsentiev and Todd Burleson, August 1991

Mike and Shelli, Mt. Everest Hotel, spring 1992

Shelli, Mike and Deborah Spencer in foreground of
Mt. Everest, 1993

Mike practicing ladder crossing,
Mt. Everest, 29,028', spring 1992

Koot's flag on summit of Mt. Everest, May 1992, Peter
Athans and Lapka Rita

One of the Dalai Lama buttons made by Shelli and
Mike and secreted into Tibet, spring 1990

Mike crossing a crevasse, Mt. Everest, spring 1993

Expedition Sherpa team wearing Koot's tee shirts and holding the Chilkoot Charlie summit flag, Base Camp, Khumbu Glacier, spring 1993

Alex Lowe proudly brandishes photo of his sons, Mt. Everest, spring 1993.

Mt. Everest massif and route to the summit from Camp IV, South Col, 26,000'

Cho Oyu, 26,906', with Pumori, 23,494', in foreground, from South Col

Camp IV, the South Col, with its notorious oxygen cylinders, May 1993

Mike, before summit attempt, takes a break from supplemental oxygen at South Col, 26,000 feet, May 1993.

Mike back at Base Camp, 17,500', with fellow climber, John Dufficy, May 1993

Mike and Shelli, 10th Wedding Anniversary, celebrating renewal of vows, 1993

Mike, Mike's daughter, Michele, and Shelli, 1994

Mike with his son, Michael, in Halibut Cove, 2002

Mike hams with Jack Kent, Las Vegas, 2008

Halibut Cove house, 2009

USF roommates Jim McCartin, the graduate, and Rick Fischer, May 2011

Mike poses in front of the big 2012 Smoke-Free Coalition sign, Concourse B, Ted Stevens Airport.

Mike stands in front of Chilkoot Charlie's shortly before retirement, 2015.

19th Anniversary Climb
1970-1989

Chilkoot Summits
Mt. McKinley!
In Memory of Curt Sorenson
5-15-64 – 4-19-79

Cachet Carried By
1/141

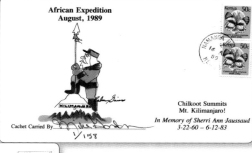

African Expedition
August, 1989

Chilkoot Summits
Mt. Kilimanjaro!
In Memory of Sherri Ann Jaussaud
3-22-60 – 6-12-83

Cachet Carried By
1/158

South American Expedition
December, 1989

Chilkoot Summits
Mt. Aconcagua!
In Memory of John E. Tegstrom
6-2-42 – 5-7-69

Cachet Carried By
1/205

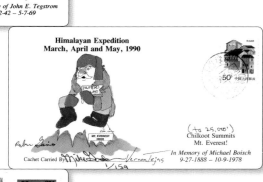

Himalayan Expedition
March, April and May, 1990

(to 25,000')
Chilkoot Summits
Mt. Everest!
In Memory of Michael Boisch
9-27-1888 – 10-9-1978

Cachet Carried By
1/159

Antarctic Expedition
November, 1990

Chilkoot Summits
Vinson Massif-16,864 Ft.

In Memory of
Red Fuller 1-20-1918 – 8-29-1989
and Tommy Fuller 6-6-1919 – 2-16-1990

Cachet Carried By
1/172

Australian Expedition
March, 1991

Chilkoot Summits
Mt. Kosciusko
In Memory of
Clyde Sherwood
3-21-25 to 1-27-87

Cachet Carried By *Shelli Gordon*

Australian Expedition
March, 1991

Chilkoot Summits
Mt. Kosciusko
In Memory of
Clyde Sherwood
3-21-25 to 1-27-87

Cachet Carried By

Russian Expedition
September, 1989, ~~1990~~
Aug. 1991
MT. ELBRUS

Chilkoot Summits
Mt. Elbrus!
In Memory of Harry S. (Whitey) Gordon
12-15-10 – 2-8-77

Cachet Carried By

Everest Expedition II
The South Col - Spring, 1992

Chilkoot Summits
Mt. Everest!
In honor of my wife, Shelli,
for her love and support.

Cachet Carried By

Everest Expedition III
The South Col - Spring, 1993

Chilkoot Summits
Mt. Everest!
In honor of my wife, Shelli,
for her love, support and
PATIENCE.

Cachet Carried By

Politics

When I ran for a one-year term to fill a vacant seat on the Anchorage City Council, Skip Fuller rallied the industry behind me and raised enough funds to put me on television. At the time, Chilkoot Charlie's employed Jack Kent, an audio/video expert with access to sophisticated equipment, as the club's main entertainment. We made a couple of outstanding television spots with me talking directly to the viewer from alternating angles—campaign ads way ahead of their time in 1971. I won by a landslide, garnering more votes than all my competitors combined.

Anchorage was a first-class city within the Anchorage borough and had all the privileges of a first class city, whereas the Anchorage borough had only those rights specifically given to it by the voters. The borough had been granted taxing and zoning powers, though Anchorage was as yet un-zoned outside the city limits, and it did not have police or fire powers which it had to contract for from the city. There were eleven members on the borough assembly. Five of them were selected from within the Anchorage City Council by its members. The other six were selected by voters from six districts within the borough, but outside the city limits. I was chosen to sit on the borough assembly, a dubious honor, the entire three-plus years I served on the Anchorage City Council. The city and borough were always at odds, and we city assembly members always bristled at our one-vote disadvantage. As a borough assemblyman I tried to represent the community at large, while simultaneously remaining loyal to my city constituents. It was a daunting task.

The big issue I faced initially was the controversial A Street/C Street couplet of one-way streets designed to increase traffic flow north and south. Those streets now run through the center of town and, in retrospect, the detractors' claims that they would forever divide the city were an obvious over-reaction. Mayor George Sullivan and his camp were on the side of the unions, including the powerful Teamsters Union, who wanted the couplet built as soon as possible in order to create jobs. Some council members, who were not part of George's inner circle, wanted to hold up awarding the bid, ostensibly to wrestle concessions from the state of Alaska, but mostly to defy George—often referred to as "King George" because he ruled with an iron fist, the way a big city mayor might. He sent Jim Campbell, another city councilman, to talk to me. Jim basically warned me that I was either with them or against them, and I replied that I had not been elected to the city council to take orders from him, George or anyone else.

George sent Skip Fuller next.

I said, "Skip, there is hardly a thing I wouldn't do for you, but you're asking me to change a position I've already committed to—to go back on my word. I'm sorry, but I just can't do it."

He reported back to George: "You know these kids today have got minds of their own."

It was a serious let-down for Skip, who told me later over drinks at Chilkoot Charlie's, that it had marked the end of his political clout in Alaska. I was stung by Skip's assertion. We tend to idealize our mentors, and when they show their human side it's easy to become unfairly disenchanted with them. He was only reporting things as he saw them; he and George were both old-school, hardball politicians, playing the game the only way they knew how.

Next, I got a call from the Teamster Union guys, who invited me to a lunch meeting from which I wasn't sure I would return. They didn't convince me to change my vote either. During the fracas over the couplet, George would refuse to give me the floor, gaveling me down when I would try to express an opinion. In response to such heavy handedness, our group of five members—opposed to the four in George's camp—voted to make him officially a part-time mayor. Now we had a real battle on our hands. George took the issue of his position to the residents of Anchorage and, being the popular guy that he was, he won. So, by the will of the voters, we had a city manager form of government with a full-time mayor—maybe the only one in America.

It wasn't long after this stressful episode that Wilda Hudson, a council member who had tutored me during my early days in office, said to me, "Mike, I'm proud of you for being your own man." Coming from Wilda, those ten words made the many sleepless nights worth it in spades.

At the end of my one term, when I had to run again for a three-year seat, George and his friends ran a previous councilman pal of theirs, car dealer Dick Silber, against me. Again, I received more votes than all my opponents combined. Once seated for a full three-year term with obvious enormous popular support, others on the council, and George, were forced to recalculate their political relations with me.

Though we had our disagreements, I learned a lot from George Sullivan. We respected each other and were friends until his death in 2009. George did not hold grudges like some politicians I've known. He might fight like hell with you, but when it was over he would shake your hand. George had a great sense of humor and a devilish gleam in his eyes.

Once, when we were in executive session pouring over job applications for the position of city manager, George looked at the portfolio of the man we eventually hired, Douglas Weiford, and said, "This guy's a member of Mensa. Anyone know what that is?"

Ben Marsh said, "It's an organization of geniuses."

George said, "Hell, no wonder I didn't know what it was!"

During council meetings I sat between Gordon Hartlieb, a lawyer who owned First Federal Savings and Loan and First Alaska Title Company, who constantly spat his chew into a Styrofoam cup, and Ben Marsh, who constantly dozed off. To their mutual credit, I don't remember Gordon ever missing his cup or Ben ever missing an important issue.

Serving on the assembly and the council simultaneously, I literally went from one meeting to the next seven days a week at a time when the borough assembly had no mandated hour to end its proceedings. One year—probably my last—we passed a budget at 5:00 a.m. We passed some pretty amusing ordinances early in the morning, which is why there is now a time limit.

I am most proud of supporting Lanie Fleischer's efforts on behalf of our marvelous green belt system. Today, the green belt and the bike trails that crisscross Anchorage, bordering its creeks and other water features, are the very heart of the city. As I sat there in meetings drinking coffee, puffing on cigarettes and voting for the land purchases, I never would have dreamed that I was destined to be one of the most frequent users of those trails for daily training, sponsoring the Chilkoot Charlie's Snow Goose Marathon and personally completing three Mayor's Midnight Sun Marathons.

The toughest job I experienced on the assembly was zoning the Anchorage bowl area, the natural basin that holds the city between Knik Arm to the north, Turnagain Arm to the west and south and the Chugach Mountains to the east. The Planning and Zoning Commission presented the assembly with a pretty, multi-colored map of Anchorage the way it ideally should look from the perspective of an urban planner. We were charged with a multitude of responsibilities, from defining the limits of downtown business property that wouldn't be required to provide parking, to inserting strips along either side of arterials for smaller businesses that would have to provide parking, without allowing them to encroach into adjacent residential areas. Further, residential zones were arranged so that the locations of densely-zoned residential properties were closer to the arterials and downtown than those of single-family zoned properties. In zoning properties on the hillside (the foothills of the Chugach Mountains), consideration was given to the space required for water wells, cesspools and percolation. Meanwhile, institutional lands and park lands were set aside, and light and heavy industrial zones were positioned along railroad corridors and away from residential areas.

It was our job, as an elected assembly, to deal night after night and week after week with personal appeals from residents and business owners who found themselves covered by the wrong color on the map. With a push of the button, we decided whether to acknowledge the historical legitimacy of their claim or impose upon them the new map, which might turn their business into a non-conforming use or downgrade their residential property's permitted usage, killing future plans. Outside of going to court, we were the final arbiters and, of course, there were winners and losers; there was no way we could make everyone happy. It was agonizing.

We held the meetings in a large meeting room in the old borough building on Tudor Road. They were heavily attended. If a landowner was fighting for a land use his neighbors objected to, they all showed up too. Or residents might show up *en masse* to support a specific zoning proposal or general concept applied to their neighborhood. Most people showed up and represented themselves individually. Others, particularly those with big stakes in the game, showed up with their lawyers. Some lawyers represented their clients well, while others just annoyed the assembly members and sometimes everyone else in the room, too. Some cases were slam-dunks. Some took all night to bring to a vote depending on the number of questions by assembly members and the number of people testifying.

We could always count on a smooth and effective presentation from Joe Cange, a young, successful self-made developer who had acquired significant parcels of property all over the Anchorage bowl. I had known Joe since my family moved to our Illiamna Avenue duplex out past Turnagain by the Sea, and remembered him bagging groceries after school at Andy's Turnagain Food Fair on KFQD Road (now Northern Lights Boulevard), above Fish Creek. Joe, by now a big developer, always represented himself, carrying a roll of his plans under his arm as he approached the assembly. He was very polite and low-key, never asking for too much but always something, and just about always getting it. But Joe had built a house of cards, like a lot of other developers and real estate speculators at the time, betting that Anchorage real estate values would always go up. When things went sour for the Alaskan economy in the mid-1980s he folded his deck and left the state.

In the end, when faced with a close call, I usually, but not always, came down on the side of the property owner instead of the pretty map worshiped by the planning department. I knew I had an obligation to do the right thing for the future of Anchorage, but above that I had an obligation to the citizens—the taxpayers and builders—of Anchorage.

Fortunately, I was able to occasionally come to someone's assistance, such as when some zoning enforcement folks were of a mind to "purify" the types of businesses that could operate on the land around Merrill Field airstrip. They were giving Lynn Cunningham, owner of Merrill Field Upholstery, a problem with his lease extension. I saw no reason why it should not be renewed, as ninety-five percent of Lynn's business was airplane upholstery, and his clients appreciated that he was conveniently located right next to them. His lease was indeed renewed.

Having taken part in laying out the plan for sewers, zoning the entire Anchorage bowl area, purchasing land for the Chester Creek Green belt and planning for the coming expansion that would result from the North Slope oil lease sale and the impending construction of the trans-Alaska pipeline, the citizens of Anchorage wisely voted to unify the city and borough. I could have run for the new unified body, but I was struggling with my Chilkoot Charlie's operation in Fairbanks, which had been opened a year before construction started on the pipeline, when everyone in town was chasing the same dollar. Also, my marriage to Tiffany was unraveling, so it was a perfect opportunity to make my exit and end my short political career.

Serving in local government is a great learning experience and also one of the best ways possible to make a meaningful contribution to your community. I was only in my twenties back then and now that my political mentor Wilda Hudson has passed, I find myself in the position of being the last surviving member of the last Anchorage City Council; the last surviving city councilman to have taken part in the design and approval of the city's logo.

I considered moving up the political ladder, but I wasn't really a politician. I was a businessman who ran for office for a reason, put in my time and got out. After I left, I missed being in on the action and knowing what was going on in the community, but I didn't miss living in a fish bowl and feeling like I had to answer to everyone, all the time—though, as the holder of a liquor license, I've never really escaped that circumstance entirely. I subsequently played a more limited role in public life, serving as a board member and chairman of the Alaska Alcoholic Beverage Control Board on two occasions, appointed first by Governor Steve Cowper and then by Governor Frank Murkowski.

I can certainly attest to the city's vibrancy. People participate. People show up. And they are passionate. I would recommend the experience of running for and holding local office to anyone so inclined. It's an awful lot of work and responsibility and it's mostly thankless, but you don't know how the system really works unless you've participated in it. There are a lot of folks from all walks of life who just don't know what is and isn't possible, or what distinguishes a worthy fight from a waste of time in local government, so they end up frustrated, beating their head against the bureaucratic wall. Having spent time on the other side, I'm not one of them.

Expansions

Still smarting from the loss of Gordo's, I could not let go of my stake in Fairbanks, where I had bought The Wonder Bar on First Avenue from Fairbanks businessman, Larry Wike. Remodeled with the Chilkoot Charlie's theme, it was successful by any measure but financial, since we had opened too early. Then when pipeline construction actually started, Fairbanks was even crazier and more out of control than Anchorage. After operating for a couple of years—when it looked like we just might survive the insanity— one of our competitors burned us down. Arson. Again. And I don't think there was even a token investigation. Still, I didn't see it for what it was: a message from the universe to leave Fairbanks and focus all my efforts on a single establishment.

I don't like to give up on anything. So instead of leaving town, I stood knee-deep in water in the basement, under the charred remains of my investment of time and money, and negotiated a deal with Larry for the Howling Dog, a rustic bar he owned in Ester, almost nine miles south of Fairbanks. We easily converted the Howling Dog into another Chilkoot Charlie's. After a couple of years and more red ink, I reflected on another of Skip's adages, "Never ride a loser." So, I sold the place back to Larry and left Fairbanks for good.

The Chilkoot Charlie's in Girdwood didn't fare much better, never turning a profit in five years. Finally, I did the sensible thing and unloaded that one too. The location is now Chair 5 Restaurant. My plan had been to build a franchise in Alaska and then export it to Washington and beyond. I tried to institute ideas and principles I had learned from working for large corporations, but my associates, whom I made officers and shareholders, were incapable of the necessary level of performance. My challenge was managing management in other communities, and it just didn't work. Franchises are easier to maintain with restaurants because they don't present the same degree of temptations and pitfalls that you encounter in nightclubs and bars, especially in pipeline and post-pipeline Alaska. Restaurant employees also tend to be more career-oriented. In the end, I decided it was okay to own more than one bar as long as they were under a single roof, where I could keep my eye on them.

In 1974, business booming in Spenard, I purchased the Barry's Motorcycle Shop property, our neighbor to the south, which nearly doubled our floor space. One of our bartenders and managers, Jim Ables, a capable artist and carpenter, used his skills to remodel the new south side of the club, soon to be decorated with our signature motif. He had a snaggletooth incisor on the right side of his jaw and delighted in opening Schlitz cans with his teeth. I can remember him standing on the stage before a film crew from some national travel organization opening a six-pack of Schlitz in a matter of seconds.

They also filmed Jim opening the new South Side to the public with a chainsaw while boasting, "This is how we do all our finish work."

Until we could afford to enclose the fenced-in yard on the southwest corner, the bands in that bar played to an L-shaped dance floor without much space directly in front of them. We weren't able to contract the quality of entertainment I wanted because of the limiting room arrangement, so we built an addition to enclose the fenced-in yard, which expanded the dance floor, and we threw in a second story featuring a wine bar.

Jack Kent, the most talented musician I've ever worked with, took over the house band entertainment reins from Mr. Whitekeys and played the new stage, which we renamed the Meat Rack—inspiration for his new nickname: Jack Cunt. To this day, he still refers to me as Rocky (the Flying Mutherfucker) and I call him C-Man. Jack and I are still such good friends that he was kind enough to fly to Anchorage and emcee my seventieth birthday bash at the club.

One day, as I cut the check for his weekly pay, just for fun, I wrote Jack Cunt not only on the envelope, but on his check too. He cracked up, and being the character that he is, he actually took the check to the bank to cash it. He waited patiently for the young female teller to become available, sauntered over to the counter, put the check down in front of her and said, "I need to cash my check, please."

The young teller, glancing at the check, said, "Sure, Mr. ...C, uh, Cun__.

Jack, a professional entertainer playing the role as straight as can be, said, "Yes, that's my name, Jack Cunt. I just need to cash my paycheck, thank you."

"Okay, Mr. Cu__, uh, sir."

Jack, of course, didn't have any identification for that alias, but the teller didn't ask for any because things were looser in those days, Jack was so insistent, credible and persuasive, and she was flustered and embarrassed. She just gave him the money. Jack came by my office and casually mentioned that he had just returned from cashing his check at the bank and said, "I was pleased to find that the funds were available," while giving me that sidewise glance of his.

"You what? You actually cashed that check?"

"Yep." Perfectly straight face.

Jack can play more than just that challenging role; he can also play piano, trumpet, trombone, guitar, bass guitar, flugelhorn and drums—and sing with the best of them. I have a recording Jack made called "Love Songs," that I like to play for guests at our home across Kachemak Bay. I offer large rewards for anyone who can guess who the vocalist is. The guesses range from Frank Sinatra to Perry Como, from Engelbert Humperdinck to Dean Martin. He's that good.

I continued to buy properties to the south of Koot's, right across Twenty-Fifth Avenue, in anticipation of a much-needed parking lot. Then in 1985, I purchased the two-story Spenard Bingo Hall, which sat on two adjacent twenty-five-foot lots to the north of Koot's. Adding the two-story bingo hall space—doubling our capacity again—was a massive undertaking. I thought I could remodel it for $250,000, but ended up being required to install a new foundation, as well as new plumbing, electrical and mechanical systems. Then right in the middle of the project—my building suspended in the air by two one-hundred-foot-long steel beams over the partial basement—the mayor, Tony Knowles, pulled the entire inspection staff from the borough for over a month to solve a big engineering problem at the construction site of the new elementary school in Birchwood. We were hemorrhaging money. On top of that, my contractor had to hire a new crew by the time we could get started on the job again. As part of the expansion, the building department also required us to upgrade the parking lots to the south—a virtual Koot's Lake during breakup—which included paving, fencing, landscaping and installing storm drains. I found myself staring at a $900,000 price tag.

Another of our acts, Tommy Rocker, had approached Don Fritz, my manager, more than once about playing at Koot's, but I wasn't convinced a solo entertainer could handle the large new stage on the north side of the club. We had started out with local acts on the North Stage then discovered a great musical XXX-rated comedy duo named Bird and McDonald that we used off and on for an extended period. Bird and McDonald used to say, "In Alaska you don't lose your girl, you just lose your place in line." In desperation, Tommy Rocker told us he would play for nothing just to get on our stage. I agreed, but I didn't have high hopes. Boy, was I wrong.

Tommy played for me for so long and I paid him so much money that he bought his own club in Las Vegas and now has three, including two in Henderson. Tommy would get on stage with just his guitar and a rhythm machine and his various get-ups. He was extremely entertaining—very funny—and he brought in a great crowd that packed the dance floor. He had different personas. Everyone's favorite was Daryl Green, a cowboy redneck asshole. He'd play the "Rodeo Song" and flip off the crowd, which would then throw balled-up napkins at him. He could be a surfer dude, or a Rasta man, and he played a lot of Jimmy Buffett material. He never took a break; he wasn't about to let his crowd leave and have to rebuild it again. He would play right through from start to close, without fail. I've never been able to convince another single entertainer or group to try that, and Tommy's the only one I know of them who owns three of his own clubs—or even one. He also had a fictitious agent named Irving Green. I hated the guy.

Tommy would say, "Irving says I need a raise."

Unbeknownst to most people, Tommy has a law degree and he really didn't need an agent. The agent was simply Tommy's way of letting me hate someone else for the squeezing I got. But Tommy was worth the money, outdrawing four-piece bands on the competing stage, getting paid as much or more than the other four together. Of course, the others took breaks.

Next we built the Patio Bar, at the back end of the structure, adjacent to an open area with horseshoe pits and an outdoor fireplace, where we hosted free feeds on Sunday afternoons for many years. I appreciated those Sundays for the way they brought our patrons together during the day. It was like welcoming my customers into my own home. Some pitched in with the cooking chores. I could sit and break bread with them, and forget about the headaches and craziness of the night before.

Safaris

Even though the early '70s were actually more dangerous than the pipeline construction era, nothing could have prepared anyone for the chaos that swept the state during pipeline construction.

It was hard to keep good help during the boom because everyone, understandably enough, wanted to get their hands on some of that big money. Guys and gals who had never had a good wage in their lives were now driving a bus or engaging in some other menial labor, making $1,000 to $2,000 a week plus room and board. They were mostly out of control. The good times would never end. They'd line up at the bar to see who could out-spend the other. They bought new cars. They took vacations to places they'd never heard of a year before, and they drank and snorted and stayed up all night at any one of the many "massage parlors" along Spenard Road, or threw their money over the tables at the numerous after-hours gambling dens.

The down side of all this for me, though the money was flowing agreeably enough, was the fact that everyone was out of control. There were fights every night, and I needed a crew of the toughest sons-of-bitches north of Seattle on my door and on my floor just to keep the peace. There was "Big Bruce," an amiable enough giant until provoked; there was "Cowboy," a short, balding Texan built like a fireplug; and there was Richard "Dirty Dick" Stevens, a tall, very capable lady's man, with a big black Afro hairdo. All were bikers, none to be trifled with, at a time, ironically, when motorcycle club colors were *verboten* in the club.

The worst problems were the aimless assholes from the Lower 48. It was as if someone had pried a rock loose in California and released every shiftless, no-good jerk-off to slither up the Alcan and immediately appear at my front door.

We'd say, "I'm sorry, sir, but you can't take that drink out with you."

"Fuck you!"

And, wham! The fight was on. It was us against them. Although we never lost a fight, we did eventually get into some trouble for heavy-handedness, settling out of court with a patron named Cameron that my doormen had handled with less than kid gloves. Hell, we didn't throw them out the door; we threw them through it, and I am totally unrepentant. They begged for it. I worked the floor with my doormen, wearing a black western-style hat, a black vest with armbands and a light-colored long-sleeved shirt. I never wore hand jewelry because I knew I was going to get in a fight every night. We were just trying to protect our clientele, employees and premises, but if you insisted on a fight, you got it—in spades. I thought more than once about selling the place and going back to school, but I was making a lot of money and I was caught up in the madness like everyone else.

During the chaos I had an uncommonly good janitor named Mike Stanton, nicknamed Big Foot, for obvious reasons if you ever noticed them. When you wanted to get Mike's attention, you could just holler, "Hey, Boot!" and he'd invariably appear from somewhere in the recesses of the bar, covered in peanut shells. I have a vivid memory of Mike sitting on his haunches on the floor of the Show Bar around 6:00 a.m. sifting the shells of our signature free peanuts into a nice clean pile. Part of Mike's job was to sweep up the shells each morning after the bar had closed at 5:00 a.m., sift them through a hand-held wire screen to remove debris, spread them throughout the club again and douse them with fire retardant.

Big Foot was territorial. Bartenders and waitresses had their tips and he had his: anything he found on the floor. Anything dropped was pretty hard to retrieve, with everyone standing shoulder-to-shoulder in three inches of peanut shells. Foot would come up with hundred-dollar bills, jewelry and grams of coke almost every night. Occasionally a brave, careless or uninformed bartender or doorman would venture around the bar, flashlight in hand, in search of treasures in Foot's domain. If they got caught, their ass was his and everyone else stayed out of it, including me.

One night after closing, wandering around the place, nosing here and there as I'm prone to do, I came across a .22 rifle lying on a stack of beer in the storage room. When asked about it, Foot began to shuffle those huge namesakes of his in the freshly sifted peanut shells. I offered an assurance or two but insisted on knowing what the deal was with that rifle.

I was afraid it was contraband, perhaps part of a drug deal—maybe even a gun that had been used in some foul play—but it was nothing of the kind. You see, Chilkoot's had not only become very popular with people, it had become a world class hangout for mice—a small game preserve, of which Big Foot was the game warden, committed to thinning the herd. Whenever they got the time, between 5:00 a.m. closing and 10:00 a.m., when the bar reopened for business, Foot and his buddies would load up the .22 rifle with birdshot and go on safari.

A mouse running across the back-bar in front of a row of glasses could be killed with a blast of the bird shot without breaking a single glass. Of course, there would be other unpleasantries spattered around, but they could always be cleaned up. I suggested in the name of health concerns and, of course, keeping the herd trimmed that I should accompany Foot and his buddies on a safari some night. He reluctantly and bashfully agreed, but before it could ever be scheduled Foot went to work on the pipeline along with everyone else. At one time I had a photo of Foot with the .22 and another employee, Buzz—proud sportsmen—standing on either side of a half dozen rodents lined atop the South Long Bar. Eat your heart out, Ernest Hemingway.

What happened to all those mice is another story. By now Jimmy Carter was president of the United States and inflation was on—big time. You may recall that Jimmy was a peanut farmer. If you ever want to have a shortage of peanuts and the corresponding jump in their price just put a peanut farmer in the White House. I had been buying forty pound boxes of goobers from a wholesaler in Oregon and before long I was searching the local grocery stores for one pound bags. You can imagine the difference in price. So, I did what I had to do. I bought a popcorn popper and started putting cedar chips on the floor.

There isn't enough nutrition in popcorn, much less cedar chips, so the mice migrated *en masse* back across the street to the Sunrise Bakery. What a reunion party that must have been!

Belize

The marriage to Tiffany was the make-over that didn't work. I was the one that was made over, not her. I had noticed how cavalierly she treated others, but she treated me differently. Once we were married that changed and I was now treated like everyone else. Tiffany was tactless. Once she was trying to create a costume for Halloween and asked my mother, "Ruth, can I borrow some of that gaudy, red lipstick you always wear?"

My sister, Pat, and I were astounded—not so much by what Tiffany had said—but by the fact that she got away with it. Mom was really a sweet person. She must have sensed that Tiffany wasn't being intentionally insulting. Otherwise that invisible line of hers might have been crossed, instigating the catfight of the century. My money would have been on Mom.

Billy Joel surely had someone like Tiffany in mind when he wrote the lyrics to "She's Always a Woman to Me":

"And she'll promise you more than the Garden of Eden

Then she'll carelessly cut you and laugh while you're bleeding

But she'll bring out the best and the worst you can be

Blame it all on yourself 'cause she's always a woman to me."

Six months after coming up for air in the aftermath of the pipeline boom, in the spring of 1977, business was tanking and a guy froze to death overnight in his car in our parking lot. At 5:00 a.m. on a frigid January morning, one of my bartenders, Tom Biss, and I closed down the bar and drove to my condominium in Woodside East. I grabbed an odd assortment of belongings: skiing equipment, a coin collection, my camera, a photo of my dad holding a football in 1942, my borough assembly and city council plaques, a down jacket, rifles, a few personal files, a case of my best wines, and my Anchorage High School letter jacket. Tiffany woke up, annoyed.

"What are you doing?" she asked.

"I'm playing a practical joke on someone," I said. "Go back to sleep."

We went to Tom's apartment to get his stuff—skis, black handbag with personal effects, a suit, a bag of dope—and returned to my place for $500 in my dresser drawer, scuba equipment, and ski clothes.

By now Tiffany was screaming at me, "What are you doing?!"

"Calm down," I said. "I'll be back shortly."

I watched her staring out the second floor window of the family room as we drove off.

We stopped at the bar, where I took all the money from the safe, then visited the credit union and First National Bank of Anchorage, where I withdrew whatever I could.

It's easier to justify my actions if it's understood that the business owed me more money at the time than any amount I could lay my hands on that morning. My problems were not just with Tiffany. My lawyer partner, Bill Jacobs, had built an ill-advised triplex in Bootlegger Cove. Most of the time Bill was either drunk, stoned or both. He was going down and he was taking me with him. I kept thinking back to our banker, Jack Hansmeier, leaning over his table for effect and forcefully proclaiming, "Bill, don't build that triplex. If you do, you'll end up having to sell a lot of things you don't want to sell." No truer words were ever spoken.

Tom Biss and I drove north, mostly laughing, but on the verge of crying all the way to Glennallen, where we checked into the Athna Hotel. The water was brown. The room was like a furnace and so dry you could hear, and feel, the air crackle as you moved around.

We unloaded the Blazer, hauling in the money, the wine and Tom's overnight bag. I felt like a bank robber. Tom kept telling me that I was doing the right thing and that my real friends would understand. I dumped and sorted the money on the bed, a little surprised at the amount; it just kept coming out of bag after bag. Then I realized I didn't even have a change of underwear or an extra pair of socks.

We showered. Unable to sleep, we finally just checked out of the hotel and headed toward the Canadian border. Passing into Canada was routine; I reported my .38 Smith & Wesson revolver, which they put into a plastic bag with a sticker on it. By the time we got to Whitehorse it was after dark, so we settled into a room at the Yukon Inn.

The next morning, while Tom shook the roof with his snoring, I arose early and wrote a long letter to my attorney in Anchorage, Ted Burton. Then I called an attorney in Whitehorse, Don Kidd. I told him essentially what I was doing and that I needed a couple of powers of attorney, which he said he would have ready for me when I showed up for my appointment. After breakfast I went to a bookstore and bought a Spanish dictionary, Spanish thesaurus, and a book of conversational Spanish.

At 2:30 p.m. I arrived at Don Kidd's office. He handed me the completed documents, not the least bit alarmed by what I was doing. Who knows—maybe he dealt with crazy Alaskans running away from home every other day. I signed a power of attorney that he'd send to a friend of mine and gave him my letter to Ted Burton to mail with another power of attorney. "If you ever get to Costa Rica," I said, "look me up."

Tom and I managed to make it alive all the way to Lake Tahoe, passing through the border with half an ounce of cocaine we had scored in Vancouver, BC hidden in Tom's hat band. In Tahoe we parted company because my intention had always been to team up with an ex-manager of Koot's named Howard Pumpelly, aka "How Weird," who owned a chalet there. He and his girlfriend Peggy were glad to see me. Howard was to sell his chalet and buy a trailer. I was to buy a boat. Then we would both drive to Costa Rica.

In late January and early February, Howard and I spent a lot of time skiing and researching in the Tahoe City Library, studying Central and South American countries. Instead of Costa Rica, we began focusing on Belize, previously British Honduras, which operates under British common law, where the official language is English, and along the eastern shores of which lay the second longest barrier reef in the world. Per capita annual income was about $500—a significant circumstance for a guy with a little money but no income.

The tethers of our lives are hard to cut all at once. On February 15, I had to fly back to Anchorage for three weeks to deal with a legal action against the club. The action arose from an incident where someone on our clean-up crew had, against my explicit instructions, left open the trap door to the basement at the end of the South Long Bar. A good customer named Reich had fallen in the hole, severely injuring his leg. I felt sorry for Mr. Reich. The incident never should have happened. The employee was fired, the South Long Bar was extended to the east and the trap door was rebuilt to fit behind the bar, and Mr. Reich received a $10,000 settlement he fully deserved.

Evenings were spent hanging out with old friends. During the days I visited with Bill Jacobs, other attorneys, our CPA, Clyde Sherwood, and collected, packed and stored my belongings. Tiffany was cooperative—temporarily—and more worried than she let on. She kept talking about losing her "status," that being the wife of a prominent nightclub owner and former city councilman. She could see "the good life," which she had taken for granted, slipping away.

Then Tiffany hired a new attorney—Jim Christie—her third, and efforts at reconciliation and cooperation came to a screeching halt.

I said, "Tiffany, if you insist on retaining Jim Christie he'll drain us both dry and there won't be any property left to settle."

After following Christie's advice not to let me into our house anymore, she left to spend a couple of weeks in our condo on Maui. I first went to Able Locksmiths and assured them that what I was doing was legal. I then called Alaska General Alarm where a girl told me that I had been removed from the approval list, so I asked for Jerry Woods, who actually looked at the contract and finding that I was signatory, agreed to let me in. I took my time and got everything I wanted including some business records that Bill Jacobs needed.

I spent some time with my kids skiing, taking them to *Close Encounters of the Third Kind* and, of course, in the process dealing with their mother, who couldn't resist a few digs. "If you hadn't left me, you'd have a nice family, and a beautiful wife, blah, blah, blah." Jesus Christ! I was reminded of the quote penned by William Congreve (1670-1729): "Heaven hath no rage like love to hatred turned, nor hell a fury like a woman scorned." However, I must say my first wife, Lilla, was in fact a beautiful woman, and a fine one despite our inability to get along while married. She has been nothing less than saintly in dealing with our schizophrenic son, Michael. Today our relationship is a friendly and loving one.

I began preparing for the trip to Belize. I paid off the Blazer and procured a new registration, along with proof of insurance. I acquired a Proof of No Criminal Record document for me and for Howard. I scheduled inoculations against smallpox, typhoid, diphtheria, tetanus and cholera.

In March, I flew back to Reno. This time a small group of friends saw me off at the airport. By now, Howard had sold the chalet and bought a trailer. We were ready to go. Before leaving, he drank a half bottle of gin and said goodbye to Peggy, who was taking it pretty hard.

"Let's not have a scene," he said. "Christ, it's just a little adventure."

It was snowing so heavily that even residents of Buffalo, New York would have been in a panic. I easily cruised through the pass, headed toward the Bay Area in the Blazer, as Howard brought the trailer skidding around corners, undaunted. Several times the highway patrol ordered him to put chains on all tires, but he'd speed off as soon as they turned their attention elsewhere.

I stayed in San Francisco with Marion Shepardson, widow of the man who had recruited me to New York Life, as Howard and I got our affairs in order. We visited the British Consulate for a fact sheet on Belize and secured Mexican visas. Howard purchased a CB and radio for his truck and I bought a tape deck for my Blazer. I traded a couple of pistols for a .30-30 lever action Winchester at a pawn shop, which I fancied using to hunt jaguars in Central America. I visited a clinic for an oral polio booster and the rest of my shots for cholera, hepatitis, yellow fever and the plague. I opened a savings account with Barclays Bank at 111 Pine Street and received a letter of introduction to a banker in Belize.

Marion threw a send-off dinner party for us at her beautiful Tudor-style home in Saint Francis Woods. We drank, among other things, a bottle of my 1968 Heitz Cellars, Martha's Vineyard cabernet and a bottle of my 1970 Sonoma, Alexander's Crown. We all got pretty drunk. Howard and I had a big, loud argument over the age of Muhammad Ali. He screamed and carried on something terrible, really pissing me off. It was a harbinger.

The next morning I found myself in Huntington Beach at the home of my USF friend Pat Lonergan. Pat and his new wife had gone to work and her two boys had gone to school. The birds were chirping outside and their big sheep dog was barking at the patio sliding glass doors wanting inside. I sat alone in the dining room, consumed by a persistent anxiety about Tiffany that had been dogging me for weeks. I figured I would get over it, but it was disconcerting nonetheless. I had an archetypal love/hate relationship with her and I cursed her frequently and loudly in the most vulgar fashion. It mattered little that I detested her. I was in love with her. And I was regularly in excruciating emotional pain. I had, after all, literally ripped myself away from her—and everything else.

I drove to Redondo Beach and bought a twenty-one-foot dive boat and trailer for $3,000. At a dive shop I purchased three aluminum dive tanks and a cut-off dive suit for warmer waters. When I returned to the local Chevy agency, where I had taken the Blazer to have the radiator flushed and cleaned, the wheels packed, transmission oil changed and exhaust pipe tightened, my credit was refused and the card was confiscated. I called the credit card company and was told that I owed $255.00—three months overdue. So much for my arrangement with Bill and Tiffany, who had agreed to cover my monthly expenses while we negotiated a settlement. Howard called me and said he was crossing the border and would meet me at the beach in Mexico. After I had a new trailer hitch put on the Blazer, I was ready to join him.

At 7:00 a.m. on the 18th of March, I parked, exhausted, next to Howard's trailer in the KOA Campground in Rosarito Beach, Mexico. It had been a major challenge getting through Tijuana at night, lost in a maze of terrible roads. Thank God for cab drivers. I slept on a mattress we pulled out of Howard's trailer and placed on the floor of the boat. It was more comfortable than it sounds.

As we drove south we encountered washed out bridges two days in a row. It took us seven hours to cross the first. The second one was worse. I went right across in the Blazer, but Howard had to tie up with several other vehicles, then—drunk—had an accident soon after. His truck was half on and half off the road, high-centered on the edge. The trailer was still on the road. We built a bridge of rocks under the downside wheels, then I hooked onto the trailer with a towrope and pulled the whole works out.

It was Benito Juarez's memorial birthday holiday, and I had problems finding an open bank. A *federale* officer that Howard had befriended was admiring my Blazer, and he and Howard both busted a gut laughing when I complained to him about everything being closed because of "Bonito" Juarez's birthday. Howard was fluent in Spanish, growing up as the son of a United States military attaché to the dictatorial right-wing Nicaraguan government of Anastasio Somoza. I knew very little Spanish at the time and didn't realize I had complained about "Beautiful" Juarez, as if he were a woman. Fortunately the *federale* thought it was funny.

My first boating experience, however, wasn't so funny. I had never owned a boat and hadn't a clue what I was doing. After launching from the beach with a young couple we had just met I realized I had forgotten to insert the two stern drain plugs. We were soon standing in ankle-deep saltwater. Then the engine overheated halfway to a nearby island. The fan belts were ruined. It took a while but we shut the engine down and made the repairs. Fortunately I had brought my tool kit and had extra fan belts. We returned to the beach, where Howard then decided he would join us, so we cruised out to a beautiful lagoon by the island, went for a swim and trolled for fish.

By now it was 2:00 p.m., and I returned to the beach to clean the boat, dirty from the road trip. The cable broke as I was loading it. Then, as I tried to pull the trailer out of the water, the Blazer wouldn't budge. The water was getting rougher and the Blazer was sinking into the sand at the water's edge with the tide coming in. Fortunately some locals came to our assistance, responding to my frantic calls of "Helpo!"

First, we pushed the boat off the trailer and Howard drove it to deeper water. With considerable effort, I disconnected the Blazer from the trailer and with sticks, cardboard and manpower from two nations, drove the Blazer out of the sandy quagmire. Finally, I hooked a chain onto the trailer and pulled it out of the water. We found a stretch of rocky beach, backed the trailer in again and loaded the boat using nylon rope on the cable winch. When I pulled the boat and trailer back to the beach I got an ovation from the locals who had assisted us. They invited us to join them for boiled shrimp with limes and hot sauce, and some of the beer I had given them to cool off after their exertions on my behalf.

The next day, I couldn't locate Howard. His truck was at the hotel, but he was nowhere to be found. I assumed he was out somewhere getting drunk, and I was right. Around midday he showed up and told me about thirty-six acres he had seen for sale, a piece of property in the middle of town that belonged to a female friend of one of his drinking buddies. We walked it, through groves of olive trees, citrus and figs, irrigated by a pump in a hand-made well. It could have been made into a nice trailer park, but it wasn't nearly thirty-six acres. In fact, the For Sale sign said 3.6 acres. They wanted $50,000, way too much in my mind, and Howard lost interest as quickly as he had gained it.

Fifteen miles further down the road, in Escondido, Howard started talking about dropping his American citizenship. Then he said he was going to call Peggy and have her meet him in Mexico City. The guy never ceased to amaze me. Of course, it's pretty hard to keep your shit together when you're drunk by noon every single day. I stopped drinking altogether for days in the hope that it would help the situation. It didn't. Howard's idea of responsible drinking was not spilling any. Next he told me he was thinking of going back up the highway, selling his truck and flying down to Belize because he was so upset with his truck and trailer, which spilled out a mess every time he opened it. The problem was he never packed it properly and drove too fast over the rough roads.

While in Escondido, Howard did aggravating little things, like taking his hose and brush out of the boat and putting them back into the trailer, as if I were planning on stealing them. We stayed away from each other most of the day. At dinner we talked about some of our issues. I told him I frequently had second thoughts and was just too proud and stubborn to turn back—that I was going through with the plan no matter what before I ever went back to Alaska. I went to sleep thinking how appropriate his nickname was. "How Weird." I had never realized what an asshole he could be.

On March 25, Howard and I left Escondido early for the drive to Cabo San Lucas. Again, we didn't communicate well all day. I figured his problem was not having Peggy to order around and generally treat like shit. Howard stopped for lunch thirty minutes out of La Paz and I went on in, driving all the way out to the ferry terminal to check it out. Minutes after I had doubled back with him to get auto permits for the mainland, he told me he had decided not to take the ferry.

"I'm going to go back north to sell this rig and buy something better," he said. I grimaced, but didn't say a word.

I followed him to the trailer park we had spotted, fuming. Nothing was easy with Howard. As we approached the park, he stuck his arm out to signal a left hand turn. His turn signals hadn't worked since I pulled his truck and trailer out of the sand in Loreto. Just as he was going into the turn, a kid in a Mustang roared around me and collided into the left side of the trailer and truck, badly damaging both.

Howard called the *federales*. They showed up at the scene with a captain. A number of Americans from the trailer court walked over to observe while the kid tried fabricating his way out of the mess. The captain took all the information and insisted on impounding both vehicles. Howard left with the *federales*, saying he would call in an hour, but he never did. I registered in the trailer court, took a shower and washed my clothes. I went into town and searched in vain for the police station. After dinner I tried again, but by the time I found the station it was closed.

I went to a rip-off discotheque, had one drink and returned to the trailer park. I laid my sleeping bag out on a concrete slab under a *palapa* and spent the night attracting the curiosity—and cool, wet noses—of mongrel Mexican dogs. I fully expected never to see Howard again, though I went to the police station again before lunch and discovered he had retrieved his truck and trailer. After lunch I returned to the trailer court and found him registering.

Howard said, "The kid was driving someone else's car and doesn't have any insurance. He's agreed to give me a camper cover for my pickup and repair the damages to the truck." The trailer, which looked like something in a hurricane newsreel, would have to be abandoned.

I couldn't find him anywhere the next day, so I went to the beach, read *The Eagle Has Landed* and thought about my circumstances. Ross Perot certainly wasn't going to fly in a team to help me. I had dinner alone at La Perla along with a couple of beers, and curled up on the concrete slab under the *palapa* with my four-legged amigos again. The next morning I committed the following to writing:

1) *I don't want to be married to Tiffany anymore.*

2) *I don't want to be in the bar business anymore.*

3) *I don't want to leave Alaska.*

4) *I want to maintain my credit, reputation and investments.*

5) *I thought I didn't want to be single, but I do.*

6) *I still love Lilla, but I don't even like Tiffany.*

7) *I want to be near my kids.*

8) *I need to get as much rest down here as possible before I return to deal with matters in Anchorage.*

9) *Bill is an incompetent businessman and a financial liability.*

10) *Howard is a complete asshole.*

11) *I can go to Belize later—freedom of movement being single.*

I placed a note for Howard on his chair before driving north at noon on March 28, 1978:

Howard—

I am returning to Alaska.

At this stage I don't feel I owe you anything, least of all, an explanation.

If you feel otherwise, you know where I'll be.

Mike

Wednesday morning, March 29, I was sitting again at Lonergan's dining room table. I had undergone a rather thorough inspection while coming back into the country, though the inspector was pleasant enough. Fortunately, he didn't find any remnants of Tom Biss's marijuana. Pat and Jeannie confessed they were disappointed they weren't going to be able to visit me in Belize, but were entertained by hearing about the past two weeks, especially my maiden boating adventure.

Wednesday evening I called Bill Jacobs. He was out of it and it seemed I was interrupting a television program. The situation was worse than I had imagined. Though he claimed things were going well, he admitted he had not been able to get any money from the bank and had not renegotiated a note with K & L Distributors, our main liquor distributor.

I made up my mind to at least fly to Belize and check it out before returning to Alaska. I flew down on Monday, April 5, 1978, just less than ten months before I was to first meet Shelli. I was amused by the sight, as we landed, of British Harrier jump jets along the runway covered with camouflage netting. The British provide for the country's foreign policy and its defense since the peaceable citizens there would be helpless against a sometimes belligerent and aggressive Guatemala, which in fact was at the time posting signs all over the place that read "Belize is ours!" in Spanish.

I got a room at the Fort George Hotel. Later that evening I found myself naturally enough, at the Hotel Continental, a whorehouse and favorite hangout of British soldiers. During another raucous night at the Big "C" I became pals with a Scottish sergeant who, at the end of the evening, when I was too drunk to realize what I was doing, hooked me up with one of said prostitutes. I was supposed to spend the night with her, so we held hands and walked to a little hovel behind the bar with pornographic pictures all over the walls, a room so small you couldn't stand upright. Once in the light of the one bare bulb I could clearly see how ugly she was, rotten teeth and all, though as sweet as could be.

I said, "Look here. I'm married, yada, yada, yada. I really shouldn't be here, and I'll never forgive myself if I go to bed with another woman."

She believed me. I gave her $20 in Belize dollars and got the hell out of there. As I was departing I stepped off the board leading to her hovel, immersing my bare, sandaled foot into the foulest liquid putrescence perhaps anywhere on earth. I momentarily contemplated amputation—well, at least sobriety.

By then I had struck up a friendship with Winston Smith, a twenty-eight-year-old waiter at the Fort George. I was amazed that Winston had lived his entire life in Belize and never been out to the Cays, so I volunteered to take him out there for a few days. Meanwhile, hung over and feeling depressed about the previous night's experience, I was again dealing with thoughts of calling Tiffany, apologizing and asking if she would take me back. It was demoralizing. The idea was like an annoying song playing over and over in my head that I battled with one of many "erasure tunes," my favorite being Elvis Presley's "Be-Bop-a-Lula."

I absolutely fell in love with Ambergris Cay. Everybody was friendly, tourists and locals alike. The water was crystal clear. The beaches were pristine and only a quarter mile from the barrier reef. Winston flew back to Belize City after two nights and I stayed an extra night to go diving, but the water was too rough the next day.

I spent a lot of time at Ramon's lodge, enjoying wonderful food and company. Ramon, a Spanish expat thriving in the Cays, showed me the property I wanted to buy: five acres smack on the beach with a dock, a nice building, water well and boat, just beyond his own place. It was perfectly suitable for a lodge operation, owned by a dentist in Baton Rouge who was asking $125,000 for the whole kit and caboodle.

I spent my evenings at a rustic place called the Navigator Bar, where I met some interesting people that I'd never see again. There was Corry McDermott and his stunningly beautiful fiancée, Mary Anne; Harold, a young guy from Texas who was going to go to law school and volunteered to drive the Blazer and boat down or accompany me; Bubba, another Texan who took care of a forty-six-and-a-half foot fishing boat for some rich guy who invited me out on the water for free when I returned; and the most beautiful little blonde I've ever seen anywhere. I chatted with John, from New Jersey, who ran the Navigator Bar, and Henry, an ex-stock broker who owned a resort beyond Ramon's. They were living the dream, free of the rat race. The bank on Ambergris Cay was the Bank of Nova Scotia, open from 9:00 a.m. to 1:00 p.m., Mondays only. I was smitten.

On the 17th of April I was back at Pat's dining room table again, now on the phone with Dr. Thomas, who verbally accepted my offer on the beachfront property. The deal was $90,000: $25,000 down with the balance of $65,000 payable at $500 per month including 9% interest starting November 1, 1978 plus a $10,000 balloon payment on March 1 of the second, fourth and sixth years. I would send him an earnest money agreement along with a check and then we would set up a closing date.

The time to return to Anchorage was upon me. I took the trailer to a welding shop for some repairs, withdrew the rest of my money from Barclays, stopped at Pep Boys and presciently bought a four-way lug wrench and four spare tires on rims for the trailer, which I then picked up with its repaired fender and step. I went to bed early, got up at 5:00 a.m. and headed for Redding, planning on a short stop in San Francisco to get some things from Marion's house before heading north to the Alcan Highway.

One hundred miles out of Los Angeles, I blew a tire on the trailer and replaced it in twenty minutes, feeling quite pleased with myself. Thirty-five miles later, the rear end of the Blazer went "sproing," froze up, and I stopped like a plane landing on an aircraft carrier. I had a sinking feeling this wasn't something I'd be able to fix myself.

Hitching a ride a mile and a half up the highway to a Texaco station, I had the trailer and boat towed to a storage yard, and the Blazer towed fifty miles or so to Bakersfield, where the manager at Three-Way Chevrolet prepared a work order estimate of $400. The service was superb but the problems were, in the short term, insurmountable. I watched while they dismantled the rear end and saw with my own eyes the damage to the drive shaft and casing. Casings had to be ordered from the factory, and took up to two weeks for arrival. The estimate was now $1,000. We spent most of the afternoon trying to figure out how to resolve the problem, passing on a used casing we found up north due to quality concerns. Finally, I rented a station wagon, loaded up all of my belongings, left the Blazer with the Chevy dealership, the boat in the storage yard and drove back to Huntington Beach. When I appeared on Lonergan's porch again that night, he suggested, not unreasonably, that I should consider buying the house next door.

After stashing my stuff in Lonergan's garage, I drove to the Orange County Airport, returned the station wagon to Avis and flew to Alaska. Terry Pfleiger, a realtor friend of mine at Jack White Co., had found someone interested in purchasing the liquor license from the Girdwood Chilkoot's operation. But I discovered Bill Jacobs had given Krenick Realty, an exclusive right to sell, for six months, running into October. So no deal. I also discovered he had missed the appeal deadline on the rezoning application for our parking lot.

I was tired of playing games with Tiffany, who was again vacationing at our condo on Maui, and declared total war. I cleaned everything out of the house and stashed our Mercedes. I wanted to force her hand in selling both the house and car to create some liquidity, while relieving her of her "responsibilities" at the club—which had mostly involved lording it over the employees. I had a long conversation with John Reese, later to become Judge Reese. I retained him as my divorce attorney and planned to deliver divorce papers to Tiffany as soon as she returned to Anchorage.

Meanwhile, I was out every night in the clubs with my buddies. I was seeing a young girl named Shannon who was pretty, and sweet, but hung up on downers. That girl could sleep more than a cat. I got a kick out of taking her out to see *Coma*. She could have starred in it. One night someone broke into her apartment while she was asleep on her couch, dumped dirt into her eyes, hit her over the head with a shovel and stole her rent money. I convinced her landlord, a friend named Buster Newton, to forgive her rent for the month. Then she got drunk that Saturday night, fell, and broke two fingers. I'd finally had enough.

I was encouraged by recent developments. Krenick Realty had assured me of a lot of interest from downtown Anchorage in the Girdwood liquor license. And Tiffany appeared to be coming around to the idea of selling our Woodside East condominium. John Reese put together a listing.

In an inchoate awareness of the necessity of redefining myself,

I realized I needed to find a decent woman. But first, I needed to learn how to live on my own without a relationship—and enjoy it—something I had never done as an adult. It began to dawn on me that in order to have a good relationship with anyone from the opposite sex, I needed to be completely comfortable inside my own skin, not need a relationship to feel fulfilled, and hence have something meaningful to give up—and contribute—going into one. I also needed to quit drinking and carousing with my buddies every night.

Finally, after taking care of a host of personal and business matters, I found myself again in Huntington Beach. After another night with Pat and Jeannie, I arose early the next day, rented a car, loaded up my stuff and drove to Bakersfield, where Three-Way Chevrolet had my Blazer ready to go. I drove on to Lost Hills, hooked the trailer onto the Blazer and headed north. When I got to San Jose I called Kathy Goyne, Tiffany's mother, in Milpitas. She said she wanted to see me, so I ended up spending the night with her and her husband, Bob. Neither of them had any problem at all understanding why I had left their daughter. The general feeling in her family was that she was a spoiled, overbearing female and that I had lasted longer than anyone else could have. They expressed their fondness for me and felt that Tiffany had screwed up a good thing—all very reassuring.

My second day in Canada I drove 635 tedious miles, through a lot of construction work, arriving at Muncho Lake well after midnight. I had a flat on the trailer and was almost carried aloft by mosquitoes while changing it. One of the other wheels made a clanging noise like a dragging brake shoe; the next day a bearing went out just before I reached Coal River Lodge. I lost the wheel, hub and tire, so I placed a 4 x 4 under the axle and dragged the trailer and boat to the lodge. The end of the axle was damaged, so we cut it off and I drove to Watson Lake—100 miles each way—for parts and repairs. I spent the night at the Sportsman's Lodge, relieved to have everything functioning again. The next morning I headed again for Whitehorse.

I was driving along in my Blazer, hauling the boat and tandem trailer, doing sixty over the washboard gravel road that was then the Alcan Highway, about twenty-two miles out of Teslin Lake. Through the passenger side window, I saw a tire speeding past me going maybe a hundred miles an hour as it bounded across the muskeg. I checked the rearview mirror. The truck and trailer were still kicking up a dust storm, cruising along unabated. Where the hell did that tire come from? What did it have to do with me?

In fact, it spoke volumes about my recent life. I had become disconnected from everything, pushed away by the pressure of keeping it all together. I had broken away from two decades of labor, a successful business, a set of relationships and just about everything else, instinctively aware that none of it was worth the price I was paying.

The boat was too heavy. The road was too bumpy. The wheel sprang loose and things would never be the same.

I stopped and searched for that tire, but couldn't find it. More repairs were needed. I drove on in fits and starts, tending to the fragile trailer, forgoing a night in Whitehorse in favor of Glennallen, within striking distance of Anchorage the next day. I didn't stop for anything but gas and a couple of hitchhikers, driving into Anchorage, on Sunday, June 18, 1978, just short of five months since the morning Tom Biss and I slipped out of town.

Sometimes you have to burn a few bridges to keep the craziness from following you. My runaway to Belize was the looniest thing I've ever done, but I've never regretted it. In fact, it probably saved my life. Intuition is sometimes more powerful, compelling and insightful than intellect. Having the courage to break the ties that bound me, I took over my life again and in the process learned that none of the trappings of success, and none of the possessions we've accumulated, are worth a plugged nickel if we're not happy. I regained my freedom, restored my self-confidence, reset and refocused my life. I thought I had learned who my real friends were too, but have since found that it was only an illusion. The fact is, you never know.

I had sent an earnest money agreement to Dr. Thomas, as per our agreement, with a self-addressed, stamped envelope and a copy for him to sign and return to me. Almost a month after returning to Alaska I had received nothing, so I called him.

He said, "I talked with my accountant. He said I should only do a cash deal."

This, I was unprepared to do; nor was it what we had verbally agreed upon. I was furious, but there wasn't anything I could do because I had nothing in writing, so I just hung up on him. It was a beautiful deal that had gotten away from me and, in the process, severed any remaining ties I had with Belize. I have never returned.

As Howard had explained to Peggy, it was "just a little adventure."

Kosciuszko

On March 16, 1991, Shelli and I, on our own little adventure, picked up Vern Tejas at the Sydney Airport. He and I had become friendly on the north side of Everest and Aconcagua and Shelli and I had agreed to let him accompany us to Australia to save on his expenses. I had gotten so much attention in the Anchorage press regarding my Seven Summits bid, it never occurred to me that I was assisting the one person in a position to beat me to it—and he intended to. We arrived late that afternoon in Canberra, a town resembling middle-to-upper-middle-class American suburbia, and home of a beautiful parliament building rumored to have cost one billion U.S. dollars.

This time around, I was more excited about sightseeing with Shelli than I was about the climb. Climbing was never entirely what it was all about anyway. At least that's what I told myself, and in retrospect it was a great excuse to see a lot of the world I wouldn't otherwise have seen, to make new friends, some for life, and to stay in superb physical condition all the while. On this trip, we had carved away more quality time together than we had since our separation began. I couldn't have been happier.

Arriving in Thredbo the next day, we checked into the Alpine Hotel and had dinner with Vern in the hotel restaurant, where he received his first warning from a local about his plans to parasail from the summit of Kosciuszko. He laughed it off as Shelli and I rolled our eyes at each other.

In the morning we all had breakfast in the hotel and were at the post office when it opened at 9:00 a.m. Julie, the postmistress, was charming and helpful. We got all the cachets done, which seemed to take forever, and started up the mountain about noon, boarding the tram across the street from the hotel for the six-minute ride to the lodge, our starting point for the climb. Locals at the lodge and on the tram were the next to react negatively to Vern's questions about parasailing.

One man said, "I'll tell you, mate, it's a bloody bad idea!"

One of the YPO guys in Antarctica had told me a tale about a rather nasty day on Kosciusko with unexpectedly severe weather so I wasn't of a mind to underestimate it, especially with Shelli along. Mentioning this to her, I also explained the mountain's namesake, Tadeusz Kosciuszko (1746-1817), a Polish revolutionary who fought in the American Revolution as a member of a French volunteer contingent. In 1777, he served as chief engineer under General Horatio Gates at the Battle of Saratoga. Returning to Poland in 1794, Kosciuszko led his fellow countrymen in an ultimately unsuccessful but valiant revolution against their ineffectual King Stanislaw II Augustus Poniatowski—an effort to forestall the partitioning of Poland by the Russians, Austrians and Bavarians. The mountain was named in his honor by the Polish explorer Strzelecki in 1840.

An intense debate about whether 7,310-foot Mt. Kosciuszko is the tallest mountain on the continent of Australia was most recently initiated by Patrick Morrow, who lost his bid to be the first to complete the Seven Summits to Dick Bass. To his credit, Morrow did climb more difficult routes than Dick Bass and, instead of Kosciuszko, climbed Carstensz Pyramid in Irian Jaya, Indonesia, which he suggests is the highest peak on the Australian *subcontinent*, at 16,023 feet. Some people climb both Kosciuszko and Carstensz just to make sure their accomplishment is indisputable, though you would have to look long and hard to find anyone who does not feel Dick Bass deserves the credit for being the first. Learning how to articulate and spell the names of both mountains presents more difficulty to most people than climbing them, especially Kosciuszko.

Then there's the intellectual debate about what kind of mountain Mt. Kosciuszko is. In *Volcanoes of the World*, Lee Siebert, Tom Simkin and Paul Kimberly have recently described it as a satellitic shield vent on the larger Andrus volcano.

The debate about Australia's geography is not a new one. In *The Devil's Dictionary*, Ambrose Bierce 1842-1914?, defines Australia as only he could: "Australia, n., a country lying in the South Sea, whose industrial and commercial development has been unspeakably retarded by an unfortunate dispute among geographers as to whether it is a continent or an island." I had decided if it was good enough for Dick Bass, it was good enough for me, and I could always go climb Carstensz Pyramid if I ever felt it was warranted.

I was wearing a poly-pro top and bottom, a pair of shorts, hiking boots and a Chilkoot Charlie's baseball cap. In my small backpack I had some water, a pile jacket, Gore-Tex bib overalls and Gore-Tex parka, gloves and a balaclava. Vern was dressed the same, only in his standard blue and red colors. In that urban environment we looked like a couple of escapees from the North Pole. Shelli wore jeans. Not knowing much about the mountain, Vern and I had simply prepared for a climb as we would anywhere else. We certainly didn't know about the metal grated walkway that ran almost the entire distance from the top of the gondola to the summit. Not long into our ascent we passed a guy descending with his little five-year-old daughter in hand.

He gave Vern and me a quizzical look and asked, "Where do you chaps think you're going, Victoria?"

It took about two hours to make the summit, moving leisurely at Shelli's pace, as fast as her ankle, severely injured in a high school auto accident, would allow. It was a beautiful day, so we stopped to take a lot of photos. That morning in the post office, we had met a couple, Ralph and Diane, who were from Palmer, Alaska of all places; we met them again on the summit. It was great to stand on one of the Seven Summits with Shelli. It made me feel like she was really supporting my effort. She started back down first to make sure she could catch the last tram to Thredbo, which departed at 4:45 p.m.

Vern dug out his parasailing gear as I surveyed the boulder-strewn mountainside, a murder of crows playing in the thermals overhead like floating black omens. Among other things, he had been told that the local parachute gliding organization had stopped using Kosciuszko altogether because of a number of serious injuries. All these warnings simply added up to an unavoidable challenge for the indomitable Mr. Tejas.

The gusts, strong and unpredictable, dragged him careening through a field of boulders the size of VW Bugs, bounding off one and then another like a pinball. He would ascend fifty feet, then get slammed down to earth and hauled around from boulder to boulder until he managed to get the chute collapsed again—no small task. When I had seen enough I took off to meet up with Shelli. We kept looking over our shoulders to see if Vern would appear in the sky heading for Thredbo. Instead, he caught up with us on the trail looking noticeably worse for wear.

We made it down with time to spare for the last gondola. All-in-all the "climb" had been an enjoyable experience. When we got back to the hotel, Shelli spent the better part of an hour ministering to Vern's cuts and abrasions before dinner.

In the morning we drove to Cooma to get the Mt. Kosciuszko summit postmark on the cachets, then wandered around the small country town of about eight thousand and said goodbye to Vern, who was going to hitchhike back to Sydney, pack on his back and fiddle case in hand. We spent the night in Albury on our way to Melbourne, where we visited one night with friends, turned in the Avis rental and picked up a motor home for a trip halfway up the east coast of Australia to Brisbane.

We spent an entire sunny afternoon in the company of dozens of kangaroos at Pebbly Beach, south of Sydney. We were completely alone on the grass, just above the white sandy beach and bluish-green water. The kangaroos ate carrots from our hands; the smaller ones sat in our laps. They jostled with each other over the hand-outs and took naps with us under the shade of the eucalyptus trees, snuggling up next to us as if we were extended family members stopping by for a visit. It was magical—one of the most memorable experiences of my life.

Next, we visited friends in Sydney and continued on through the Hunter Valley wine country, touring vineyards, sampling wines and dining in local restaurants. Driving cross-country in the motor home was pleasant, being mostly insulated from the outside world in close but comfortable and intimate surroundings, seeing places for the first time—together.

On our meandering way back home, somewhere between the Waitomo Caves in New Zealand and our property in Fiji, I blurted to Shelli something that had been nagging at me—I wanted to have another child—a child with her. We had lived together for three and a half years before our marriage, four and a half years as a married couple and apart for three years after our separation in July, 1988. We had known each other so long and been through so much, I wanted to share everything. I wanted to share a family.

It went something like this: "Honey, I've been thinking and I've decided we should have a baby." First, I got the look. Then, day one: silence. Day two: silence. Day three: silence.

Mt. Everest, Second Attempt, South Col Route, 1992

After my post-Kosciuszko revelation, Shelli broke her silence on day four, saying, "Our relationship has always been grounded in our mutual desire not to have children together."

She added, "It hardly bears mentioning that we could have been halfway through raising children by now and I'm thirty-four—beyond my best child-bearing years."

I said, "I know. I'm sorry, but I'd still like to give it a try." She was missing out on parenthood. I felt our marriage was somewhat incomplete without it, and that it was my fault for having had a vasectomy years earlier, preferring not to raise a family with Tiffany.

Thus began the long road of fertility work-ups for Shelli, sexually transmitted disease testing for both of us and a vasectomy reversal operation for me. Shelli's gynecologist, Tina Tomsen, MD, tried to keep things light as we embarked on our journey; during a pelvic exam with me in attendance, she exclaimed over her shoulder, "Mr. Gordon, there's your target!" Shelli, looking up at me from the exam table, wasn't sure whether I was interested or merely queasy.

A few days later, Shelli stepped into my office to ask how my STD exam had gone. She had just recently been tested at the municipal clinic on L Street and reported that it was a breeze. My experience was way different. I had been assigned a number to ensure anonymity and, after spending an hour flipping through *Family Life* and *People* magazines, my numerical identity and I were led into a tiny cubical sporting the same number. A doctor or medical assistant came in, had me lower my pants, producing a super-sized, extra-long Q-tip with absolutely no lubrication and began jamming and twisting it into the end of my penis while chatting pleasantly and asking, "Aren't you Pat's brother?" Somehow I managed to nod affirmatively, making a guttural sound while gritting my teeth, standing on my tippy-toes and breaking into a cold sweat, as pale as Uncle Fester of the Addams Family. I should have bolted from the building and abandoned the idea of renewed parenthood right then and there. My new friend now explained to me that the first swab had only been to clean out the urethra; the *next* one was for collection purposes. The whole experience was like a sign from the Almighty that unfortunately went unnoticed.

That winter I saw the guy again, across the room at my sister's Christmas party, though I didn't recognize him right away. When I did I said, "Oh, shit! I forgot to feed the cat!" and made a hasty departure.

We contacted a doctor specializing in delicate vasectomy reversals who had appeared on *Oprah*. The doctor was located in St. Louis, where my friend Jack Kent lived. The fee for a reversal was $20,000 and there were no guarantees, but he was operating with a significant success rate, so we flew to St. Louis, where I had an interview and a physical exam. We were then ushered into a room to watch a video recording of a reversal being performed, which left us *both* feeling queasy. We had another session of fertility reviews by a specialist who said that Shelli's fertility work-up by Tina Tomsen was the best he had ever seen outside his own office. And, finally, before the surgery, I was told that I absolutely must not vomit after the procedure because it would wrench apart the microscopic surgery reconnecting the vas deferens and ruin the repair.

After the surgery I was returned to my room where Shelli had been provided a cot and I was told I was allowed to have a meal. I was so hungry I ate mine and most of hers. Since I was beginning to drift off to sleep, we agreed that Shelli might as well indulge her passion and go to the St. Louis Public Library to do some genealogy research. When she returned three hours later I was retching over the side of the bed into a series of those little tubs provided for personal hygiene.

Shelli explained, "When I left you looked like a sleepy man who had just had surgery; when I returned you were bloated like a woman well past her delivery date."

Why I had been allowed to have a meal, I'll never know—it was ill-considered at best. My digestive system had shut down and the results were disastrous.

Back in Alaska, the night before receiving my first post-surgery sperm count, Shelli had a dream that it was fourteen—not fourteen million, or fourteen thousand, or even fourteen hundred. In fact, the count was just seventeen sperm, total, most of which were not motile. Shelli put away her basal thermometer, stopped keeping temperature charts, and gave up looking at baby furnishings. I suggested we could adopt, but Shelli wanted to either have our baby or no baby, so we agreed to let nature take its natural course and not become obsessed.

Flying to Nepal again for my second attempt at Mt. Everest, Shelli and I stayed a few nights again at the Oriental Hotel in Bangkok. After deplaning I discovered a couple of blisters on my left shoulder and, thinking I'd been bitten by a spider, I had Shelli prick them with a needle when we got to the hotel room. I still have the scars.

The blisters spread and were so painful, I couldn't bear wearing a shirt or walking around in the heat and humidity of Bangkok. I all but refused to leave the air-conditioned hotel. The Thai hotel resident doctor visited me in my room and seemed baffled by my affliction. He asked me lots of questions about mountain climbing but offered no diagnosis. By the time we got to Nepal I had broken out all over with little red spots. Shelli said my skin looked like dotted Swiss fabric. We visited an emergency clinic where the young American doctor blurted without hesitation, "You've got shingles!"

Suffice it to say, I couldn't carry a backpack to Base Camp, and if it's true that an outbreak of shingles can be stimulated by stress, I was perhaps more worried about making another attempt at Everest than I realized.

However, on March 23, 1992, I left the Everest View Hotel at noon with Todd Burleson, his cousin Lorraine, and a Sherpa guide. We arrived at Tengboche (13,000 feet) at 3:00 p.m. My heartache was registering eleven on a scale of ten from saying goodbye to Shelli for two whole months. I had started my Seven Summits quest when we were separated and estranged. We had been through a lot, had reconciled our problems, and now wanted to set our lives in order again—together under the same roof. But I was committed to my quest, and too far along to abandon it. I had sunk my teeth firmly into the Seven Summits. So here I was again in Nepal, this time in the Khumbu Valley on my way to Base Camp on the other side of Mt. Everest—the south side.

I waved until Shelli was out of sight then waved in the direction of the hotel when I got to the other side of the valley.

From Base Camp I wrote, "I keep picturing you standing on the hill in your red, white and black sweater, North Face jacket and green corduroy pants, waving and blowing kisses to me. I swear the whole first day I was on the verge of turning around, running back to you and forgetting all about this expedition…Honey, you mean everything to me. You've stood by me when I've been down and you're allowing me to find myself in my own way, though I know it's been hard on you. I look at your photos often, and you're my last thought before I go to sleep at night. You're in my heart and in my soul. I love you dearly.

Your faithful and loving husband, Michael."

After departing Nepal, Shelli sent me a letter: "I was totally miserable all night before you left, waking up and thinking the night would never end and our parting was going to drag out forever. You must have felt a lot of pressure about starting off on such a huge undertaking. I'm proud of you for going after your dreams and making them come true. That is part of what brings happiness to any person: finding what their goals/dreams are, then following through with action. I keep thinking and believing that there is a lesson in my fear about your climbing and that it is to trust that each moment holds all the happiness I'll ever have, that I have to search each moment of my life for that happiness and hold onto it as if it is my last. I believe that you are doing the same thing. It's a hard lesson for me, yet I know it is an important one."

As I read the letter, tears ran down my face like melting glacial water.

We were traveling with a half-dozen trekkers who were part of Todd's overall expedition. They had separate supplies and utensils, and the Sherpas were very fastidious, or should I say territorial, about keeping everything separate. The trekkers were going to climb Kala Pattar in Gorakshep, the last stop on the way to Base Camp. From that summit one can see the upper portion of the south face of Mt. Everest, the Khumbu Icefall and Base Camp. After reaching Base Camp, they would overnight and return to Kathmandu. We were all camped in a small rock-walled compound across the trail from a tea house, where we took our meals in the large dining room. I was comfortable, sleeping well and adjusting to the altitude, though I discovered a slow leak in my Therm-a-Rest sleeping pad, so I negotiated with one of the trekkers to purchase his when he returned to Kathmandu.

The climbers in our expedition included Frank Fishbeck and Keith Kerr, an inseparable duo from Hong Kong. Frank was a publisher, originally from Namibia. Keith worked for a large real estate development corporation that also owned Cathay Pacific Airlines. My tent mate, Ken Kamler, was an orthopedic surgeon specializing in hand surgery. Marge Chippen, whom I had met in Antarctica as I was leaving, was a recovering alcoholic with an eating disorder who was writing a book about her Seven Summits attempt. Everest was her seventh mountain and she had mortgaged her home to be there. It was also my seventh, since I had summited both Kosciuszko and, finally, Elbrus in 1991.

Arriving in Pheriche, a real outpost at 14,000 feet—about as high as people can live for extended periods—I was depressed and wondering about my abilities. Besides the high altitude clinic there were a few tea houses, a small area for erecting tents, an outdoor shower and a filthy, smelly outhouse. Spring colors hadn't arrived yet, so the surroundings matched the drabness of the facilities.

I also had diarrhea and felt lousy, with stomach pains and slight chills, but I refused the antibiotics Ken proffered and took acidophilus instead. I didn't want to start a round of antibiotics so soon. I skipped dinner, took some Diamox and Benadryl, and slept well, waking up the next day feeling much better. On Thursday I caught my stride and paced everyone I wanted to. During lunch I thought how I was going to miss the trekkers who, since they weren't intensely focused on climbing the highest peak in the world, were providing the only levity in the expedition. I sensed that without them, the group was simply driven and not particularly compatible.

When we arrived at Base Camp on the 28th the weather was balmy, with clear skies; I had to open both ends of my tent to cool off in the middle of the afternoon.

Vern reported to me about the Khumbu Icefall looming in the background, saying, "It's really in pretty good shape considering what it is. We've used a couple dozen aluminum ladders on the route; sometimes it takes fifty or sixty."

I visualized the photos I had seen in *The Seven Summits* of Bass and Wells crossing gaping crevasses on ladders while wearing crampons.

Our Buddhist prayer flags flapped in the breeze as Sherpas and guides installed Camp I above the icefall. There wasn't much planned for climbers for the next week except for sorting gear, acclimatizing and doing a few exercise climbs in the vicinity. The Kiwis I had met in Antarctica, Rob Hall and Gary Ball, had established their expedition's camp right next to ours.

Instead of the 8:30 a.m. leisurely breakfast we had planned, Bob Matthews, one of the trekkers, came around next morning at 6:30 a.m. to report that they were leaving right away, much earlier than scheduled due to weather. It was snowing, and the Sherpas were dismantling the trekkers' tents with them still inside. Ken and I clamored out to see them off, only to find ourselves waiting around for two hours. When they had finally departed, I looked about at the much smaller and much more serious group.

We downed a breakfast of scrambled eggs and pancakes. Then we had a roundtable discussion about strategies for the climb. I didn't learn much I hadn't already known, except that the Russians and Spaniards, who did not to our knowledge have a permit for the South Col route, appeared to be using it. The Russians had purportedly already reached their Camp II.

We took advantage of the trekkers' vacant tent spaces and shifted into a more comfortable long-term arrangement. I now had all my belongings in my own tent so I could spread things out and get organized. After lunch, the leader of the Indian Border Patrol Expedition came by for a visit. He was a dignified gentleman who knew Todd from the embassy rounds in Kathmandu. They talked about the condition of the icefall for a while; the two Indian expeditions on the mountain—the other was civilian—were responsible for maintaining safe passage over myriad crevasses for the next week. We were skeptical of the outcome. They had only wire ladders and a supply of rope, and the civilian group was short on experience. By comparison, the well-outfitted Dutch had fifty aluminum ladders.

The Sherpa were burning aromatic juniper branches under prayer flags strung out from a tall pole in the middle of camp when Vern and Pete Athans left early in the morning of March 30 for Camps I and II. Pete, who had summited our route, was knowledgeable about Nepalese and Tibetan cultures and fluent in Nepalese. I told Vern, to assess his plans, that I felt comfortable with him and thought it would be nice to stand on the summit with him and be the first two Alaskans to finish the Seven Summits.

"I'd like to take my two Hong Kong buddies up first," he said, "but I'll talk to Todd about your feelings."

Vern was a paid guide on the trip and I worried he intended to use his position to beat me to the top. He had just, I learned—at the last minute—flown over to Africa to climb Kilimanjaro, leaving Everest the last of his seven as well. His position in the climbing world was perfectly well established with his first winter solo of Denali, but I was the one who had built the local interest in the Seven Summits. I asked Todd over to my tent that afternoon.

"I've spent four years and $200,000, at least half of it going into your pockets, to be the first Alaskan to complete the Seven Summits," I said, "and I'm not going to stand idly by while a guy who is working for you—and me—tries to cheat me out of it!"

"I'll keep it in mind," he said.

It took the turmoil of an accident to jolt me to other thoughts. A young Sherpa in the Kiwi expedition, returning from Camp I, had slipped and fallen eighty feet into a crevasse. He had not been clipped into a safety line. Many young Sherpas thought it unmanly to do so. Now he had suffered a serious head injury and perhaps a broken hip. I sat on a rock in the sun beside the mess tent writing postcards, watching the tragedy unfold.

Our expedition sent a radio up to the site of the incident and Ken set up an IV in the medical tent, but the Sherpa was hustled into the Spanish Camp, closest to the bottom of the icefall. A helicopter had been ordered from Kathmandu, though by 6:00 p.m. it had not arrived. Our Sherpas burned juniper branches and chanted all night for their fallen comrade. That evening, amidst our concerns for the young Sherpa, John Helenek, our youngest member at thirty-four, showed up and immediately added some life to our group with his outgoing personality and sense of humor.

Thursday morning, the Alouette helicopter arrived before breakfast. The craft and crew stayed on the ground only a few minutes and refused to take anything or anyone onboard except the injured Sherpa, because of weight concerns at 17,500 feet.

Ken had been up all night at the Spanish camp and said, "If he wasn't such a tough kid, he might not have made it. He probably has a subdural hematoma. He needs a CAT scan, and probably a hole drilled in his head to release pressure from fluid build-up. But what do I know? I'm a hand surgeon."

Before dinner another member of our group, Lewis Bower, arrived bearing some mail, including another letter from Shelli that he was kind enough to dig out of his bag before I went to bed. After the two days of drama at Base Camp it was nice to retreat to my tent with my letter, soaking up her loving words, best wishes from family and friends, and news that business was good. On a long expedition, nothing trumps getting mail.

Most of us arose early Saturday, had breakfast, and walked into the icefall for some ladder practice. We made up three different rope lines. It was a beautiful day and I thought it was great fun. We went as far up as the fourth crevasse crossing, two ladders tied end-to-end over a deep abyss, and practiced going back and forth in our crampons from one end of the ladders to the other. We were getting accustomed to finding the "sweet spot," the wide middle area of our crampons with no spikes that fitted comfortably over the ladder rungs spanning the yawning, cold darkness below. Afterward, I returned to my tent to prepare for the 4:00 a.m. departure to Camp I, feeling like I had needlessly worried about crossing the ladders in the icefall, much as I'd done with traversing Denali Pass on my first climb.

It snowed that night during dinner; the wind started to blow by bedtime. Todd came around to our tents at 9:00 p.m. and said, "Sleep in. We won't be going up in the morning."

Instead, we left on Monday morning at 5:15 a.m., arriving at Camp I six hours later. It was another nice day spent crossing two dozen crevasses, some so wide they required three twenty-foot ladders tied together—bouncy in the middle, like a trampoline designed by a masochist with limited material. The ladders proved to be no problem for me, though I did consciously avoid looking into the blue-black darkness below, deep enough in places to harbor independent weather systems. I dropped a spare carabiner into one crevasse, just to see if I could hear it hit bottom. Nope.

I was more apprehensive of the huge, ugly ice hunks hanging over our heads in places. I spent most of the day ascending behind John, patiently following him through some pretty scary spots under large, unstable formations. After several hours I ended up in front of him, when he jerked hard on the fixed line and stopped me in a particularly harrowing area. I had waited patiently behind him on numerous occasions while he caught his breath as ominous building-sized formations of ice loomed over my head, and never over-reacted. He just got scared and lost his nerve.

I said, "John, just go by me. I don't want you behind me anymore because I'm afraid you'll flip out and pull me off the mountain."

At Camp I, he said, "You were being patient behind me because you couldn't catch me."

"Then what was I doing in front of you when you jerked on the rope? You're full of shit, John," I said.

By that time Frank and Keith had established their Hong Kong-style aristocracy at Camp I, inviting the "chosen" into their tent, including John. Those of us among the "un-chosen" had to somehow survive in the other tent. They played a game of exclusion that reminded me of what teenage girls might play—not that I cared one bit. I thought it was moronic. After a pretty good dinner of freeze-dried lasagna, we went to bed and slept well in spite of our low social status, awakening to a lot of condensation—or was it condescension?—in the morning. Later we hiked about a third of the way to Camp II. The weather was pristine, but uncomfortably hot. Having made our way up 2,000 feet through the Khumbu Icefall, we were entering the Western Cwm, or valley, situated at 19,500 feet at its lowest point, above the icefall, and gradually rising to around 22,000 feet at the base of the Lhotse Face. It's a huge box canyon, with 29,028-foot Everest on the left, 27,939-foot Lhotse straight ahead and 25,791-foot Nuptse on the right, all towering more than 4,000 feet above the floor. Snow and ice slowly works its way down to the narrow opening at the bottom, forming the icefall we had just ascended. From there it gradually morphs into the Khumbu Glacier, location of Base Camp, then splinters into moraines and, finally, flows into the turgid, silty waters of the Khumbu River.

At midday, when the sun is shining down on the Western Cwm, it's like a solar oven, intensified by the thin atmosphere and almost totally white surroundings. You can feel the heat acutely in the absence of any kind of breeze. When the sun is obscured by clouds or passes beyond the walls of the canyon, the temperature plummets.

There are two climbing seasons on the South Col Route, generally accessed by the Western Cwm and Lhotse Face with Camp IV being situated at 26,000 feet in the South Col itself. Spring is the preferable season since there is a period of time in early May when the jet stream over the peak of Everest tends to abate momentarily, providing access to its coveted peak, and after which there is a comfortable amount of time to remove oneself from the area before the seasonal monsoons. Very heavy snows in the Western Cwm and on the Khumbu Icefall would be problematic to an expedition, to say the least. The fall season is at the end of the monsoons and shorter and the end of the fall season is even more problematic because it means the onset of winter.

The geologic drama of Mt. Everest is both sedimentary and tectonic. It started thirty to fifty million years ago in the Tertiary period, halfway back to the time of dinosaurs, at the bottom of the Tethys Sea. The Indian sub-continental plate started pushing relentlessly into the Eurasian continental plate, creating Mt. Everest. The process continues as you read this, forcing the highest mountain in the world ever higher. When I attempted to climb Mt. Everest in the early '90s, it was 29,028 feet high. It is now 29,035 feet high. When you observe the Lhotse Face and the massif of Everest you see clear evidence of sedimentation all the way to the top. The Yellow Band, formed of limestone from the bottom of the ancient Tethys Sea, is the most obvious. You traverse the Yellow Band while climbing between Camp III (24,000 feet) and Camp IV (26,000 feet). Beneath this shallow marine rock is the highly metamorphosed and layered black gneiss of the Precambrian Era. This hard, ominous-looking rock is the actual remains of when the continental plates first collided, eventually creating the Himalayan mountain range.

We shed layer after layer in the blistering heat of the day as we waited to climb the fifty-foot vertical face of a crevasse in our path. Just beyond the crevasse sat the remains of a large avalanche that had recently fallen from the Nuptse face, where we had a lunch of smoked oysters, kippered sardines, crackers and candy. Looking up the Western Cwm toward Everest we could see the tents of Camp II and someone walking down in our direction. It turned out to be one of our high-altitude Sherpa, Chuldim, bringing us Sherpa tea and pineapple slices.

On Thursday, a couple of us walked farther into the Western Cwm past the Indian, British, Kiwi and Spanish camps, all crowded together above us and emitting the unpleasant odor of latrines. Our camp was not as close to the Lhotse Face, but it was better protected and did not share space with other camps in the immediate vicinity, so we didn't have to endure the smell of multiple open latrines. From the high point of our walk we were able to get some real perspective on Pumori, looking back down the Western Cwm; it wouldn't be long before we were looking down on it from decidedly higher up. The scenery in every direction was spectacular. We were now almost at the same altitude as Pumori's peak and, though it still loomed over the top of the icefall, it had shrunk beneath the much larger and taller mass of Cho Oyu (26,906 feet) behind it. Together, they framed the backdrop of the all-white floor of the Western Cwm framed in, as well, by the West Buttress of Everest on the right and the North Wall of Nuptse on the left. Now perched above some of the high obstacles, we were enjoying perhaps an hour more of daylight each day. The first night at Camp II, I was sleeping approximately six hundred feet above the summit of Denali, yet there was still another 7,000 feet to go. I was no longer playing in the minors.

The route up the Lhotse Face was now very clear to us. The closer I got, the more doable it appeared, unlike the Super Couloir route of the previous year. The closer, the scarier, that one.

On Friday, April 10, we left for the foot of the Lhotse Face at 9:00 a.m., carrying three aluminum ladders, some rope and pitons. We installed an aluminum ladder across a significant crevasse, and fixed a safety rope over a couple of minor ones. We left the other two ladders next to the trail to be used when more crevasses appeared later or small ones grew larger. During the ascent I was right out in front the whole way. I was feeling stronger and more confident every day. At our highest we were right at the bottom of the Lhotse Face at about 22,000 feet. From there, Pumori was almost featureless in front of the giant Cho Oyu.

Before a climber could go back down to Base Camp qualified as a member of a summit team, he or she had first to go up the Lhotse Face and "touch" Camp III (24,000 feet) before returning to Camp II. The climber had to then, after a rest day or two, return to Camp III and overnight, perhaps moving up to the Yellow Band the next day, return to Camp II, and then move on down to Base Camp. When the climber had been to the altitude of Camp III once, the return would be easier, with the overnight stay reinforcing his or her acclimatization at that altitude.

Our whole group began the ascent to the fixed lines on the Lhotse Face on Monday, the 13th. Ken turned around first, followed by Marge, Frank and John. The Lhotse Face was certainly steep enough—about forty-five degrees and covered with hard ice, mixed in places with rock. We were on the fixed lines for almost an hour when Pete announced it was time to return to Camp II. Several members of the Indian Border Police Expedition passed us up on the fixed ropes, and I was feeling a little uneasy about the number of people on the lines. It seemed to me that one person up high could fall and possibly take out everyone below like so many pearls on a strand. Returning to Camp II, I discovered the mess tent was full for dinner and lively, with a sociable atmosphere, but I bailed out early to get a good night's rest.

The next morning, we moved up the Western Cwm again to see if we could "touch" Camp III. I was climbing along by myself, feeling good about my performance at the highest and toughest climbing I had ever done, when around noon I had a close encounter with a sizable rock of the high-velocity, downhill-flying variety. Roughly the size of a cannon-ball, I surmised from the sound of it. It certainly shot past me like one, no more than two feet distant. I never saw it, only heard the sound of the thin atmosphere parting ahead of it and felt its back-draft.

It was a damn sobering experience. What had separated me, I wondered, from that parallel reality where the rock takes my head off? I didn't have a better answer than the next person, but I did have a rudimentary appreciation for the concept of fate and a deep, abiding feeling of gratitude.

Mid-afternoon, I was perhaps a half hour short of Camp III and moving along well, when Todd, coming back down the face, said, "We've got to go back down, Mike."

The rule in play was that the group needed to leave Camp III for Camp II by 2:00 p.m. in order to have a safety margin in case something went awry on the descent. It was 2:15 p.m. Turning around so close to my goal was the last thing I wanted to do.

Todd assured me: "You've gotten close enough to be part of the overnight contingent."

He and Perry had reached the camp and turned around immediately, and Hugh had not reached the actual camp site either. Vern and Keith, perhaps forty-five minutes behind me, turned back when they saw us coming down the ropes. At the bottom of the face we all took a break and then continued on down to Camp II.

Vern told me along the way, "Todd was impressed with your efforts and feels all four of you are summit material."

I said, "Vern, I appreciate you sharing that with me."

More and more members of our expedition were contracting respiratory ailments; the mess tent sounded like a tuberculosis ward. I was suffering only from blistered lips, a sore throat and sinus congestion. I assumed the climbers who had left days earlier for rest at Base Camp would continue to try to get up to Camp III, only on a more extended schedule than our group. Frank, Keith and I seemed to have relaxed somewhat with one another. And I liked Lewis, their friend from Hong Kong. Marge appeared to be on the mend though she was getting on my nerves, talking nonstop to anyone or anything, anywhere, at any time. She was an expert on everything and involved herself immediately in every conversation, invited or not—mostly not. Conversation requires two participants, a concept that was totally alien to Marge.

Thursday, I walked by myself about forty-five minutes uphill, returning for a lunch of ham, boiled eggs and Tang. All the guides, Todd, Peter, Vern and Skip, were now in Base Camp. Those of us at Camp II sat around the mess tent and chatted for a while about the permits, or lack of them, on our route. Todd and the other legitimate permit holders had been meeting to discuss the Russians and Spaniards and had made a formal complaint to the Nepalese ministry in Kathmandu. Though I didn't appreciate them using our route and guessed it was a Spanish-speaking rock that had almost beheaded me, I thought it also amusing that the guy who had the Super Couloir route on the North Face two years earlier and took over the "Crazy German's" West Ridge route was making such a fuss now that the shoe was on the other foot.

The physical health of the expedition was becoming a major issue. Marge had developed a particularly nasty cough and, to her, if you have a cough but are in denial, it's okay to cough without turning your head, covering your mouth, or taking other socially or medically appropriate measures. Go ahead and cough on everything and everyone in range, and never let it interrupt your incessant jabbering. In an attempt at sanitation control we were instructed to regularly wash our hands in a basin with iodine water, but it was pointless when Marge insisted on serving meals and then coughed mightily and directly onto each and every plate she handled. It was done so blatantly you couldn't help but wonder if it was intentional. The basin disappeared after a few days. There was some discussion about quarantining those with health problems (Marge), but nothing ever came of it.

I coughed all night before we left to overnight at Camp III. Going through the motions of getting ready to leave was the hardest thing I had done thus far on the trip.

It was tempting to say, "To hell with it. Lee, Steve, John and Ken have already gone down to Pheriche. I'm going down too."

But that morning, March 17, Todd, Vern, Keith, Hugh, Lewis, Perry and I ascended the Lhotse Face to Camp III. It took an hour and a half to reach the fixed lines and then four to five hours of strenuous climbing on hard ice in cold and windy conditions to reach Camp III. We spent the night in a pair of little yellow conical Himalayan Hotel tents on a narrow ledge so precarious that walking out at night in boot-liners to urinate would surely have been your final act.

The climb, though arduous, was uneventful except for passing a Russian on the line and waiting an interminably long time behind another with whom Todd had a shouting match.

Todd screamed, "You've lied and lied and you're going to end up in jail in Kathmandu!"

Perry and I organized the tent for the four of us. Vern was busy melting ice to cook dinner. He was coughing a lot and obviously didn't feel well, but went about his chores without complaining. Lewis had a huge appetite for both water and food, while Perry and I didn't require much. We were in Tangerine Dream sleeping bags that had been carried up by the Sherpas; nice, soft bags, but not nearly as warm as my Snowy Owl. Once in our bags we coughed all night in unison.

Just before dark one of the Russians we had encountered came by, searching for his camp. Vern hollered directions through the tent walls. An hour later the Russian was back, now in total darkness, with no headlamp, saying he had been unable to find the Russian tents. Vern directed him to Todd's tent, which was occupied by only three people. After a lengthy discussion and more than a little swearing, the Russian joined them for the night. He would certainly have perished otherwise, but the irony of Todd being his savior and roommate was not lost on those in our tent. Of course the Russian didn't have a sleeping bag either, so they had to allow him to wrap himself in their down clothing. No one from the Russian camp ever came looking for the guy, he was not invited to breakfast, and he was gone as soon as it was light enough to move.

In the morning Vern cooked and served breakfast, in good spirits despite his obvious ill health. It was near noon before we started up to touch a high point above Camp III. Not long after Todd signaled us to turn back, the weather overcast and the wind picking up. We stopped at Camp III to get our personal gear and continued on down the face. I struggled to descend the fixed lines as it started snowing. My glacier goggles became encrusted with snow, obstructing my vision. I cursed myself for leaving my ski goggles back at camp, along with the heftier Salewa crampons. My Light Fang crampons were perfect for walking over the ladders in the icefall, offering a convenient open space at the arch. But here on a forty-five degree face of hard ice and rock, it was much better to have points on the ice rather than open spaces.

I slipped once. Though my jumar held, the fixed rope was wrapped painfully around my left arm as I dangled in mid-air—pivoting on my crampons, perpendicular to the face with no foothold whatsoever, toe points only touching the near vertical ice—looking straight down the nearly 2,000 foot face. It was an awkward, vulnerable moment, swinging on that line—the only thing holding me to the Lhotse Face—and in that moment, I decided to leave the Light Fangs in Camp II on my summit attempt. I wasn't badly shaken by the incident, but I can't say I enjoyed it either, swinging and swaying back and forth like a dangling piece in an Alexander Calder mobile.

Back in Camp II, I began organizing my gear for the return to Base Camp and Pheriche. Marge started babbling her two or three words of Nepali at some newly-arrived Sherpas, carrying on as only she could.

Frank said loudly, "Oh, look! Marge's got some more faces to talk to!" I couldn't suppress a smile.

The next morning we started another beautiful day with the long descent to Base Camp through the blistering hot Western Cwm. It felt more like being in the Sahara Desert than in a snow-filled valley at 20,000 feet of elevation. There had been movement in the icefall and repairs; some crossings required a gnarly-looking contrivance of three or four ladders lashed end to end. Many of them leaned one way or the other as they crossed huge, gaping, dark voids from which you could feel the rising cold air like the breath from a heartless, subterranean siren. We worked quickly under those huge blocks of ice jutting skyward at odd angles. They were going to fall; it was simply a matter of when. One such huge pinnacle had a tent imbedded in it about three-quarters of the way up its face. Other, more disturbing things have been known to appear. It was like walking under a frozen Stonehenge rock held at a forty-five degree angle by some mysterious force that might let go at any moment. I would look at a huge protrusion from an uphill vantage point then hastily make my way along the ropes, barely breathing, until I stopped at a safe resting place—only to look up and find that the same protrusion was now even more immediately and threateningly over my head. Nonetheless, the icefall was eerily beautiful.

Near the bottom, we were stalled behind a group of Spaniards carrying their leader down on a stretcher after he had suffered a heart attack. It proved to be a very time-consuming process. I felt so wretched I would have readily occupied the stretcher myself. Not only had I not had a bowel movement in two and a half days, but now my body was urgently announcing its intentions.

Finally, one of the Spaniards motioned for us to pass and Frank, who was happily taking photos of the drama, said, "Oh, we're okay."

I didn't say a word but took immediate advantage of the offer, passing around the group thinking another drama would unfold if I didn't get to Base Camp and some toilet paper soon. Two of our

Sherpas met us near the bottom of the icefall with lemon tea. As I enjoyed the refreshment I patted a block of ice, thanking the Everest gods for allowing me safe passage through the Khumbu Icefall once again.

Since our doctor, Ken Kamler, was already in Pheriche, those of us with health problems—most of us—paid a visit to the Kiwi's doctor, Jan. Perry, who was showing early signs of high altitude pulmonary edema (HAPE), was put on supplemental oxygen and visited every hour all night by Skip. Vern was in bad shape from "Marge's Crud." Though practically everyone was now taking antibiotics I still steadfastly refused, preferring to use them as a last resort.

Jan, Rob Hall's pretty fiancée, suggested, "Mike, perhaps you should reassess your condition immediately upon reaching Pheriche, and then start taking antibiotics right away—if you decide to start taking them—so they'll have a chance to have an impact before your summit attempt."

First thing on the morning of the 20th, Skip, Vern and Perry started off to Pheriche. I had breakfast and washed most of my dirty clothes. Then I bathed myself from head to toe in the warm 17,500 foot Base Camp sunshine. The rest of the afternoon I spent socializing with my friends in the Kiwi camp. I had become very fond of Rob, Gary and Jan, but I'd be remiss not to admit that, unlike at our camp, they also always had a lot of tasty snacks lying about—things like quiches and fresh-baked cookies.

I wrote a letter to Shelli saying, "I know how hard this Everest business is on you, but I know in the long run that it'll bring us a lot closer and it is the last one. I feel like we're so fortunate to have each other and that we've really earned some future happiness. I'm so proud of you and want to hold you in my arms forever. I love you more than anything else in the world, and will be as careful as I can be, knowing how much I have to come home to. See you soon. Your loving husband, Michael."

At 8:30 a.m. I had my gear ready in front of the mess tent. Marge arrived on the scene and asked, "Is this where we're supposed to put our stuff?"

"I don't know, Marge," I said. "It's just where I decided to put mine."

It was a "we" kind of morning for Marge and I figured she thought it was going to be a "we" kind of day. I had determined otherwise. Lewis had prepared in advance; he said something about some business he had to attend to in the Kiwi camp and high-tailed it out of there.

Lapka Rita arranged for four Sherpani to carry our larger bags down—little girls, big bags, no problem. Provide them with a perfectly good backpack and they will take everything out and re-sort it so it fits nicely into one of their conical, woven baskets with a strap that runs over their foreheads.

The Sherpani were in no hurry to be underway, so they stopped and chatted often. Marge went through the Kiwi camp stopping at every single tent and calling loudly for Lewis. Of course, he was nowhere to be found. She was out in front of our procession, motioning the Sherpani to move on, and they were motioning for her to move on. I was standing way back, keeping my distance.

Marge hollered, "Mike, do you know where the trail is?"

"No, Marge," I said. It was clearly visible in front of us.

Not far from Base Camp, with Marge out in front of me, I could see that a couple of Sherpani had to make nature calls and didn't want me in the vicinity. I tried my hardest to move on without catching up with Marge, which proved impossible. She claimed to have lost the trail, which I soon spotted. I took off in the lead and got to Gorakshep in time to enjoy a Coke and depart before she arrived. I reached Lobuche in time to gulp a Sprite and leave just as she appeared, though it didn't stop her from barging right into a conversation I was having as if she had not missed a word, offering unsolicited advice on everything and anything, including the weather, the condition of the trail, circumstances at Base Camp, and even Camp III, a place she had never been.

I just said, "Goodbye."

After a couple of wrong turns, I arrived in Pheriche mid-afternoon, a bit chilled from the wind and increased humidity. I found our group at the Himalayan Rescue Center. It was like a movie scene of the New York General Hospital emergency room. Perry lay in the Gamow bag with the atmospheric pressure inside already pumped up. Vern sat hunched over, a towel covering his head and his face in a vaporizer. Everyone else sat about, coughing and gagging. Ken was there, John was there and Lewis was there—the rat! So were Skip, Karen (Todd's girlfriend), and Karen's friend Gayle, who was obviously infatuated with Perry, Gamow bag and all.

The physicians had decided that "Marge's Crud" was viral and since my lungs were clear and I did not seem to have a sinus infection, I didn't need to start a round of antibiotics. Perry was in the worst condition, battling HAPE. Vern was next, diagnosed with a super infection, followed by Marge, who was moving no oxygen through her lungs—only huge volumes of nonsensical words. Matt Reese, one of the young doctors at the clinic, asked around about the history of the contagion, suggesting parallels to Legionnaire's Disease. Marge immediately volunteered a view that didn't have anything to do with reality. Later, alone with him, I explained why we had labeled it "Marge's Crud."

Had Marge been sent back to Base Camp after a couple of days at Camp II, when it was obvious her health would not improve, she might have been able to recover and make it to Camp III and join a summit team. The body doesn't heal at altitude; it's too busy keeping you alive. Even farther down the mountain at Base Camp you burn as many calories each day as if you had run a marathon.

On Denali, I had suffered from high altitude sickness at 14,000 feet. But upon arriving at Pheriche, also 14,000 feet, I felt like I was at the beach and my appetite knew no bounds. At dinner I ate a pile of yak steaks, an onion omelet, egg fried rice, and some chips and drank three Fanta orange drink sodas. If only I could have enjoyed all my meals so uninterrupted. Later, at lunch in the hotel with Perry, Marge walked in, stood immediately over our table and coughed all over us. I managed to shield my food from the deluge with a magazine.

Marge asked, "Is there anything interesting in the magazine, Mike?"

A couple days later, when I stopped by the clinic again to get some Robitussin, Dr. Matt listened to my lungs and said, "They're still clear, Mike. No indication of trouble."

My oxygen saturation level was ninety-eight percent. Still, I had coughed so much, and for so long, there was no area around my torso that didn't hurt. I guess the doctors were so focused on pulmonary edema, pneumonia and "Marge's Crud," they were prone to miss chronic bronchitis.

On Sunday, March 26, I learned that Vern was going to take Marge down a thousand feet lower to the Ama Dablam Hotel. That was the best news I'd heard since congress voted for Alaskan statehood. Finally, a break. I had spent only one night away from her in over a month, the night at Camp III.

Lewis and I returned to Base Camp four days later, stopping for visits in Lobuche and Gorakshep along the way. Ken looked much improved but said he still had pneumonia in one lung.

Skip said, "Mike, you, Lewis, John and I will be leaving as a team for the summit in three days."

The weather remained marginal high on the mountain. The Dutch stayed put at the South Col, as did our group at Camp III. We learned that three Indians from the Civil Expedition, still alive after a disastrous descent tragically shrank the team, were moving down with members of the much better-equipped Border Police. The body of the Civil Expedition leader had frozen to the mountainside, still hooked into the fixed line between Camp III and Camp IV. The Indians wanted us to remove the corpse from the line. I don't know why they didn't do it themselves, but our Sherpas would have no part of it for superstitious reasons. Besides, it was the Indians' responsibility to take care of their own dead. Our climbers at Camp III fixed a rope around the body, moved it to the side and left its eventual removal to the Indians. The whole affair was macabre and unsettling and I worried that Shelli and my mom might get wind of the incident and fear I was somehow involved in it.

In his book, *Dark Shadows Falling*, Joe Simpson describes with some detail the callous attitude of everyone on the mountain toward the Indians that spring, especially the Dutch, who did nothing to save the dying Indian climber waving his arms in the air outside their tent. He decries our summit group's inhumane treatment of the dead climber on the fixed line, but you have to be able to put yourself in the shoes of those who were there, which is not an easy thing to do. I have given it a lot of thought and I believe it comes down to having too many people on the mountain at the same time, the most vulnerable of which were improperly trained and equipped. And, to make matters worse, one Indian group did not take care of the other, expecting others to do so instead.

Mr. Simpson, a renowned climber and competent writer, has personally experienced being left for dead, an incredible survival story he relates in *Touching the Void*, so he is understandably sensitive to the issues involved. And though I sympathize with his feelings about the indifference shown toward the Indian Civil Expedition, I think he overreaches in favor of a disappointing elitism. Following Simpson's line of reasoning, people like me should never have been allowed the chance to climb Everest because we hadn't been climbing all our lives, had bought our way in, and hence, in his opinion, had no climbing standards or principles.

Climbers in our Number Two summit group, including me, were upset that Todd took all the best guides and Sherpa with him on the initial summit bid. Pete, Todd, Lapka Rita, and Chuldim all accompanied just two climbers, leaving our group of three climbers with just one guide, Skip, who had never summited Everest, and Sherpas who had not done so either. The feeling at Base Camp was that it was all about getting Todd Burleson to the top.

Ken and I walked over to visit our friends in the Kiwi camp, who were all sitting around eating a beautiful quiche. They had a camp manager named Ruth, who oversaw their kitchen operation, including the menu, whereas ours was left to Ong Chu, a Nepali, with little oversight. We were consequently subjected to a lot of lousy, spicy, inedible Nepalese food, which was no doubt also cheaper to acquire and prepare. When we returned to our camp, we complained bitterly to Karen, pointing out the fact that the clients in the Kiwi Expedition hadn't paid any more for their experience than we had. Karen graciously accepted the criticisms, acknowledging that we weren't attacking her personally, and promised to make improvements.

It was snowing and blowing at the South Col on May 4, so all of our first summit team returned to Camp II except for Chuldim, who walked all the way down to Base Camp from Camp IV in one day—a very impressive feat. We wondered if Todd and his group would now return to Base Camp as well, allowing our group a chance at the summit, or make another attempt. Vern, Perry and Marge were all back from Ama Dablam Lodge. Vern was so thin it was shocking. Marge was still coughing—and talking.

Todd and the rest of the first summit team showed up before dinner, exhausted but in good condition otherwise. We ate a wonderful spaghetti dinner that actually tasted like spaghetti. Karen had traded some cookies for tomatoes from the Kiwis. Our entire expedition was now in Base Camp. My team was to head for the summit in a day or two, and I had received a long-anticipated package from Shelli that included letters from just about everyone I cared about. I had taken a shower and paid a Sherpani to wash my clothes. My mood was positive, my spirits bolstered, though I was still coughing a bit at night.

Our summit bid began on Saturday, May 9, 1992, when we entered the icefall at 6:30 a.m. and arrived at Camp II at 3:00 p.m. By then, I had started coughing again. Talking to Ken by radio that evening, we agreed I should start taking Augmentin.

The next morning, Todd asked about my health during the 10:00 a.m. radio call. Skip said, "Mike's made a remarkable recovery since last night."

It was true. I could actually feel the Augmentin working. The rest of the day, we prepared to move higher early next morning. It was John's thirty-fifth birthday. Skip gave him a couple of candy bars. I gave him a hand warmer. The Voice of America (VOA), which is the external broadcast institution of the United States government, funded annually by Congress, played Billy Joel music because it was his birthday, too.

All day long the weather was crystal clear with hardly a breeze, offering a view of the long line of climbers high above us, probably the Indian Border Police Expedition, coming out of the uphill side of the Yellow Band and heading for the South Col. That would be us soon enough. It was hard to believe when the temperature inside my tent registered just below ninety degrees that afternoon. Never would I have imagined myself at 21,000 feet, stretched out on my sleeping bag, wearing nothing but my shorts and a light polypro top, placing my feet alternately on the frozen ground on either side of my Therm-a-Rest to combat the heat.

We left for Camp III at 6:30 a.m. on May 10. Vern and I reached Camp III at 3:30 p.m., a couple hours behind Skip and Lewis and about ten minutes behind John. Vern wore a handkerchief over his face and, though I tried to wear a surgical mask, I found it too suffocating and climbed without it, which was to cost me. We spent several hours digging out around the tents, especially the guide tent, which had leaked from the uphill side and was full of snow. Vern and Lewis argued intensely over the whole issue because Lewis had a headache and felt it was just a "make-work" job.

Vern said, "Lewis, you wouldn't have a headache if you hadn't been in such a hurry to get here."

"He's right," I wanted to say.

Around 6:30 p.m., John, Lewis and I climbed into our sleeping bags and I started coughing non-stop right through dinner, which was ramen noodles, followed by a packaged meal none of us could eat. Despite Vern's badgering, we threw it out the back door of the tent.

After more than four hours of the most violent coughing and gagging of my entire life, John and Lewis begged me to call Vern for some oxygen. The oxygen didn't stop the coughing entirely, but slowed it down.

Even so, it was a dreadful night and in the morning, with a worried look on his face, Lewis asked, "Mike, do you plan to continue?"

"No," I said, "I don't think it would be prudent for me to go any higher."

"There are a few imprudent Indians up there already," John said.

Vern hollered over from the guide tent, "Mike, what are you going to do?"

"I'm going down," I said.

Silence.

If you cannot make it down from Camp IV, or even Camp III, under your own power you are likely to be there for a very long time.

I felt I had made the right decision, but after eating some fruit cock-tail, getting dressed and moving around I started second-guessing myself. After all, by turning around I was allowing Vern Tejas to become the first Alaskan to complete the Seven Summits, something I had fought hard to achieve for four years. Rationality prevailed only because I knew I could not spend another night like the previous, 3,000 feet higher, at the South Col, and hope to survive it.

By 9:00 a.m. the remainder of the summit team was ready to proceed to the South Col and I was ready to descend. I gave my farewells and best wishes as quickly as I could to avoid an emotional scene and departed with Nawang Sherpa, who carried some of my gear. Two and a half hours later, we were back in the Camp II mess tent visiting with Peter and Perry over tea. I was despondent, dispirited and depressed. I cried. I felt I had let myself and everyone else down, but I knew I had at least one more attempt in me and Mt. Everest has a learning curve. I might not be the first Alaskan to complete the Seven Summits, but I could still do it.

Peter said, "It took me six tries to summit the first time. I had to quit once for this very same reason."

He looked hard at me. "I personally know how difficult that decision was for you but, believe me, you did the right thing."

Todd was visibly upset about my failure to summit, saying I had showed up in great shape, the best ever, and was as capable as any climber in the expedition. He agreed to carry my Chilkoot Charlie's flag, my Anchorage Fire Department hat, and my cachets to the summit for me.

The Khumbu Icefall had grown funkier as the season progressed, a route maintained by dwindling manpower and supplies over ever-widening crevasses. One ladder rested on the ice on one side of a yawning black hole, but fell short of the ice on the other side by at least six inches, held in place by a couple of ropes, sinking nearly a foot below the lip of the crevasse on the far side when I put my weight on it. Near the bottom we made a sizeable detour around large newly-formed pools of water, but managed the entire descent in only four hours, arriving at Base Camp to the popping of a champagne bottle. Our team had made the summit, sans me.

Skip, Vern and Lewis reached the summit of Mt. Everest around 11:00 a.m. on Thursday, May 12, 1992, three of about thirty altogether that made it, including the Kiwis (all of whom made it), Spaniards, Indians and who knows who else—no doubt the Russians without a permit. It was a record day; our guys had to wait at the foot of the Hillary Step for an hour due to the traffic jam. Vern became the first Alaskan to complete the Seven Summits, which was wonderful for him, but hugely disappointing for me.

I called Shelli from the Kiwi camp to let her know I was off the mountain and safe, though summitless. Although obviously disappointed that I hadn't made the summit she was happy to hear my voice, as I was to hear hers. I looked forward to returning to Anchorage, to continue restoring our relationship and rebuilding our lives together and, though I knew I was subjecting her and the rest of my family to a lot of stress every time I attempted Mt. Everest, I was already planning my next trip. At the time, I considered the Seven Summits to be the one truly remarkable thing I had ever attempted, in part for how powerfully it had pulled me out of the misery my life had become in the '80s. I was in the final inning, and I wasn't about to walk off the field.

The Rollercoaster '80s

When I reflect on the '80s, I remember how hopeful I felt after emerging—barely intact—from those tumultuous '70's. I had high hopes for the '80s. By then I had set in order the mess that had been my life when I returned from Belize, and committed to the success of my business as a stable, level-headed bachelor who finally understood a good thing when he saw it, strolling the Maui beaches with Shelli in December, 1979. I had made the best decision of my life, asking for her hand in marriage and starting a new chapter with the most caring person I had ever met.

The first half of the decade was great—a period when, because of Alaska's newly found oil wealth, money was no problem and all things were possible. I opened the Bingo Hall addition to Koot's in October of 1985, with its North Long Bar on the back side of the South Long Bar, and the new Horseshoe Bar. I was now carrying a maximum Small Business Administration loan and big loans from Alaska Continental Bank and Alaska USA Federal Credit Union. Things were going along well enough until the shit hit the fan in the spring of 1986.

In an extreme price-war move against OPEC members cheating on their quotas, Sheikh Yamani of Saudi Arabia opened the Saudi oil taps, creating a glut that sent the price of oil free-falling more than 50% and collapsing the economies of oil-producing states like Alaska. It got so bad that Alaskans were just dropping off their house keys at Alaska Housing Finance Corporation and driving down the Alcan Highway. The only guy in the state making any money was the one with the U-Haul franchise.

First, I borrowed all my life insurance cash loan values and all the money in my retirement plan. Then I took out a second mortgage on my condo on Sorbus Way, and sold two condos in Hawaii. I completed a work-out with SBA, Alaska USA and several mortgage-holders, including another bank after Alaska Continental had gone belly-up. At that point, there was nothing else I could do but hang on and pray.

My son Michael was a sophomore in high school, living back and forth with his mother and stepfather in South Anchorage or with Shelli and me, when he became disturbingly involved in a game popular with teenagers at the time called Dungeons and Dragons. It affected his school and social life, and he began to show the first symptoms of a mental disorder—withdrawal, sleeplessness and agitation. His stepfather only made things worse: he was autocratic and unloving to Lilla as well as to my children. I threatened to kick his ass if he ever called Michael a sissy or a girl again. Lilla had sought a home for her children and what she got was one for the children of her new marriage, but not for our children, or even for herself.

Michael had his first psychotic episode in the fall of 1985 when I was in Hawaii, about to fly to New York to run the New York Marathon. Shelli and I had planned on meeting in the city, and we did, after discussing Michael's condition with his doctor by phone. The doctor insisted there was nothing we could do to alter or improve Michael's circumstances so we should continue with our travel plans. We sat on the hotel bed together, exhausted and stunned.

"I'm about to crack up myself," she said, inviting the specter of what I would discover was her bipolar disorder to join us in the room.

It was too much. I neither believed her, nor felt I could deal with it, my only son having just been committed to a mental institution.

Back in Anchorage and ironically on Friday, the thirteenth, I woke up in the middle of the night for some unknown reason and couldn't find my wife. Searching through the eerie quiet I finally found her in the garage, sitting in our Mercedes-Benz in her night clothes, her Raggedy Ann doll in her arms, the car windows down, garage door closed and the engine running. I brought Shelli back into the house and called over her best friend Deborah's mother, Vivian, who lived just a few doors down the street in Woodside East. We talked to her in quiet voices, those long hours; she assured us she would be okay.

After a second suicide attempt, this time by overdosing on aspirin, I called 911 and my lovely, newly-minted wife was whisked away to Providence Hospital, where Michael was then occupying their inchoate psychiatric ward. Shelli didn't want Michael to know she was in the hospital, so when I visited, I would see Shelli first, sequestered in an observation room in the burn unit, then Michael in the psych ward via a circuitous route. He caught me in the act once.

"Dad," he said, "what are you doing here?"

I felt like my world was falling down around my head like a heavy, wet blanket. There were moments when I could barely breathe—a sensation that would, in less than a decade, feel almost normal, but not yet.

Lilla, Shelli and I had agreed to send Michael to Judson School in Scottsdale, Arizona. We hoped that beginning his junior year in the expensive private school would provide him with some structure and the chance to improve his grade point average. I had to sell a beautiful river-front lot on the Kenai River to finance the tuition, but it worked. Michael's grades improved and we received glowing reports from the school. But he didn't like it there, and he persuaded me to let him return to Anchorage so he could graduate with his friends. I shouldn't have done it, though he did graduate—barely—after suffering a serious psychotic episode during the interim. Twenty years later Michael admitted that, in the fall of 1985, on a dare, he had overdosed on various drugs—mostly amphetamines. He has since been diagnosed with drug-induced psychosis rather than clinical schizophrenia, though his symptoms are practically identical.

His friends, if you could call them that, reported that he turned blue and stopped breathing. They thought he was dead. He had, in fact, suffered an amphetamine-induced stroke—a known drug syndrome with a medical protocol for treatment—but because Michael never admitted to anyone that he had basically swallowed a bottle of amphetamines, and because he and his friends made the decision not to seek medical attention at the time of the incident, he never received the treatment necessary to help him recover from that type of stroke. Instead he was left with permanent and irreparable brain damage, setting off a chain of psychotic events that have continued ever since.

Thinking back, I did something almost as stupid when I was exactly Michael's age, only with bourbon whiskey I had pilfered from my dad's liquor cabinet. Had I been born fifteen or twenty years later I might have chosen drugs as well; the world had become a more dangerous place.

Though Michael's mental condition was unstable, hoping for the best, he and I flew from Anchorage to Seattle, rented a car and drove together to Boise, where I enrolled him at Boise State University. I had helped him get a student loan from the state of Alaska, helped him enroll in various classes, got him a room in the dorm and even met his roommate, a good kid who promised to look after Michael. But Michael couldn't endure attending classes because of his paranoia and the voices in his head, both of which were becoming more insistent, so he returned to Alaska before the semester was over.

During roughly this same period of time, my daughter Michele was failing her freshman year at Brigham Young University. I was disappointed in her, said as much, and she reacted by lashing out at me and returning to Anchorage with a conman she had met on campus. Randy was a control freak and couldn't let my daughter out of his sight any more than he could keep a job. By the time she realized her terrible mistake, he had her so ineluctably wrapped up in his web that it took a family intervention and an orchestrated plan to extricate her.

She put her dirty clothes into a paper grocery bag, grabbed her purse and told Randy she was going to our house to do laundry. We put her on a plane with her cousin, Teri, bound for Honolulu to stay in a unit I still owned in the Ilikai Hotel. A close Hawaiian friend, Henry, met the girls at the airport, took them to the condo and watched out for Randy.

I told Henry, "If he shows up, don't kill him, for God's sake. Just break his legs."

Michele and Randy had been living in a downtown apartment on L Street near Simon and Seafort's. I went there with a security guard friend of mine, aptly known as Nick Danger. Confronting Randy with Nick gleefully glaring at him from the sideline, arms crossed, I told him that Michele could do whatever she wanted. So if she, for some insane reason decided to return to him, it was her choice. But he was not to look for her, and if he did, I would hurt him.

Michele did return to Randy, exchanging her return ticket to Anchorage for one to California. She married him and ended up pregnant, living out of a car—the new Honda Civic I had given her as a high school graduation present.

Michele has never told me the rest of the details about her ordeals in California, which is just as well, but we were finally able to coordinate another escape. Pregnant again, she drove up the Alcan Highway with my little granddaughter, Courtney, and my disabled grandson, Eric, and moved in with me for a year when I lived on Sorbus Way, in Woodside East. Shelli and I were separated at the time; she was living in an apartment downtown. At the end of the year Shelli humorously gave us a "Certificate of Familial Co-Habitation" in acknowledgement of how well we had managed a difficult situation.

By the late '80s, Shelli and Lilla and I had suffered more than we could endure dealing with Michael. Michele, then living with Randy, volunteered to give it a try in California, as if she didn't have enough problems dealing with Randy who, not surprisingly, proved totally uncooperative in the effort to manage Michael. I'll readily acknowledge that Michael was more than anyone could handle, that my daughter was naïve to think she could manage him, and that I was relieved to get any sort of break from the strain of it myself.

Since things predictably didn't work out well in his sister's household, Michael moved into his own apartment—that is, until he got cold and decided to build a campfire on the carpeted floor of his room. He didn't burn the place down, but he was understandably unwelcome after the incident. He disappeared for a week soon after. We later discovered that he had been roaming around San Jose barefoot, sporting long hair and a beard, in a psychotic haze that led him to believe he was Jesus Christ recruiting disciples. He ended up in jail with burns on the soles of his feet from the hot sidewalks. He then did no small amount of additional damage to himself by throwing his body into the corner of his cell and against the sink and toilet, over and over, because the voices in his head were telling him to break his dick in three places. So he wound up where he belonged: a mental institution.

When Michael was ready to leave the institution, purportedly stabilized, he returned by plane to Alaska with his sister. He was a problem for her on the flight, bothering the passenger in front of him, getting into his space, talking too loud, moving too forcefully and disturbing the back of the guy's head. Michele passed the passenger a note pleading for patience.

Michael was a bigger problem when she got him home. The three of us—Shelli, Michele and I—could not possibly control his behavior, and he had to be watched twenty-four hours a day. Once, while we were all watching a video, Michael got up from his chair, grabbed the VHS player and started to leave the room with it.

When we jumped up to stop him, asking why he was doing it he said indignantly, "Because you told me to put it in the dryer!"

Another time we found him filling his running shoes with ice from the refrigerator ice maker because his feet were hot. More frightening, we caught him in the downstairs bathroom holding his sister's plugged-in electric hair curling iron under the faucet. He was soon back at Alaska Psychiatric Institute, where his medications were adjusted and he was able to function more or less adequately again. In his lucid moments he could joke about his insane behavior, like when he laughingly told me about what a lousy Jesus he had made, spending all those days and nights roaming around San Jose proselytizing to people but finding not a single disciple.

I provided Michael with an apartment adjacent to the club parking lot and gave him a job working for my maintenance manager, but he could not get out of bed in the morning. Anti-psychotic drugs are extremely powerful and most of them have unpleasant side effects, the least of which is sleeping more deeply and longer than normal. One night, when Michael was staying over at my condo in Woodside East, I brought home the members of the Scorpions, a big-time German rock band the club had co-sponsored at the George Sullivan Arena. Michael was distraught when he discovered the band had been in his home and he had not met them—one of them had done some doodles for him on a napkin as a keepsake—but Shelli and I simply could not awaken him.

People with mental health issues do not like to take their medications because of the side effects and so, when they begin to feel under control they will stop taking them, which generally brings on another psychotic episode. In Michael's case, it seemed that each time he experienced an episode, he would return with a little less of himself than before.

In previous years, when Michael was released from the Alaska Psychiatric Institute, he had stayed in a halfway house that was staffed by professional mental health care workers who provided structured living conditions. Then the state funding the halfway houses depended upon was withdrawn. So, after more than a year of unsuccessfully trying to manage Michael, we sent him to Washington, where his mother had recently moved with her second family.

The state of Washington's mental health institutions would not voluntarily have accepted Michael's transfer from Alaska, but once in his mother's household, it was only a matter of time before he had another psychotic episode. He would then be under their jurisdiction. Washington State has a far more extensive mental health infrastructure than Alaska, though their system is riddled with problems not unlike those seen in the movie *One Flew Over the Cuckoo's Nest*. Suffice it to say, one is wise to avoid the entire experience, if at all possible. Michael has never moved back to Alaska, though he has visited us several times in Halibut Cove during the summer with his mother.

Michael cannot hold a job and relies on Catholic Social Services, Social Security and other programs, but currently he is stable and living in his own apartment in Bellingham, Washington, near his mother. We visit him when passing through Seattle, exchange Christmas and birthday gifts, and he always sends me a present and calls on my birthday and Father's Day to tell me he loves me. He said in the latest Father's Day card that I would "always be his very best friend," something I could never have said to my father. He is a gentle soul, kind to animals and considerate of others as long as he's on his meds. Even in his worst state, I've always felt he was far more a danger to himself than to others.

I feel responsible to some degree for Michael's mental disorder. I have never asked his mother whether she feels similarly, but I wouldn't be a bit surprised if she did. During the early months of Michael's affliction, a psychiatrist at Alaska Psychiatric Institute explained to me in some detail why he thought it was all Lilla's fault. He hadn't spent more than a few minutes with her before arriving at this ridiculous conclusion—it was purely academic—and he never pointed his finger at me, but then, he didn't have to. I concluded he was clearly misogynistic and I also decided long ago, through my contacts with the mental health treatment world, that the strongest link in the chain of care and treatment— the hardest working and most empathetic—is the nurses. The weakest link is the psychiatrists themselves, many of them distant, emotionless, and flat-out wrong about their diagnoses, and better at writing prescriptions than anything else. After all, medication is, next to incarceration, the best way to control a person with a mental disorder. Every psychiatrist I've ever met needs the mantra "First care, then treatment!" Treatment without caring is inhuman.

Until recent years, the parents of schizophrenic and autistic children have had to deal with the specter of parental fault, especially the mothers of the afflicted children. In the early '80s, the reference to "refrigerator mother" and "refrigerator parents" was still widely used by psychiatric physicians, implying that the mother or both parents were cold and distant to their children, causing them to disconnect from others in convoluted, antisocial ways. Unfortunately, these mostly discredited and abandoned theories still have traction.

Michael did, and still does, have some deep-seated anger toward his mother and he has been hateful to Shelli on more than one occasion, as when Shelli, Michael and I were having lunch at the New Cauldron Restaurant in the University Center, and I didn't understand what the waitress said to me regarding the check, so Shelli repeated it for me.

Michael exploded with, "Can't you see what she's doing?" and launched into a tirade about how Shelli was trying to manipulate me.

Fortunately, most of the strain between Michael and Shelli, and his mother, has dissipated over the years. It is apparent to Michael at this stage of his life that Shelli is not a threat and that his mother has sacrificed her own life for his. I've never seen such motherly dedication with the exception of my daughter's mothering of her own disabled son, Eric.

My feelings of guilt regarding Michael's illness are the result of my decision to file for a divorce from Lilla. We were very much in love, but we had a tumultuous relationship and fought constantly toward the end. That sort of environment isn't good for anyone either —children or adults—though breaking the news to six-year-old Michele, sitting next to her on a bed at the log cabin on Sixth Avenue, was the heart-breaking experience of a lifetime.

When I broached the subject she said, "I know, daddy, it starts with a 'D.'"

Michele was so brave and I was so afraid for us all.

I wish I had been more mature. I wish I could have mustered the courage to soldier on with the marriage for the sake of the kids. I wish I had had the benefit, as in later years, of listening to the advice of Dr. Laura, who would have commanded me to hang in there. But I wasn't, I hadn't and I didn't. I tell myself that had I hung in there things would have turned out differently, that Michele wouldn't have had such a tough time as a teenager and young adult, and Michael wouldn't have ended up in one mental institution after another. Of course, had Lilla and I stayed married, in that kind of unhappy, volatile relationship, our lives might have taken an even more challenging course, if that's possible.

Time heals most things, and though it will never heal my deepest feelings of guilt, I have tried to be a loving and supportive father in spite of the difficult, uncertain circumstances I had a major part in creating. During her awkward young-adult years, Michele accused me of being "the father I never had," but I have, in fact, always been there for her. She recognizes that today, her feelings perhaps tempered by the experience of her own divorce. I always paid my child support—and a lot more. I attended her prom, graduation, basketball games, beauty pageants, took her skiing and visited as often as I could. Since her second marriage and the birth of four grandchildren from that marriage, Shelli and I have aided in the purchase and furnishing of a home, helped pay for the grandkids' college educations and a number of other kindnesses a loving father and nana would provide.

Michele made a complete recovery from her own unhappy circumstances and met Jerry Ritter, one of the finest human beings I know, on a blind date. He did not bolt when she showed up with two-week-old Jared because she couldn't find a babysitter who would sit all three children. In short order, they fell in love.

Shelli and I jokingly told her, "If you screw this one up, we're keeping him!"

Jerry was the attorney for Ahtna, Incorporated, smallest of the Alaska Native regional corporations. His family lived in New Mexico, where he had been raised and educated through law school. Michele and Jerry eventually moved south, out of the long and dark Alaska winters that proved too difficult an environment to care for Michele's son Eric, who had severe developmental issues. They may have walked away from all those Alaska Permanent Fund Dividends checks and taken my grandkids with them, much to our chagrin, but every time I visit Michele and Jerry—now a federal magistrate Judge in Albuquerque, New Mexico —and the grandkids, I leave inspired by what a loving, caring family they are.

Randy never paid a cent of child support, but that didn't prevent him from attempting to retain his parental rights from California. When asked by the judge why he wouldn't return to Alaska, he said he feared for his life, establishing for the record that at least he wasn't stupid. He also lamely tried to make that an excuse for his delinquent child support, but the judge didn't buy it. Jerry legally adopted Randy's children, yet Randy still tried to get his clutches on Courtney, his oldest, during phone calls from California to Alaska.

Courtney would simply say, "He just doesn't understand. I have two daddies now."

We all breathed a sigh of relief.

Alaska's economy was finally saved, ironically enough, by the $2 billion that Exxon pumped into the Alaskan economy to clean up the oil its Exxon Valdez tanker spilled into Prince William Sound, after running aground on March 24, 1989, at the very beginning of its trip to Long Beach, California.

Business at Chilkoot Charlie's came back stronger than ever, until the advent of the still-popular dance format—DJs and recorded music—caught us flat-footed. We were scrambling. We had been running bands in both the Show Bar and the North Long Bar and had to adjust to the new format in the Show Bar. That is when we hired Bob Lester, known to locals as DJ Bob. It worked, and saved the business, but we had to periodically redecorate the area to keep it fresh for the younger clientele packing the dance floor.

I wanted to install a theme with intrinsic value that would be substantial and varied enough to last, and I hit upon the Russian theme. I had studied Russian history at USF and by the early '90s had been to Russia three times in my attempt to summit Mt. Elbrus, so I had a few items to use for decorations to get us started before turning to eBay. The idea was logical enough; after all, the Russians used to own the place. So we installed an Ice Bar fronting a gulag theme, decorated one wall to look like the Berlin Wall, hung Soviet space program missiles and satellites from the ceiling, turned the Show Bar into a Vitus Bering-era ship's prow, and the stage area into a Tsarist-era St. Petersburg ballroom theme. The upstairs bar became the Romanov Room and the walkway between the north and south sides became the Soviet Walk, sporting perhaps the largest private display of Soviet memorabilia anywhere.

DJ Bob kept the customers entertained with his music and antics, part of which involved midget bowling with his midget buddies. In a highly creative—or misguided?—moment we even built a Midget Bar where the Ice Bar is now. We all had high hopes for the Midget Bar, where our midgets served single-serve sized drinks like you get on an airplane. But once people packed the room, no one could see their little bar over in the corner, and the midgets grew frustrated and gave up. I always thought we should have raised the bar off the floor and stuck with it a while longer, but the midgets, and DJ Bob, had short attention spans.

Nonetheless, things were looking up. I could breathe again. Run ragged by another up-and-down decade, I gazed out my window at Denali and yearned for a new start. Adventure had proven a cure-all, to be sure. But I had to do it right this time, with a regimen that demanded planning and forethought. I couldn't survive another Belize.

During 1987 and 1988, I had been struggling to save my marriage to Shelli by going regularly to counseling. It was then I first felt inspired to take up climbing, setting in motion the chain of summits—and summit attempts—that took me to Everest three times. In fact, the day I stood on the tarmac of the Talkeetna airport and witnessed the injured climbers being unloaded from the helicopter was less than two months after the Exxon Valdez ecological disaster and Alaska's economic windfall.

Mt. Elbrus

Whether standing in the Koot's Tsarist-era ballroom, the Romanov Room or admiring the workmanship in the Berlin Wall recreation and Soviet-era space program hanging overhead that I had created, I was transported to Russia. In a blink it seemed, after my return from my second attempt at Everest in May of 1992, I was back that fall at the base of another mountain that had proved difficult to conquer—Elbrus. In 1989, deep, unstable snow and high winds dismissed our strong Genet Expeditions group led by Mike Howerton from the summit ridge. The following year our group, also led by Genet Expeditions, would not fully commit itself. I was furious, sitting at Priut Hut watching a Rainier Mountain expedition on their way to the top in beautiful weather while we sat packing our bags and preparing to head down the mountain. It meant another trip to Russia.

Soviet Russia was dark and oppressive. Russia during *glasnost and perestroika* was more open, but it was still a dreary place. So the last thing in the world I wanted to do was return to that god-forsaken country a third time. The people were sad and withdrawn, the accommodations third-rate, and the food awful, but I had to get to the top of that mountain.

I had dedicated the cachet for Mt. Elbrus to my father, which is why I figured the journey was proving so difficult. I had never had a chance to reconcile with him during his lifetime, and here I was, still sorting things out more than a decade after his death.

I had Shelli convinced that I came from a perfectly normal family until we started therapy. We had a husband-and-wife team of therapists—since divorced—that we have outlasted by over twenty years. Shelli would meet with the wife and I would meet with the husband on an individual basis, then we'd occasionally get together for nasty little clashes. The sessions began to produce positive results because I felt I had someone in my corner with whom I could confide and discuss issues that I had never discussed with anyone.

I discovered my childhood wasn't everything it was cracked up to be when I started reading about adult children of alcoholics, trying anything at that point to save my marriage.

One often-heard comment that resounds in my head from my high school years is, "Don't bring *that* up if you know what's good for you."

During holidays my mom would slave in the kitchen all day, cranking out a turkey, a ham or whatever, along with a strawberry upside-down cake. We'd say grace and eat. Dad, drunk by then, would be asleep in his overstuffed chair in the living room. And that was it. Everything was rosy. Any unruly elephants in the room were swept under the carpet with a big, invisible broom and we'd tip-toe around that carpet lump roughly the size of a drunken man in a chair. God forbid you "bring *that* up."

When I was in junior high, my mother confided to me that she was contemplating suicide. Why would a mother admit that to her thirteen-year-old son? At the time, when my dad wasn't fighting with my sister at home, he was a devoted functioning alcoholic at work, hiding out in the camper he parked at school, drinking between classes. But my parents weren't divorced—everything was just fine. Right. It's no wonder I didn't hit my scholastic stride until I went to college, and got away from home. I am fully aware that there are a lot of people in Anchorage who had my mom and dad for teachers and think the world of them. I can understand why. But they were better teachers than parents.

When my sister left for Stetson University she said to me, "Now it's your turn."

She had been the main focus of my dad's relentless badgering emotional abuse until then.

During junior and high school, I had a bedroom right next to my parents' bedroom. I recall a conversation I overheard when they thought I was sleeping.

Dad said, "You spend too much time with the kids and not enough with me."

Mom replied, "Whitey, do you expect me to ignore my own children?" (As a child, my father was a towhead and carried the nickname Whitey throughout his life.)

My mother brought her own kind of turmoil to the family. She told me that once, sitting at the family dinner table with a college girlfriend, she politely objected to something her father said by saying, "But, Daddy..." He back-handed her right out of her chair—that was her idea of discipline. Presumably the message there was that when her dad did it to her it was unjustified, but when she did it to me it was. I could sass my dad and get away with it, but heaven help me if I tried it with my mother.

I was always feeling for the invisible line. When I found it, the instantaneous reaction was, "Don't you talk to me like that!" accompanied by a swift, hard hand to the face and likely as not a bar of soap to wash out my mouth.

I never had my mother for a teacher, but I know my mom was one teacher who did not have a disciplinary problem in her classroom. She loved me unquestionably, but it didn't come without a price and I'd have to spend a lot more time in therapy—which I'm not about to do at this point in my life—to unravel it all.

During my climbing years I grew a ponytail. Subconsciously I must have done it to test my mother's love for me.

She told me later, "I was *so* ashamed!"

I said, "Mom, I've done some things you could be rightly ashamed of, but growing a ponytail is not one of them."

Up into adulthood, I had low self-esteem and didn't know it. I remember my dad hounding me all the time, and calling me "Schmuck." I wonder if that might have had anything to do with it?

I played four years of high school hockey and a year of college hockey and my dad—a coach—never attended a single game. Neither did my mother.

Dad's response when I returned from San Francisco with Lilla and confronted him with it one night: "You picked a sport I didn't know anything about."

He did make an attempt to go sheep hunting with me one time, wearing wing-tip shoes and slacks; he didn't get far. He was definitely a big city guy, having grown up on the streets of Pittsburgh, but I do remember the effort—pathetic though it was.

I had covered over my problem neatly with pride, sort of like I was taught to do with that carpet for the elephant in the living room. But pride is a poor substitute for self-esteem, and creates a whole other level of problems generally referred to as denial. Hell, I didn't even know the difference. And co-dependence—no idea.

My mother told me after my dad's death in Honolulu, walking on the hot sidewalk near the Marina Condos where she lived, the very smell of life and death in the ocean air, "Mike, I know he wasn't the father you wished you'd had, but he loved you. He used to brag about you all the time to his friends."

It speaks volumes that my mother felt it was necessary to tell me that. I didn't realize at the time how seriously I had been injured or how angry I was deep inside. I didn't feel so much abused as neglected—just not worth his trouble and—of no particular value. Every time my therapist and I would broach the subject of my dad, he'd just push the Kleenex box in my direction. I didn't just cry. That injured little boy in me screamed out loud for help, convulsed with wracking sobs. I began slowly to realize that my whole adult life up to that point had been about proving that I was a better man than my dad. I also soon realized that I was unknowingly and unintentionally directing my anger with my father toward others, including Shelli, and previously Lilla. It's the reason I was a tough kid. I was the plug in a volcano of anger. Loosen that plug at your own risk. My therapist suggested I might be the first person in generations to break out of the cycle of abuse in our family. I set that as my goal.

Still, I kept asking myself: Why was it so easy for him to communicate with other kids my age and so difficult to do it with me? Part of it, I know, was that he was "coach" to them. They never saw beyond that. They didn't have to, and they didn't have to live under his constant harassment. He couldn't ask me once to take out the garbage and simply give me a chance to do it. Instead, he preferred to badger me, repeating half a dozen times, "El garbacho."

I'm also just as certain that part of the problem was generational. My dad, brought up in a very different, Depression-era world, didn't readily show or express his feelings. And, of course, by the time I reached my teens he was drinking a fifth of whiskey a day. After he wound up in Providence Hospital in a straitjacket he joined Alcoholics Anonymous, attended AA meetings every single day, and remained sober for the last seven years of his life–but by then we hardly knew each other. I watched him dissipate himself. Though I loved him, I had never felt loved by him. I never felt like he treated me with respect and, consequently, I didn't respect him. The best I could do was honor him in an undertaking I respected, and even that was proving to be difficult. But was I honoring him or me? It took me so long to figure out that I felt I deserved more—so much more. In a way, I was making up for lost time. I was doing it for myself.

At 18,481 feet, Mt. Elbrus, the tallest mountain on the European geographic continent, is actually located in Georgia, in a tourist area known as the Baksan Valley. In the late 1980s and early 1990s, the Baksan Valley was one of the tourist areas in the world that could have advertised itself as *au na-*

turel, generally meaning no toilet seats and no toilet paper. The food served at the lodges was hideous. When we were served chicken we could never discern from what part of the bird's body it came, as if they had turned the birds loose in a room with a drunken maniac wielding a dull meat cleaver. It did taste like chicken, but then, a lot of things do. When it wasn't chicken, it was meatballs of questionable origin. We nicknamed them sinkers (think fishing) and used them mostly as projectiles. I usually walked into the cafeteria, looked at the selection of fly-covered culinary delights, grimaced, picked up an apple and walked out.

From Moscow, we took a long bus ride to another airport. Staring blankly out the window at boxy Ladas stuck in traffic, I thought about the mountain and the forthcoming climb. I had stamped and postmarked the Elbrus cachet twice and simply lined through the year for each previous attempt. This year—1992—had been freshly printed on them.

I didn't give much thought to the tanks riding on the railcars on a track next to us. After all, I was in Russia, and my mind's eye swept across the years of newsreels of May Day parades bristling with armaments and columns of wooden-legged soldiers saluting dour-faced Soviet dignitaries on display in their suits and uniforms, weighted down with medals from the Great Patriotic War.

Hundreds of miles south, at the airport in Mineralnye Vody, I wasn't surprised that some of our gear was unaccounted for. Nor was I surprised that the flight supposedly carrying it had been postponed, but I was definitely surprised when they told us they didn't know where the plane was—a new international flying experience for me. At least, *perestroika and glasnost* in play, they had been willing to share that unsettling information.

We arrived around 10:30 p.m. and waved a brief hello to our bus driver, Alexis, who didn't wave back, agitated after waiting around for us all afternoon and evening. He and Oleg, the other Russian accompanying us, chain-smoked the whole three hours to the lodge, offering surly responses to perfectly innocuous questions from Bob John's wife, Jan.

The accommodations were superior to anything I had previously experienced in the former U.S.S.R. I enjoyed a private room with three beds, one on which to sleep and two on which to spread my gear. Preparing to climb is mostly sorting, packing and repacking. Then you unpack, sort and repack again, not necessarily in that order. On the mountain, the process continues. Climbing is ninety-nine percent drudgery and one percent real excitement; standing on the summit, surviving the attempt, overcoming enormous mental and physical obstacles or possibly all of the above, resulting in another kind of high. Other than that, what's the point? Why bother? There are no rare gems up there on the mountain tops, no big game to hunt, no fish to catch. The answer, I believe, is best stated obliquely by George Mallory, an early British alpinist who died on his third attempt at Mt. Everest in 1924. One day, weary of hearing the question, he famously replied, "Because it's there."

Our first morning, the weather was clear and warm—a good sign. After a late breakfast, planning on an acclimatization hike, we drove to the base of the decrepit gondola and chairlift that hauled tourists, skiers and climbers alike to within proximity of Priut Hut at 13,800 feet. We all stepped onto the open area at the bottom of the gondola, a perfectly natural thing to do, and incurred the wrath of the drunken operator, who gave Alexis and Oleg a large ration of Russian shit. For a while it looked as if we weren't going to get on the mountain at all. We finally did ride up in the gondola, then the chairlift, and walked about halfway to Priut Hut, where the climb would begin. We had to turn around early to catch the last ride down.

Back at the lodge we had a surprisingly nice lunch of watermelon, fruits, tomatoes, cucumbers, chicken soup and roasted chicken. We washed it down with some of the world's worst wines, in a selection of both red and white, the likes of which had probably provoked Napoleon to invade.

I was feeling positive about the trip. I had come in August instead of September, hoping the weather would be more cooperative, and already it appeared so. However, my diarrhea and stomach cramps were a reminder that I was indeed in the third world, regardless of the nuclear-tipped missiles pointed at my homeland and loved ones.

We awoke to an early breakfast and arrived at the bottom of the gondola at 9:00 a.m., finding ourselves at the back of a two-hour line of Russian and Eastern Block tourists. But luck was with us farther up the mountain, as we were offered a ride to Priut Hut on a big, new tracked vehicle with snow blades fore and aft. It zipped us right up to the hut with a full load of supplies. I felt particularly fortunate because I had loaded up on gear and carried a very heavy pack. With the extra time afforded us, we hiked above the hut and worked with Jan on self-arresting techniques and walking on crampons.

Todd Burleson, the leader of our little expedition, and I were first to get back to the gondola. He waited for the others while I got on, since a car was leaving at that moment. It was filled with a dozen school children aged five to fourteen, who were quite charming and very interested in me. I had a few Chilkoot Charlie's stickers left in my pocket, so I gave one to the cute girl of twelve next to me. Red and green Koot's stickers can be found all over the world. The more remote the location, the more likely you'll find one. They're my version of the Wall Drug Store campaign. They already adorned the gondola windows. And of course, once I gave her a sticker they all wanted one, so I passed them around. After very friendly introductions, during which I found out they were from Moscow and they found out I was from Alaska, the girl produced a ballpoint pen and asked that I autograph her sticker on the back. Of course, then they all wanted autographs, which I happily provided them. I don't know who they thought I was but they were all thoroughly delighted. When we arrived at the bottom of the mountain the kids waved goodbye as they walked down to their bus and I thought sadly about the conditions they were inheriting in their country.

When the last gondola arrived with the rest of our group, we hung around the base for a while waiting for our bus. I read a brochure advertising the government's proposal to sell, as well as finance the property, including the gondola, chairlift and Priut Hut—all in a sad state of repair. I thought it would be fun to buy it just to fire the drunken gondola operator, an especially appealing thought after we learned that our bus had departed for Mineralnye Vody to pick up our main guide, Sergei Arsentiev, leaving us to walk several miles on asphalt down to the lodge in unforgiving plastic climbing boots.

We moved into Priut Hut the next morning, again gladly hitching a ride on the tracked vehicle from the top of the chairlift, resting our heavy packs on our laps. Priut Hut, which looked like an over-sized Airstream trailer, has since burned to the ground. We'd venture down to the remains of World War II fortifications that supported facilities listed in 1991 by *Outside Magazine* as the "world's nastiest outhouses." They hung out over an open space that forcefully funneled the incessant wind up through two open holes in the floor. The floor was slippery, messy, dilapidated and foul. There were no seats. You'd drop your used paper down the hole only to watch in horror as it was blown right back, flying wildly around the small room while you frantically tried to dodge it without slipping and falling through one of the holes, your clothes down around your knees. In the dark, the cold, the filth, the stench—on the perilously slippery, decrepit floor— you knew you had discovered hell on earth.

The next morning we all walked up to a spot referred to simply as "The Rocks," a standard acclimatization climb for the day before a summit attempt. We did it in an hour without mishap in nice weather. Returning to Priut Hut, I took a nap and then visited for a while with Sergei, whom I found to be friendly and ready to please. I was glad we finally had a chance to chat after having met briefly—not much more than a handshake—on the north side of Everest in 1990. He had been on Jim Whittaker's Peace Climb. Sergei had become famous in his own country for being the first Russian to summit Everest without oxygen, and controversial elsewhere for the same reason. The climbers had agreed they would all use oxygen so no individual climber would hold up the others. But because Sergei had unilaterally decided not to use supplemental oxygen, the American and Chinese climbers had to wait for him on the summit. Whittaker was pissed. Sergei unconvincingly explained to me that he couldn't wear the oxygen mask because of the size of his nose, which was admittedly larger than average. I was destined to have my own unpleasant experiences with an oxygen mask the following year.

Our summit day arrived and I wasn't a bit surprised that our previously good weather succumbed to howling wind, lightning and sleet. I couldn't see the rocks right outside the hut, much less the ones farther up the mountain. Fortunately, I could laugh at those circumstances two days later, when we left for the summit very early in the morning on Sunday, August 19, 1991. Twice I felt with certainty I wasn't going to make it: during the first half hour of the climb, when I could not get my stride as every fiber in my body complained under the light of my headlamp; and five hours later, when I saw the headwall to the summit from the floor of the saddle and stopped in my tracks, overwhelmed. I had never seen it up close before due to inclement weather. In the bright sunlight it was, like the steep climb out of Base Camp on Mt. Vinson, reminiscent of the Headwall on Denali. Jan, bless her heart, took one look at it and lost her ambition.

Bob said, "Well, let's flatten this fucker!" and though I didn't share his enthusiasm, I put on my pack and started up.

It was warm, beautiful shirtsleeve weather on the summit. I had actually found myself wishing for a little wind during the ascent. We embraced each other and took some photos as Sergei lit up a cigarette.

I thought, "The creator doesn't make them any tougher than Russians, but then he's still pretty young, and someday it'll catch up with him."

An ex-smoker myself, I couldn't imagine taking a drag off a cigarette at 18,481 feet. But I had finally conquered Mt. Elbrus. Like the elite Edelweiss Division of the German Wehrmacht, who had conquered it in spite of a stubborn Russian defense in WWII, it had been a costly victory, mine requiring three attempts.

I walked mostly alone down the mountain, the weather remaining pristine all the way back down to "The Rocks," where fog moved in, restricting my vision to a few yards on a trail well marked with wands. Bob and Oleg continued on undeterred, way down below me, and in time Sergei and Todd went ahead also. I was in no hurry, savoring the victory and thinking about my father. Would he have been proud of me? Yes, but he probably wouldn't have told me. It didn't matter. I had now crossed an emotional threshold. Attempting the Seven Summits was probably beyond the limits of my dad's imagination. It had been beyond the limits of my own just a few years earlier.

But even this peaceful moment coming to terms with our relationship would be short-lived, when a Russian climber above kicked a rock loose and it hit me a glancing blow on the left side of my chest. I didn't see it coming and didn't hear it. It must have been the size of a soccer ball. Suffice it to say it gave me quite a jolt. Had it been six inches higher, it would have hit me square in the face.

I got back to Priut Hut about 5:00 p.m., completely exhausted. I cleaned up as best I could, changed clothes and went to the main room of the hut to join everyone for a beer. Oleg had brought up a couple of six-packs of Chilkoot Charlie's Sourdough Ale and we drank them all. I slept a much needed twelve hours, packed up and left Priut Hut an hour before anyone else, without any breakfast. Arriving at the top of the chairlift, I sat on my pack and watched some Russian kids skiing through a slalom course as I fretted over the chairlift, which wasn't running. It was a pristine day and I could see another Mountain Travel group walking into the saddle between Mt. Elbrus's two peaks, only this time it didn't upset me. Soon everyone else showed up. The chairlift started running and we were on our way down.

Back at the lodge we used up all the hot water, luxuriating in the showers. Sergei arranged for a wonderful lunch of watermelon, tomatoes, soup and some spicy sausage with sour cream and cucumbers, accompanied by a white wine that might have mollified Napoleon—a little.

While descending the mountain on the tram, we heard that Gorbachev had been ousted. Later, at the hotel, we heard he had resigned. It was difficult to determine how the Russians felt about it. For all their complaining about Gorbachev, I thought they weren't too keen to see him go. They were all glued to the black-and-white television in the lobby, gleaning very little hard information, according to our interpreter, Alexis, who explained the stations were playing a lot of classical music and repeating the same vague story over and over. "Such is our way," he said. Of course, the Russians expected there would be a slowdown in reforms, despite mention that "private businesses" would not be affected. I personally thought Gorbachev was an extraordinary man, but from the Russian perspective he had ruined their economy and dismantled their empire.

I was in the nicest hotel I had experienced in the Baksan Valley, and the maid had not touched the mess in my room since my arrival. The elevators worked only half the time. When I pulled on the window handle to open my window, it came off in my hand. You could not get a hot shower until the hot water was turned on at 7:30 a.m. They played moronic, obnoxious disco music from morning until bedtime, inside and outside the building, so loud you could hardly talk at the dinner table. One certainly couldn't blame that all on Gorbachev.

On the last day in the valley we took an upright portable barbecue and a feast of fruit, caviar, bottles of sherry-like wine, brandy, pivo (the Russian equivalent of beer, which tastes more like what the name implies), cheese and a freshly killed lamb to a small man-made lake by a running stream in the middle of a cow pasture. We gathered wood from the hillside and Abdul, our bus driver who lived in Elbrus Village, did the honors. We ate and ate, and drank and drank, toast after toast, attracting the attention of a young bull that became friendly enough to eat a tomato out of my hand.

I had come to associate my difficulty summiting Mt. Elbrus with my dad. But now, after three attempts I had finally conquered it, feeling emotionally unburdened and able to put all those feelings behind me. It wasn't so much an epiphany as

it was the simple recognition of a closing chapter in my life, however belated. For the first time, I felt completely at peace with myself.

"QUACK, QUACK, QUACK!"

As a charter member of the Spenard Duck and Fuck Club, I have spent almost as much time tromping around duck flats and wading through shallow ponds as I have post-holing in deep snow and crossing crevasses on ladders. Let's face it. Duck hunting is a serious Alaskan pastime.

Beginning in the early '70s—for over twenty years in a row—I would fly across Cook Inlet with a group of guys in a Ketchum Air Service plane, the afternoon before duck hunting season began on September 1. We were such regular customers we usually got first pick among the number of cabins the Ketchum family owned. There was a core group of about half a dozen of us that went every year and others that came once or twice. For the core group it was a tradition, a top priority, almost a pilgrimage to the duck flats every fall. We liked to eat well, so we took plenty of food, but even more to drink. After loading in all the beer, wine and liquor, there was hardly room left in the planes for the hunters. Suffice it to say, we were a weight-and-balance challenge for the pilots.

I had been shooting ducks for a long time. While in junior high and high school I lived on Iliamna Avenue, out beyond the Turnagain By the Sea subdivision in Anchorage. My friends and I used to walk out Clay Products Drive to Point Woronzof and hunt the flats between there and Point Campbell. We also used to hunt at Potter Flats, where people stop to photograph migrating waterfowl these days. You didn't often get good shots at geese, which were more cagy than ducks and tended to stay way out on the mud flats where it was impossible to hide from or sneak up on them.

One time there were four or five of us hunting at Potter Flats. Two of us were separated from the others by quite a distance when a flock of about a dozen Canada geese came slowly cruising in and tried to land right on top of us. Our friends watched with mouths agape from a distance as we jumped up and started blasting away. The geese were so close and we were so excited we filled the sky with holes and didn't hit a single bird. It took years to live that one down.

I didn't have anything personal against ducks. I mean, I didn't hate them or anything. That came later. I just liked the plopping sound they made when they hit the water or mud flats. I'm not a big fan of duck meat either. In fact, I don't eat meat or fowl at all anymore. Likely as not, I would give my dead ducks to someone else on the trip. One possible justification for killing ducks, depending on your political persuasion, is that they are obviously environmentalists. If you depended almost entirely on undeveloped wetlands you would be too. So, one could kill an approximation of tree-huggers without worrying about going to jail for it. And, let's face it, when you're hung over and had to drag your ass out of bed before you were ready, killing something made you feel better about yourself.

Of course, there was always the guy who had his own bird dog, could name every variety of duck and goose on the wing, knew how to call them, owned his own hand-made decoys, and expensive double-barreled shotgun, harbored secret family recipes for preparing them, and blah, blah, blah. Most of us just wanted to swat a few, savor that plopping sound, and get back to the cabin for a nap before the next raucous round of drinking, joke-telling and poker-playing.

There were others who couldn't tell a snow goose from a swan, a pintail from a teal or a mallard from a geoduck. One time two of our clueless devotees came proudly marching into the cabin after dark—one with a dead swan over his shoulder—to the trip-long derision of everyone else in the cabin.

"We got a snow goose! Wahoo! Eat your hearts out!" they told us, answered by a chorus of "That's no snow goose! That's a swan!" "Look at its neck. Its neck is three feet long!" "You guys are in serious trouble. Get that thing outta here!"

They had waited out there behind a stump in the damp and cold long hours after the rest of us had returned to the cabin for warmth and liquid sustenance. The hapless critter they shot ended up buried under a log, some distance from the cabin and was later reported in the *Anchorage Daily News* by another group of hunters. The swan's lifelong mate probably searched for him until the day he or she died.

Then there were guys who couldn't cut it. Some guys fit in nicely with a group. Some guys don't. One year, a faction of the group brought along a friend of theirs that owned a gas station. I had never met the guy before. Sadly, for him at least, he turned out to be too thin-skinned for our group of drunken, blood-lusting, foul-mouthed, poker-playing bird killers.

It started out harmlessly enough with someone referring to him as Lumpy, which he didn't like, followed with "Lumpy, Lumpy, Lumpy! Why do they call him Lumpy? I don't know, Lumpy, Lumpy, Lumpy!"

It ended with the guy moving his gear out of the cabin and arranging through another pilot for Ketchum to come get him early as he sat on a bare platform next door nursing his wounded ego. Wouldn't you know it? The weather closed in, which is good for duck hunting, but bad for people trying to escape persecution. "Ketch" couldn't fly in to rescue him and he had to move back into the cabin for the whole night to more "Lumpy, Lumpy, Lumpy. Why do they call him Lumpy? I don't know. Lumpity, Lumpity, Lump."

One guy who came on the trip a couple of times was a drug dealer. He was an intelligent, well-spoken, itinerant person that just sort of lived outside the box—a respectable drug dealer. I know that sounds oxymoronic, but we had low standards. He spent more time in the Far East than he did in America. In the middle of an alcohol-fogged, drug-enhanced debate one night while the group was preparing duck breast Stroganoff, he said something that annoyed me and I replied, "What the fuck do you know? You're just a drunk junkie." The comment brought the house down, but I guess you'd have to have been there.

Killing birds was the excuse for the pilgrimage; all-night poker was the passion. When I was going duck hunting religiously, it was before Texas hold 'em virtually eliminated all other games of poker, such as five-card and six-card draw; three-card, five-card, six-card and seven-card stud; plus Chicago and an almost endless variety of low-ball, high-ball and wildcard games.

Call me old fashioned, but I loved playing dealer's choice poker and I hate Texas hold 'em. I hate tyranny. It's like someone strolled in, leveled a 12-gauge shotgun at your midsection, and said, "Listen up. You've got to vote Republican from now on." I believe in personal choice, even when it hurts, so that sort of thing really annoys me. Today, if you're in a poker game, someone sooner or later calls for Texas hold 'em, probably sooner rather than later, and that's it. Once that's called, it's the end of any other game. I'm getting pissed off just writing about it. Incidentally, those trips were not cheap to begin with, but if you were unskilled or just unlucky at poker, the price of duck meat could rival that of Kobe beef, truffle-flavored goose liver pate or sashimi at a sushi bar a block from the Tsukiji fish market in Tokyo.

Later in life, after I'd turned around on my third attempt at Mt. Everest and hung up my ice axe and crampons, I flew to places like Uruguay, Brazil, Costa Rica, Nicaragua and Argentina to fish for peacock bass, tarpon, piranha, sailfish and marlin, and to shoot perdiz (partridges), pigeons, doves, ducks and geese. We once flew to South Dakota also, staying in a fancy lodge, and hunted pheasant. The lodge owner's wife did all the cooking and the food was the best I've ever eaten. These trips helped to fill the void I felt from not climbing anymore, and bird hunting in South America is a different kind of experience than anything I grew up with in Anchorage. I particularly loved hunting perdiz in Uruguay. I had never hunted over dogs flushing the fowl from the undergrowth before and found it exciting as hell when one, two or three birds would burst into the air from practically right under your feet. I can still hear the Uruguayan dog handlers directing their border collies with cries of, "Hut, hut, hut," the dogs slowing down, hanging back at the command so as not to flush the birds too far out in front of you. I'd like to try it again someday to down that elusive three-of-three. I was real close a couple of times, but those little birds are fast and heading off in different directions. They are also excellent eating, and the Argentinians know how to prepare them.

I had never even thought of hunting pigeons, which I also found exhilarating, though they weren't as hard to hit as perdiz or doves. We set up decoys in the sorghum fields that attracted big, fat pigeons flying in as singles or in flocks. Dove hunting is different, conducted by simple positioning of the hunter in the mornings and evenings when the birds—by the millions—are leaving or returning to their roosts. I found it best to have two sixteen gauge shotguns—an automatic and a double-barrel— and quality matters. A lot of automatics won't stand up to the punishment of firing box after box of shells until the barrel is way too hot to touch. I wore tight-fitting leather gloves to protect my hands. Your shoulder is a problem also. Don't even think about a twelve-gauge, which would kill your shoulder before you'd killed very many birds. Each hunter has a guide who loads one gun while he's firing the other one—nonstop—for a couple hours at a time. My right shoulder and upper arm were bruised and bloody after several days of shooting doves, but it was great fun and with all that shooting I got to be very accurate.

The most amazing duck and goose hunting I've ever experienced was in Argentina. We hunted a collection of ponds one morning where the ducks were so thick, I downed three birds with one shot on three different occasions. The next morning we went goose hunting. We arrived at the location, a recently harvested corn field, before daybreak. As we lay stretched out on the ground in between the rows of lightly frozen soil and the sun began to appear over the horizon, a huge flock of Magellan geese, answering the calls of our guides, made a final approach and began to land right on top of us. It was just like that day long ago at Potter Flats, only there were a lot more of them, they were larger, and many weren't as lucky as those Canada geese had been. Birds were falling everywhere, though dozens of them managed to escape, only to be—unbelievably—called back to us by our guides, turning around in mid-air to answer the avian version of, "Come back. Let's talk things over!" in Spanish, of course, then more carnage.

I mentioned earlier I didn't have anything in particular against ducks until later in life. It happened after we got a new neighbor in Halibut Cove. One spring, on our first trip across the bay, we turned the corner beyond which we'd get the first glimpse of our property to find our view almost entirely blocked by a forest of pilings, a floating dock and a ninety-foot fishing boat which, in that setting, looked as big as the *Titanic*. It was a colossal adjustment right from that moment, but the pilings and the boat were the least of it.

Our new neighbor, who had been raised in Halibut Cove, and from whose step-father and mother we had purchased our property, worked with heavy equipment twenty-four hours a day, seven days a week, fifty-two weeks a year, using dynamite not only to remake the landscape—lobbing rocks on our rooftop—but to blow up flocks of crows he had purposefully attracted. He grazed his horses on our land, after moving an official surveyor's corner marker in our direction to make it look like it was his land. We paid for a new survey to correct the situation and the surveyor was aghast at the evidence.

Our new neighbor's wife unfortunately acquired an attachment to ducks. She bought a bunch of goofy-looking, yellowish-colored morons and talked to them as she fed them each morning and evening, referring to them as her "peepers." Her ducks mated with local mallards coming and going during their normal migration cycles. Their offspring were even goofier-looking and dumber than either parents. "Quack, quack, quack," all day and all night. Non-stop yammering: "quack, quack, fucking quaaaackkk!"

You don't build a retreat in a remote and beautiful part of Alaska, a place where you can take off precious time from your business affairs and the hassle of city life for pure enjoyment, only to end smack up against such cacophony, day after day. But that was only part of it. The ducks decided that because our floating dock right next door to them was in the sun all afternoon, it would be a great place to hang out, quack, shit—mostly shit—and exhibit their stupidity. Once we motored around the "Titanic" and its moorings, our spring arrival would include four sections of floating dock that were literally covered in two inches of duck shit. It would take me all afternoon with a power sprayer to clean up the mess. While I did so, the duck-nurturing proprietress next door would cheerfully and cluelessly announce, "They love your dock! They think it's theirs! Quack!"

Shelli and I were so upset with our new neighbors that we referred to them as the "Fuck Heads." My grandkids—preteens and teenagers at the time—visited during the summer, and we couldn't very well refer to our neighbors as such while the grandkids were around. So we modified their nickname to the "Duck Heads." It was perfect. The kids loved it. They knew what we meant, and were able to participate in the "Duck Head" reference without repercussion.

Sometimes circumstances require action. I started shooting at the ducks with my pellet gun when they got near my dock. They would quack and scatter back to "Mommy," but they—with their five seconds of memory bank—never understood that I didn't like them and that they were not welcome on my dock. In my years of running nightclubs I met a lot of people like that. Usually they're drunk. Ducks come by it naturally. Their mother next door never got the message either. "Stop shooting at my ducks," she'd yell at me over the water. "Mind your own business," I'd yell back. The relationship was all downhill from there.

Returning to the duck flats there was a string of years when we experienced what one of the core group of hunters referred to as "blue bird weather." We did some marginally successful hunting early in the mornings—jump-shooting—but otherwise the birds were either absent or flying too high to bother shooting at unless you had a high-powered rifle with a scope. It was a no-brainer to be back in the cabin napping, drinking or playing poker when the sun was high in the sky, it was sweltering hot outside, and the only birds flying were in the stratosphere. Once I started climbing I became totally focused on completing the Seven Summits, and because of the new focus and the run of lousy hunting years, I forwent the annual pilgrimage.

The group drifted apart and I did no more hunting until I stopped climbing and began traveling to South America with a new set of somewhat more mature companions. Our duck-nurturing neighbor came home unexpectedly one night from her partying rounds in Homer to find her husband in their bed with another woman. "Quack!" It was real quiet after that. They got divorced, moved away and, gratefully, so did the goofy-looking, stupid, endlessly noisy mongrel ducks—as well as the "*Titanic.*"

Blub, Blub, Blub!

Things were quieter before the "Duck Heads" showed up in the cove and after they left—especially before. When Shelli and I first bought acreage in 1980, Halibut Cove was a real wilderness experience. Only a handful of homes and summer cabins dotted the shores and hills of the tiny fishing and art community, and the public dock provided the only commercial activity—the small fishing fleet. Phone service was not yet available but we did have the luxury of electricity. People communicated with one another by CB radio and everyone had "handles." Alex Combs, a well-known painter and ceramist in the community, went by Potter. We used *Shelli Bird*, after the name of our boat.

We had no slip in the Homer small boat harbor and no dock in Halibut Cove for several years, so we hauled our new twenty-two foot Boston Whaler Revenge back and forth from Anchorage, using a running line and a skiff to off-load people and supplies to the property. A running line is a continuous rope run through three pulleys in the shape of a triangle, placed so that one pulley is anchored out in the water away from shore far enough that you can leave a boat floating, even during a minus low tide. The other two pulleys are tied to the shoreline. Once you tie the skiff to one side of the line near shore in such a way that it doesn't slip up or down the line, you then pull in on the other side, which hauls the skiff out into the water where it will wait for you to retrieve it by pulling on the side of the rope to which it is tied.

In the 1980s, the spruce bark beetles had not yet decimated the spruce trees on the Kenai Peninsula and our property was covered with huge, healthy specimens. Some friends of mine came down one weekend and we built a crude platform on a prominence over the water amongst the aforementioned trees, erected an eight foot by ten foot frame and placed a wall tent on it. We built bunk beds, and installed electrical extension cord "wiring," indoor/outdoor carpeting, a small refrigerator, a microwave, and gravity-fed running water. Our hot water came from a banquet-sized coffee dispenser. We even had a small wine cellar. Approaching from the water, however, you couldn't see anything but the trees.

After a few years we were able to install steel pilings, a four-piece floating dock, and an aluminum ramp, with stairs running up to a stationary dock and on up to a deck, and yet more stairs to the porch in front of the tent. Locals nicknamed our spot "The Stairway to the Stars" because from a distance, all you could see was the dock and stairs leading up to the woods and the sky above.

Until the 1990s, there was an incredible abundance of protein in the waters of Kachemak Bay. It was an amazing and colorful biomass offering up king crab, Dungeness crab, tanner crab, shrimp, soft shell clams, steamer clams, octopus, halibut, king salmon, red salmon, pink salmon, silver salmon, Dolly Varden trout, rock fish, flounders, blue mussels and more. There was so much life it appeared as though the bottom of the bay was moving.

It's ironic that Homer, a community well known for its liberal politics and environmentalist tendencies, would allow such mismanagement and looting of its resources, accepting it as a *fait accompli* without so much as a whimper of recrimination in the local press, city council debate, the Homer/Kachemak Bay Rotary Club, or anywhere else of which I am aware.

I witnessed the decimation. First it was the king crabs. Then it was the shrimp. Then it was the Dungeness crabs. Then it was the tanner crabs. I'll never forget the day in the early 1990s when a commercial Dungeness crab boat came through the narrow passage between Ismailof Island and the mainland plopping down crab pots every hundred feet, one just off the end of my floats. Prior to this event I could always harvest as many Dungeness crabs as we needed by hand from my skiff, right out of those narrows. I haven't seen a single one in the narrows since.

State agencies who manage the fisheries let the commercial interests "harvest" everything they want in order to make the payments on their boats and to protect their sacred lifestyles. Then they close the fishery to everyone, even for personal use. This is called resource management. The result is predictably what you would expect from an industry that self-regulates. Remember when President George W. Bush said Wall Street would self-regulate? Within a few years we had the Great Recession.

Many of my neighbors and friends who reside around Kachemak Bay are commercial fishermen. I listen with keen interest when they rail against the oil companies with a certain amount of legitimacy. But believe me, there is no more rapacious group of people on the face of the earth than commercial fishermen, who would rather blame sea otters than take responsibility for all those missing crabs. Now I'm no game biologist, but I surmise that sea otters had inhabited Kachemak Bay for hundreds of thousands of years and there was no shortage of crabs when the commercial fishermen first showed up in the twentieth century.

But I digress. When there were lots of crab and shrimp and we lived in our little wall tent in the woods, my sister, who had not as yet found her current husband, came to visit for a few days with a male friend of hers. He was a big, funny guy who readily saw humor in the foibles of humanity and I was about to present him with a perfect set of circumstances.

I had been on the hunt to replace some old shrimp pots and had recently located some newly-made ones at Kachemak Gear Shed on the Homer Spit, the location of the harbor from which I would, and still do, travel to and from Halibut Cove. I was thrilled. I bought six traps and a couple hundred feet of new rope, along with stainless steel clips to attach the traps spaced about ten feet apart to the line at the end of which I would tie my buoy. Traps could be unclipped from the line when not in use.

Shrimp traps are usually made of rebar, heavy-duty landscape fabric and netting material with holes too small for adult shrimp to swim through. They are typically rectangular boxes covered on all four long sides with the landscape fabric and with a conical, concave see-through net structure on either end, but only open at one end via a round hole at the apex of the concavity that's large enough for an adult shrimp to swim through. Once having entered the trap to feast on the bait attached to the inside, the shrimp tend to swim to the corners of the box to escape rather than going for the entrance hole that protrudes into the interior of the rectangle. The shrimp don't get to devour the bait because it is enclosed in a container punched full of small holes so only the odor escapes. Shrimp traps need to be collected regularly because once one of the shrimp chances upon the hole through which it entered it's just a matter of "follow the leader," and out they all go.

And so, with about $1,500 invested in the pots, rope and fittings and a fair amount of time spent putting everything together, I was eager to put some fresh shrimp on the table. My sister's boyfriend and I loaded all this brand new gear on the stern of the *Shelli Bird* and headed out into the middle of Kachemak Bay. It was a beautiful summer morning and the water was perfectly calm.

We arrived at a location near where I had placed shrimp pots previously. I had no GPS at the time and would just go out, look back at the mainland, line up a feature at the water line with a mountain in the background and I was good to go.

The first new baited pot hit the water as the *Shelli Bird* motored slowly ahead, soon followed by the remaining five, and I continued paying out the line as my trusty assistant skipper kept us moving in a more or less straight line. When we got to the buoy I confidently tossed it overboard and watched in utter disbelief as it was pulled under water by the weight of my beautiful new pots, line and gear, never again to be seen by the human eye. Numbness settled over me as the small, diagonal wake of my boat quickly filled the dimple in the water's shiny surface—all that remained of my new shrimping gear. Alas, my new line had been too short for the depth of the water.

There was a hole in the pit of my stomach. I was in shock. From behind me, as I stared open-mouthed at the empty surface of the water, I heard, "Blub, blub, blub!" "That Gordon!" "What a big spender!" "He sure doesn't sweat the small stuff!" "He just heaves it overboard and he's on his way!" "Blub, blub, blub!"

I felt that I had momentarily cornered the market on stupidity. What could I do after such a blunder but laugh at myself? It was either that or follow my beautiful new traps overboard into the inky abyss. So, we had a good laugh and motored back to Halibut Cove, my companion absolutely salivating in anticipation of relating our misadventure to the audience awaiting us at "The Stairway to the Stars." When we got there I proceeded directly upstairs to the sleeping loft and flopped down on the bed while my assistant entertained my wife and my sister with all the fascinating details. It understandably took a while for me to recover enough composure to return to sociability, which of course happened to the accompaniment of a multitude of more "blub, blub, blub" jokes.

The next day while visiting The Saltry, a recently opened restaurant in Halibut Cove, for a beer, I ran into proprietors Dave and Marion Beck. Dave was, and still is, a commercial fisherman as well as a very accomplished builder. When I mentioned to Dave what I had done and how stupid I felt about it he looked me directly in the eye, smiled, and said, "We've all done it."

Mt. Everest, Third Attempt, South Col Route, 1993

"We can't afford to remodel the downstairs bathroom," Shelli said, "but you can afford to make another attempt on Mt. Everest?"

The bathroom again. I said nothing. What could I say?

"If you insist on going over there again, you'll just have to take me and Deborah with you. I'm not walking out of the Khumbu alone and returning to Anchorage *yet again* to anxiously wait for your return, and then I want to go to England to do some on-site genealogy research."

"Okay," I said. And so it was.

Shelli and I were reconciled and she was planning on moving back in with me—once I remodeled the downstairs bathroom for her, of course. We were still working through a couple of issues; climbing was becoming one of them. I was now addicted to international travel and high altitude adventures. Shelli was growing weary of it.

Deborah MacInnes Spencer is Shelli's best friend from the ninth grade on and was her best lady for our wedding. On the day Shelli and Deborah departed from Pheriche in March of 1993, the three of us walked to a hilltop that overlooked the valley below, which wasn't nearly as deep as the chasm in my chest. After some photos and a tearful goodbye, I watched the girls walk slowly down the valley and out of sight. It was suddenly as if they'd never even been there, but for the empty feeling inside me. Chuldim, who was to accompany them all the way down to Lukla, had left Pheriche after us and, racing to catch up with the girls, discovered me lost in my emotional turmoil in front of a large rock trying to hide from the wind.

He said, "Mike, I'll take good care of Shelli and Deborah and I'll see you again in a few days."

I had become closer friends with Chuldim after the previous year's expedition since I had bought him a roundtrip airline ticket from San Francisco to Anchorage for a visit.

Before Shelli left Pheriche, Chuldim had promised, as well as Alex Lowe and Andy Politz—two of our new guides of whom I was very fond—to get me to the summit. Expedition leader Todd Burleson made the same promise. This was to be my year. All agreed.

I walked back, fiddled around in my room, and went to the dining room table to catch up on my journal. Shelli and I had both caught a cold and cough in Kathmandu, which is why I found myself alone, biding my time in Pheriche, now that Alex and Andy had gone on to Lobuche that morning. Having just started a series of Augmentin at Namche Bazaar, I wanted to linger at a lower altitude to better combat my infection. The filth in the air and everywhere in Kathmandu seemed to get worse every year and I wondered what would eventually become of the place.

Pheriche hadn't changed one iota. I was lodged in the same bunk in the same drafty room staring at the same knot-hole faces in the wall. The wind still blew all afternoon, coming right through those same walls, and it was still impossible to get warm, even in my sleeping bag.

The morning of April 3, 1993, after overnighting in Lobuche, I departed for Base Camp. I was welcomed by Peter Athans, Alex Lowe, Andy Politz and Lapka Rita. Pete helped me set up my nice, large tent in a location of my choosing and I was soon spreading my gear all over inside. By the time our lunch of yak meat and rice was ready, I was ravenous.

Base Camp was more spacious and comfortable than the previous year and right next to the Kiwis again. The guides had built a rock enclosure for showers and a stone double-wide crapper a short walk down the hill. I was still fighting my cold with Augmentin, and that evening, after taking a couple of slugs of cough medicine, I slept like a baby. The next morning Sherpa tea was cheerfully delivered at 7:30 a.m., a service I noted ought to be instituted at home.

I wrote a short letter to Shelli in which I said, "The Kiwi group, with Marge, is a little ahead of us. They're going up to touch Camp I and return today. Give my love to everyone. I think of you every waking minute. I replay the picture of you walking down the valley over and over and over. I love you. Michael."

Having arrived so early, ahead of the rest of the group, I did what I could those few days to stay busy, visiting with other early arrivals, including Todd Burleson, and keeping in shape. Alex and I walked into the icefall and up to the first ladder, where he took photos of me walking across a crevasse. My resting pulse was sixty-four and I felt great. Alex seemed to be committed to getting me to the summit and I definitely wanted to be on his team. He was easy-going, considerate and funny. He was also the strongest climber there or probably anywhere, for that matter, hence the nickname, "Legs and Lungs Alex."

The rest of the expedition straggled into Base Camp on April 6. It was great to see everyone, especially Jonathan Lee, one of the YPOs who'd been with me on Mt. Vinson and had later stayed with Shelli and me in Anchorage when he came to Alaska to climb Denali. When we all assembled in the mess tent it was apparent what a large group we were, even considering that the six trekkers would be leaving next morning. Frank Fishbeck was there again and actually cordial, commenting on how good I looked. I was pleased to see another YPO from the Mt. Vinson expedition, Don Casto, and another climber from Anchorage, Daryl Bennett, who had invited me to his Hillside house to critique his training equipment and regimen and answer a mountain of questions about Everest. Unfortunately, we'd grow cold toward one another on the mountain and not get along at all. I met a sixty-three-year-old gentleman from Chicago named Al Hanna and his boisterous adopted son, Brock, who was my tent neighbor. I chatted with Bob Cedargreen, a doctor from California, coincidentally the brother-in-law of my property manager at the time. And, after a brief introduction, I could see it was best to keep my distance from Susie Somebody, the New York socialite wife of Bob Somebody—"Bob this and Bob that"—who had founded a media empire.

Dinner that evening, in spite of all the promises, was nearly inedible spaghetti. I would describe it if it were possible. Suffice it to say that Ong Chu didn't have a single molecule of Italian in him. He may never even have met one. During the awful dinner John Helenek introduced me to his father, who was one of the trekkers, and also proudly showed me a photo of his wife and new baby. I learned that Perry Solmonson's wife was pregnant again, and I found an appropriate moment to show Ken Kamler my codeine prescription and letter from Dr. Peter Hackett regarding its use at altitude. I had made a point of visiting with Peter, an Anchorage doctor who had summited Everest and been one of the founders of the high-altitude clinic in Pheriche, between seasons. Peter told me he would never have been able to summit himself without using codeine tablets to subdue the coughing caused by bronchial irritation due to heavy exertion in the thin, dry air at altitude.

The next morning I showered in the fancy new rock enclosure with hot water supplied by the kitchen. The trekkers had already departed, one of them carrying mail out for me. John Helenek's dad said he would call my mom and Shelli. I was feeling strong and positive, I was impressed with our guiding team and I felt that 1993 was definitely going to be my year.

That night we had an excellent dinner of cold bean salad with artichokes, baby corn and kidney beans followed by seafood pasta with pine nuts. I was one of several who thanked Pete's wife Liz profusely, yet the meals continued to be alternately wonderful and awful. The day ended well when Chuldim returned and handed me a long letter from Shelli that I read and reread.

She and Deborah had spent an uncomfortable night in Thengboche at Tashi Delek Lodge, sleeping right under the kitchen to the sounds of scratching, crawling rodents behind the woven mats on the walls and ceilings. They went on a shopping binge in Namche Bazaar. They met the rest of our expedition wending its way to Base Camp and watched our gear being hauled up the mountain for two entire days. She wondered how I could eat camp food for two months (I don't know how I did it either) and said she and Deborah were already talking about having a feast in Bangkok, then again back in the U.S., downing chips, guacamole, salsa and margaritas at their favorite Mexican restaurant in Portland, Deborah's home. Everyone had wanted to know what Chuldim was doing with two beautiful women. They were both pleased with Chuldim's patience with them because they were so slow and found out he would be in London in September when Shelli and I were planning to renew our vows. She wanted me to make sure he came.

The letter was in two parts—April 2 and April 3—both penned while in Lukla. In the first Shelli wrote: "Walking away from you at Pheriche was miserable—I just wanted to crawl up somewhere and cry and sleep. Every time I looked back and saw you waving I started crying all over again. Please take care of yourself and get to the summit of this mountain so we can get on with our lives! I love you and miss you already." It was signed "Yours always, Shelli."

In the second part, Shelli went on to say, "I really think Alex and Andy are great! I'm sure they will help to get you up to the summit! Also Chuldim is very positive about you reaching the top—Todd also! So JUST DO IT! Can't wait for you to get home and for us to finish working on the basement! We're pretty close to having the bedroom done. Chuldim told Debbie he thought it was pretty strange that I lived out where the tall buildings were and you lived by the trees! Someday, we'll get that fixed!

"You take care of yourself and concentrate on a successful climb—no negative thoughts—make two attempts if you have to! Watch over Daryl Bennett! He seemed like such a green horn on the trail! I'll be having TONS of positive thoughts for you until you get safely home! Speak your mind if there are problems—you don't have to try to run the show—just voice your opinion as a <u>veteran climber!</u> You'll benefit not only yourself, but also the entire group. Write the story about Eric the goose and lots of others also! Stay healthy and strong. I love you TONS and GOBOLAS! Thinking of you every day! I LOVE YOU, I LOVE YOU, I LOVE YOU! Shelli."

We tweaked our basic climbing strategy from the previous year. This time, we would take one more round trip through the Khumbu Icefall since we would go to Camp II and up to the ropes, then all the way back to Base Camp, making another trip up to sleep at Camp III, then return to Base Camp again and Pheriche before summit attempts. Though it would mean another trip through the icefall it would reduce the amount of time spent at Camp II, where everyone got sick the year before. If everything went according to plan, we'd make the first of several summit attempts on May 7.

Group A, which consisted of me and a half-dozen people I didn't know, climbed about a third of the way up the icefall on Saturday, April 10. We practiced walking over a couple of fairly gnarly ladder crossings—three ladders lashed together, four ladders lashed together—and were back in Base Camp before 10:00 a.m. I had sized up the group and felt I was the strongest member. I couldn't imagine how Susie Somebody was going to get her fat butt up the mountain. Inexperienced with crampons and fixed lines, neither did she seem very fit. In that regard, she was in good company with Al's adopted son, Brock, an overweight smoker who didn't even want to be there—nor should he have been. The others, however, all appeared to be up to the challenge.

The next day we held our *puja*, the nicest I had ever attended. We all sat around our pole strung with prayer flags, eyes fixed on burning juniper branches, as one of our Sherpas, who was a monk, presided over the ceremony. Buddhist or not, anyone who is about to attempt Mt. Everest enthusiastically participates in the *pujas*, and not just out of respect for the Sherpas. It is hard to overestimate the seriousness of, and the dangers inherent in, the task that lay ahead.

At the top of the icefall in Camp I, I found myself in a two-man tent with John Dufficy and Susie Somebody, neither of whom I knew very well, though I liked John. He was a powder ski-guide from Aspen who also guided float trips down the Colorado River, where he had met Al Hanna, who was sponsoring him on the Everest trip. He was actually appreciative, unlike some of the others. The first night in the tent was miserable. The floor sloped diagonally downhill with John at the top, Susie in the middle and me on the downhill side, pushing Susie away as she rolled and coughed on me. The worst part of the experience, however, was listening to her talk to John. She was constantly name-dropping, interested only in how much money you had and whether you might have something she wanted.

"We had dinner with Tom Brokaw the night before we flew to Paris. I travel four weeks out of five."

Good, I was thinking. When are you leaving again? I had brought along a copy of Ambrose Bierce's *The Devil's Dictionary* and was disappointed he hadn't included a definition for socialite, so I thought of one myself: *socialite, n., a person with more money than common sense, an utter absence of moral fiber, and lacking the skill, education, intelligence or ambition to be anything else.*

The morning of Wednesday, April 14, we walked about a third of the way up the Western Cwm toward Camp II, Bob Cedargreen and I leading the way.

The trail was essentially the same as the previous year and I felt very strong. Bob asked, "What do you think of Susie Somebody? She's always cozying up to the guides and never says a word to me."

"Consider yourself lucky," I said.

One such guide, on whom she'd been working all morning, had had enough. On the ridge of a steep hill, clipped into a fixed rope halfway back to Camp I, she hollered to Alex, "How should I go down?"

"Forward, backward, take your choice," he said and walked off.

Susie decided to move into a tent with Scott, another guide, which left John and me more room and a tolerable environment, though it was hot enough in there to bake bread.

The next morning at 7:00 a.m. we left for Camp II. I was the first to arrive, Bob Cedargreen close behind. I wore my plastic Asolo climbing boots because they were lighter than my One Sports, but my feet were cold the whole way even though I stripped down to a light polypro top because my upper body was so overheated from trudging uphill through that solar oven.

At lunch, all the guys were in the mess tent when someone announced as if he were a master of ceremonies, "And here comes Susie Somebody in a matching set of stunning mountain wear by Versace."

We all cracked up. You would have thought she was in a mountain fashion photo shoot for *Town and Country* magazine. She wore a very stylish and expensive-looking multicolored pastel climbing outfit with perfectly matching gloves, boots and scarf, while sporting bracelets, earrings, a necklace and large pendant. *Why on earth would someone have the Sherpa haul all that crap to 21,000 feet?* I wondered. I had never seen the likes of it, but then I had never before climbed with a socialite.

The day we started out for the fixed lines, I occasionally had to stop and swing my feet in the air to regain circulation to ward off the cold. Bob admitted he was cold too. Then the wind started to blow like hell. Alex and the rest of the group up ahead turned around, moving quickly back toward us. Soon we were all literally running back to Camp II. The beautiful weather at the outset had lulled us all into a false sense of security and none of us had anticipated—or dressed for—the extreme weather suddenly upon us. By the time we got back to Camp I felt I had never been closer to frostbite on my hands and feet. Bob was particularly worried to feel his feet so cold in his One Sports, which he planned to wear all the way to 29,026 feet.

Susie had started treating me like a human being. She could turn it on and off like a faucet. I was told she had a conversation with a couple other members of the expedition the day before concerning, of course, who in our expedition had the most money. She had guessed it was me. Boy, would she have been disappointed.

We left Camp II at 6:15 a.m. on Sunday and literally blasted down the Western Cwm to Camp I, where we were held up for a while because of repairs underway in the icefall, which was proving more problematic than the previous season, with more numerous objective dangers—challenging trails and gnarly ladder crossings. The one large ice face at the top that we jumared up and rappelled down was obviously going to separate and topple at some point. The crack running horizontally across the top, a few feet from the edge, would only widen in time and separate from the floor of the Western Cwm like a row of ice cubes in a refrigerator ice maker that were about to fall into the ice bucket. But even a danger this ominous was hard to keep in mind, scrambling up and down a vertical wall over two sets of eight twenty-foot ladders roped together, stretching straight up its face from top to bottom.

Bob and Mike and I made it to Base Camp in five hours. Banging my feet inside my boots on the long downhill journey, I regretted not clipping the nails on my big toes, which would later blacken and fall off. I needed a pick-me-up, so I immediately located Ong Chu, ordered a six-pack of sodas and drank four of them one after the other. Soon we were all taking showers. The Sherpa donned the Chilkoot Charlie's T-shirts I had brought for them, and posed for photos in front of a large mound by the mess tent with the icefall in the background. Chuldim had bragged to them about visiting the world famous Chilkoot Charlie's, and it was wonderful to see all of them proudly displaying my logo.

That afternoon, Todd stopped by my tent and said, "Mike, I've heard nothing but positive remarks about how you're doing this year."

"Thanks, Todd," I said, "but I'd sure like to summit with someone I've known longer than a couple of weeks." Most of my friends were in Group B.

He said, "Hopefully, it will be me," followed by his signature chuckle.

After visiting the Kiwi camp to send a fax I retired to my tent and began reading a paperback copy of Jurassic Park that was making its way around camp. I read right through dinner, finishing it at 10:30 p.m. It was the latest I had been awake since leaving home and, being more prone to having strange dreams at altitude anyway, I hid in crevasses from velociraptors prowling the Khumbu Valley all night long.

We had a breakfast of porridge and juice on Thursday, April 22, and started out for Camp II at 3:00 a.m. I set the pace through the icefall and we made it to the top in exactly four hours. The sun hit us before we got very far into the Western Cwm, slowing us down with oppressive heat during the four and a half additional hours it took to get to Camp II. I slept for twelve hours Thursday night, and the next morning dawdled over a breakfast of pancakes and scrambled powdered eggs for a couple of hours with what was left of our Group A.

We left for Camp III at 6:00 a.m. on Saturday, reaching the general vicinity at 1:00 p.m. I had almost forgotten what a bitch it was to go from Camp II to Camp III and back in one day. John Dufficy, Alex Lowe and Pete Athans, out in front, were the only ones to actually reach the camp. The rest of us were almost there when we were told to turn around because of deteriorating weather.

I was determined to make it to Camp III, but Wally said, "It isn't necessary, Mike."

"I'm not turning around unless you guarantee it won't be held against me," I said.

"It won't be. I promise," he replied.

It was cloudy and blowing so hard on the way back to Camp II that we could hardly make out the trail. As soon as we arrived, Alex told Todd that John Dufficy was the only one of the climbers to make it to Camp III. Meanwhile, Scott and Susie had gone down to Gorakshep and there was considerable joking about whether we would ever see them again.

On Monday, our Group A left for Camp III again. John, Mike and I made it in seven hours and Bob came in about an hour later. It was so hot I stripped down and opened clothing vents. Gloves were not even needed for working the ropes—a fleeting memory when the sun disappeared behind the horizon and we retreated into cramped quarters. The sleeping bags provided at Camp III were insufficiently insulated and spread on thin pads put directly down on the ice; I spent most of the night trying to stay warm, keeping a cough in check with sips of codeine syrup.

Bob and Mike went directly back to Camp II Tuesday morning, while John Dufficy and I climbed about an hour further up the face behind Camp III. It was the highest I had ever been, about an hour below where we would later cut diagonally across to the Yellow Band. I could distinctly make out the mixture of earthy colors in it, as well as the details of the craggy, horizontal mass of rock surrounding Lhotse's peak directly above us.

Below Camp III, as we descended, we encountered members of

Group B moving up to touch it. It was a relief to be moving lower with no schedule, taking my time, snapping photos and chatting briefly with those of our group who were still struggling upward.

We started down the icefall at 5:15 a.m. on Wednesday, arriving at Base Camp at 9:15 a.m. We passed Jan and Rob Hall on their way up. Jan mentioned that Marge, who was now with the Kiwi expedition, had bronchitis and was on her way to Pheriche. Many others had departed as well; there weren't many people in camp. Brock was smoking hashish in his tent, awaiting Al's return. Perry, who had pneumonia, was about to descend to Pheriche too. I dumped my gear in my tent and headed for the mess tent, where I devoured a massive helping of fried eggs and pancakes, then followed breakfast with a heavenly hot shower. My face was sunburned and frostbitten, but I figured it would be healed up and be ready for another round of abuse after a week in Pheriche. I was depending on cough syrup at night, and, at higher altitudes, the judicious use of half a codeine pill at bedtime.

Chuldim stopped by my tent, visiting for about an hour. "I'd really like to leave," he said, "but Todd won't pay me if I do."

I was tempted to just give him the money and tell him to go if he wished, though I was hoping he would join me on the summit. He and the other Sherpas were planning a meeting with Lapka Rita to demand more money since Todd was paying them substantially less in summit bonuses than the Kiwis or other groups. I was on their side. For the size of our expedition, an extra $1,000 in expenses was peanuts. I felt Todd should collect what he needed from his rich clients instead of squeezing it from the Sherpas but, admittedly, I had heard only one side of the story.

It appeared there would be two summit teams of five climbers each. Todd called a group meeting Friday morning and announced the first summit team should plan to depart Base Camp on the sixth for a summit attempt on the tenth. We immediately started peeling out for Pheriche and Dingboche. Since Pheriche was the last place I had seen Shelli, she was on my mind day and night and my feelings were so intense I could see her, smell her and feel her long dark hair and warm body when I closed my eyes.

At this point, we had seen the last of Al, Sal, Daryl, Frank, Brock and Jason. Having rested for a few days in Pheriche, John Dufficy and I departed for Lobuche on Monday, May 5, arriving in about two and a half hours. I was glad to get out of Pheriche, where young boys served us with dirty hands and the cook had somehow managed to mix kerosene into her cooking oil.

We had anticipated seeing members of Group B on their way to

Pheriche, but only ran into YPOs Don Casto and Jonathan Lee out for a walk a half hour from Base Camp. Soon after our arrival the socialite and Scott left for Gorakshep. The rest of their team had elected to remain in Base Camp. John Helenek, at his request, was now a member of our team. Andy Lapkas was added as a guide.

We had a delightful dinner Tuesday night sans Frank, Daryl, Sal and Susie and departed for Camp II early the next morning. For whatever reason, I couldn't summon much energy, arriving last into camp in about eight hours.

Bob Cedargreen came by my tent to tell me he was leaving the expedition, saying, "I got into this because of a gut feeling and I'm getting out for the same reason."

What could I say? There was nothing wrong with him. He was perfectly healthy, but he wished us good luck and left. One can hardly argue with a negative foreboding on Mt. Everest. Bob did return to the mountain, reaching the summit in 1994.

After breakfast on Friday we picked out our oxygen masks and regulators in an unsupervised and disorganized exercise commonly known as a cluster-fuck. The masks themselves supposedly came in three sizes and looked as appealing as vintage WWII equipment. I disassembled mine as much as I dared to clean it with Wash 'n Dri wipes.

We were preparing to depart for Camp III the morning of May 8 when Scott showed up, to everyone's surprise. He was intent upon joining us after having squandered his trip so far—on Al Hanna's dime—by hanging out with the socialite. Alex, not unreasonably, told him he was welcome to accompany us as far as Camp III, but not beyond.

It was another very hot day on the Lhotse Face, and I felt particularly strong during the ascent. After a long night crammed into two tents on a narrow snow and ice ledge hanging precariously over the face, we struggled to eat and dress the next morning, May 9. Andy Lapkas complained that he had experienced his worst night's sleep ever.

In response, John Dufficy said, "Andy, you kicked me in the head all night long."

John and I waited patiently for Andy to get ready, snow blowing into the tent. He had no sooner gotten dressed, when the Sherpa showed up, intent on carrying the sleeping bags to the South Col at that instant, and began yanking the bags out of our tent with John and me still inside them, snow now blowing in through both doors.

We started up the Lhotse Face at 9:00 a.m. Right off the bat, I had problems with my oxygen system. A long line of climbers were already crossing over the Lhotse Face toward the South Col, passing me as I struggled unsuccessfully to breathe through my confounded face mask. I arrived at the Yellow Band demoralized.

Alex said, "I don't know what to tell you, Mike. Some people can't handle them. Just take it off." And he was out of sight in nothing flat.

At fifty, I was in better condition than ninety-nine percent of the people on earth at that moment, but I was no Alex Lowe, so he might just as well have told me to turn around and go home. I struggled on across the Yellow Band without oxygen, dropping farther and farther behind until Andy Lapkas caught up with me and switched out my new regulator for an older model. Presto! As the oxygen flowed through my mask, I moved on up to the South Col at 26,000 feet with no further difficulties, arriving around 3:00 p.m., one of the last people to trudge, exhausted, into camp.

Not long after assisting me, Andy had to return to Camp III with Paul, who had given up on his summit attempt. Unfortunately, this left us short of guides on the upper mountain. Only Alex and Wally remained. Alex was focused on his own first Everest summit and fixing the lines on the Hillary Step, and Wally could not cover all of us by himself. Todd Burleson, who had said, "It's your year, Mike," and "Hopefully it will be me," wasn't even on the mountain.

Camp IV offered spectacular views of Lhotse, Nuptse, and the south face of Mt. Everest, but no protection from the weather. I stumbled through the Kiwi Camp over rocks and debris and into our camp at 4:00 p.m. Settling quickly into a tent, I nestled uncomfortably between John Dufficy and John Helenek. At least my rubber sleeping pad offered some respite on the bed of rocks and empty oxygen canisters. But even so, I could stretch out in only one position—on my back—and not very comfortably.

We ate some Ra Ra noodles, drank some tea, and tossed around in our sleeping bags, sucking on oxygen bottles, wide awake. Prior to our midnight departure, we drank some lukewarm tea and crawled out of our sleeping bags already fully dressed. We were allocated two oxygen bottles apiece. A Sherpa would have a third for each of us. The first bottle would last until the South Summit; we had nine hours to reach it before turning back.

Exiting our tent into the bitter cold, crisp darkness, I saw a few headlamps bobbing around on the way up the South Face. I told myself: *This is it.* The group scattered immediately, crampons squeaking loudly in the hard, brittle ice and snow. In the time it took me to adjust my oxygen mask that first time, I had lost track of everyone. I guess I shouldn't have been surprised. I felt like I was on the surface of an alien world—alone.

Proceeding toward the south face of the massif, I marveled at the steepness of the ice and rock and thought of the difficulty of descending, exhausted, without fixed ropes. Miraculously, in three or four hours I found myself in the midst of our "group" again. Don't ask me how.

I listened to Wally talking on the handheld radio to Todd, back at Base Camp. It appeared a storm was moving in. The climb was called off. Then it was called back on again, when Alex announced from up above that he was pushing on. So we all pushed on. Almost immediately, I was alone again. John Helenek and John Dufficy were out in front somewhere, perhaps with Chuldim, whom I never saw once all morning. I eventually found myself in the company of the Kiwis, who were now debating whether or not to continue to the top—and moving as an actual group. Rob Hall told their Base Camp he planned to keep going for another half hour, but that if the weather deteriorated any more they would call it quits. Having a great deal of respect for Rob Hall, I determined to just do whatever his group decided.

It was becoming light. I don't know what time it was, probably 5:00 a.m. I remember seeing Makalu plain as day, off to my right, sticking up through the clouds like a dark, pointy thumb. It appeared lower than me, though it wasn't, quite. I had been falling behind the Kiwis, still moving as a properly guided unit, unable to match their pace. I watched them move around the Southeast Ridge and out of sight on their way to the South Summit. I was utterly alone again and exhausted: no Alex, no Wally, no Andy, no Chuldim, no Todd, nobody, not even the Kiwis anymore. I sat down below the crest of the Southeast Ridge to protect myself from the wind and drank some water, which I had been carrying in the front of my down suit to keep it from freezing.

My expensive, custom-made down suit, that I had never before needed until this ultimate summit attempt, had become a huge problem. The manufacturer had chintzed on the hood, which wasn't deep enough for my head and wouldn't stay far enough forward to properly protect my face. I had spent all morning adjusting my oxygen mask and goggles, constantly pushing my balaclava up out of my eyes. Over and over, I pulled the oxygen mask out in front of my chin to keep it from fogging my goggles. After dealing with these problems for hours while wearing big, cold-weather mittens, I suffered an uncomfortable case of tendonitis in my hands for months thereafter.

I was not thinking all too clearly, trailing behind, and hardly able to move upwards. It occurred to me that if I continued up, I was perhaps moving beyond my ability to get back down alive.

"The summit is only half way," resounded in my oxygen-starved brain.

"Lots of people make fatal decisions at this point," I told myself. "The summit will always be there."

Still, it was my third attempt on Mt. Everest, the last of my Seven Summits, and I had spent four years and a hell of a lot of money to get to this point. My family, friends and business associates all had big emotional investments in my success. Doubts fogged my thinking as my breathing fogged my goggles. Question after question hit me like gusts of freezing wind.

"What about your reputation?"

"Are you a quitter?"

"Will you hate yourself?"

"Will you ever get another chance?"

"You promised Shelli this was the last time."

"How could you possibly expect her to understand?"

"You are fifteen hundred vertical feet from your goal. Do you really need to turn back? You carried seventy pounds up forty-three hundred vertical feet on Aconcagua."

"What's the matter with you?"

"You are *so* close!"

I sat there by myself and made the toughest decision of my life. I was curiously unemotional about it, perhaps due to my exhausted state and the effects of the thin atmosphere. I quit, turned around and started down, walking away from my dream. Had there been any number of people present who had promised to be there, things might have been different, but I will never know and I don't choose to go through the rest of my life blaming others for my failure to summit. The responsibility was mine. Someone might just as well have come along and assisted me in achieving a permanent high altitude residency.

Future groups might have said, "There's Mike Gordon over there. He should have turned around but, like so many others, he expended all his energy getting to the summit and didn't have enough left to get back down. A summit doesn't count for beans if you don't survive it."

The emotional impact I'd deal with later. This was no place for emotions. I needed to concentrate on living. Going down the steep rock and ice un-roped would take concentration. It is way more hazardous to move down, especially when exhausted, than to move up.

After taking a couple of photos of Makalu, I noticed a Sherpa watching me, off to my right and slightly below. I hadn't known there was a single person on the mountain with an interest in me until that moment. It turned out to be Gopal. When I started back down, he followed me. I wasn't doing well. I kept running out of breath, hyperventilating and having to sit down in the snow, so Gopal came over and checked my oxygen supply, which was empty when it should have lasted me to the South Summit. I probably would never have noticed the depleted state of the tank and had no idea how long it had been empty. He switched my tanks, which admittedly didn't do much to energize me at that point.

I had a very difficult time descending, keeping my footing on the steep rock and ice terrain; I could barely see my hands in front of my face through my fogged-up goggles. Gopal stayed with me the whole way as I struggled back to camp at the South Col. I vividly remember the last one hundred feet to the tents—both the relief of seeing the tents and the extreme effort involved in crossing that short distance, utterly exhausted and brain-starved for oxygen. But I was alive.

I crawled into my sleeping bag sometime between 10:00 a.m. and 11:00 a.m. Ang Passang brought me some tea. I don't remember thinking much about anything other than being alive until the rest of our "team" began arriving, safe and sound from the summit. My tent mates John and John returned around 4:00 p.m. John Helenek was suffering from snow blindness. They crawled wearily into their sleeping bags and we all began a miserable evening dominated by wind that rendered communication between the tents nearly impossible. It soon became apparent that the oxygen we had would not last through the night, but none of us had the energy to find more. I gave what was left in my tank to Helenek, who was in pretty rough shape, but around 9:00 p.m. he ran out again, as did Dufficy.

After some prodding, Dufficy, nearest the door, hollered over the increasing winds to the guide tent for more oxygen. I believe it was Wally Berg who hollered back about tanks in a bag next to the cook tent.

"Take the blue ones!" he suggested at the top of his lungs.

Dufficy geared up, sprinted out of the tent into what was now a raging storm, and brought back four blue canisters. Sucking on oxygen again, we were as comfy as you could be at 26,000 feet in a small, unprotected igloo tent in the middle of a raging storm. Did the word "vulnerable" catch our attention as it blew by at a hundred miles an hour?

As they used to say on *Laugh In*, "You bet your sweet bippy!"

At first light, Wally stuck his head into our tent in panic mode.

We were snuggled deep into our sleeping bags like three giant cocoons, but Wally insisted we get up, get dressed and get going. He finally completely entered the tent—crampons and all—and screamed at the top of his lungs, "You guys need to get the fuck up, get dressed and get the fuck out of here or you're all going to fucking die!"

As Wally hollered, the gusts caved the tent in. I sat up and put all my body weight against the tent poles to keep them from completely collapsing, worrying that the tent would implode or just get blown apart before we could get dressed. Once outside, we began the hellish job of putting on our crampons. How I managed it without frostbiting my fingers is one of life's mysteries. I added to the clutter of the South Col, leaving my ice axe on the other side of the tent. I didn't need it enough to bother putting it on my pack or carrying it down, much less fighting my way fifteen feet around the tent to retrieve it.

Wally said, "Mike, you go down with Alex."

"I don't want to go with Alex," I said. "He'll leave me!"

But I did go with Alex and, to his credit, he stuck with me. My goggles fogged up immediately as I started over the edge of the Geneva Spur. I couldn't even see my carabiner, so Alex clipped me in and out until I got so frustrated I just removed my goggles and we began to make some real progress. Alex was concerned I'd get snow blindness, but I didn't care under the circumstances, nor did I think it would happen during the time it would take me to get to Camp III.

Reaching Camp III was a major relief. I needed to vacate my bowels, and quickly. John Dufficy was already there; we told Alex he could go on down to Camp II. It was blowing like hell, but John and I managed to clear accumulated snow away from the front of the tent, remove our crampons, and get inside. As we organized our things John found some material he had planned to use for summit flags but had left behind, so I spread the material on the floor and let the vacating begin. Then I rolled the material up, tossed it over the ledge and began organizing my lower-altitude clothing to take back with me.

Wally arrived, still in panic mode, hollering, "Get the hell out of there, now! I would never have let you stop here!"

I hollered back, "Wally, I had to take a crap, badly, and neither you nor anyone else would have been able to stop me!"

"How can you justify shitting in one of the tents?!" he shouted.

"Wally, I did it on some flag material John had, rolled it up and threw it over the ledge. Now leave me the fuck alone!"

Next we argued about descending right away. He seemed to relish yelling at the top of his lungs. I was just trying to figure out how I was going to manage the Lhotse Face when I couldn't see through my fogged-up goggles. In the end, I replaced my mask and oxygen apparatus with my ordinary aviation glasses, and left the problematic equipment, which had contributed so effectively to my failed summit bid, in the tent.

We descended the Lhotse Face relatively quickly and without incident, despite the wind, which calmed near the very bottom. Wally stayed with me until Lapka Rita and another Sherpa met us with tea a short distance outside Camp II. Jonathan Lee came out to greet me with a big, warm hug. He fully understood how I felt. As we embraced each other, I cried and cried and cried, wracking sobs that poured forth from every fiber of my body and deep within my soul. Todd and the others came around and told me how proud they were of me for getting so high, but it was small succor for my overwhelming disappointment.

Todd said, "Mike, you've been all over this mountain." Signature chuckle. I just cried some more and thought to myself: *Yes, everywhere but the summit.*

I gathered my belongings and moved in with Jonathan Lee. He, Susie and Scott were to climb to Camp III next morning with Todd, Pete and Andy Lapkas, but hearing the horror stories from those of us that had just come down, he didn't know whether to go up or return to Base Camp with us. He remarked that he had never seen people age so much in only two days.

The next morning, Wally and I had an enjoyable time together walking back to Base Camp, talking a lot along the way, the last of our group through the icefall.

As we walked to the spot where crampons were removed, I said, "Wally, in spite of your screaming sessions, I think you are the best guide of the bunch. You're the most consistently professional and caring in spite of your fits of screaming."

He said, "Thank you, Mike. That means a lot to me, especially coming from you."

There had been considerable movement in the icefall during the season and it was a wonder no one was killed in it. Higher up, however, the first Nepalese woman to summit died on her way down and was retrieved by an all-Nepalese expedition. Later, a Sherpa working for the Australians fell near the Indian Camp V and, though he had organized and trained the Indian Women's Expedition, was not even missed for a couple days after his death. The news of the recovery of his body had just reached the Kiwi camp—overtaken by tangible gloom—when I walked over to call Shelli and let her know I was off the mountain.

Shelli had really gotten behind my third attempt, having trekked in with me, met the guides, and received promises from almost everyone, knowing full well I had the ability to summit.

I said, "Honey, I had to turn around at 27,500 feet. My regulator failed. I was practically the last climber to make it to the South Col, and I ran out of oxygen during the summit attempt."

She asked, "Where was Todd? Where was Chuldim? Where were Alex and Andy? *They all promised me—and you! This was supposed to be your year!"*

"Todd was in Base Camp, I don't know where the rest of them were. I never saw them on summit day, except by chance, early in the day. It was totally disorganized."

I was disappointed, but Shelli was angry—very angry. Chuldim was never invited to the ceremony in England, and Shelli won't talk to Todd to this day.

Later, after everyone had eaten and the gloom had lifted, Mike Sutton, John Dufficy, Alex Lowe and I walked back over to the Kiwi camp with a bottle of champagne and proceeded to have a hell of a party that lasted well past midnight. We told jokes, danced on the table and wrapped up the season in a festive fashion. I was very fond of Rob and Jan Hall and promised to visit them in Christchurch to do some climbing in New Zealand as soon as possible. The next morning our yaks arrived at 9:00 a.m. and John Helenek, John Dufficy, Paul, Mike Sutton and I headed down the trail toward civilization.

As we headed down from Pheriche to the Ama Dablam Lodge to spend the night, John Helenek and I walked together, discussing the expedition.

"Perhaps a fifty-year-old bar owner who smoked for fifteen years was just not destined to summit Mt. Everest," I said, adding: "As you know, there are only two people in history fifty or over, Bass and Bonington, who have ever reached the summit of Everest."

"Mike, you were in great shape—one of the strongest climbers in our group. Your age had nothing to do with it," he said.

After a while, as we walked down into the ever-thickening atmosphere, he said, "Someday I plan to come back and revisit old friends and the mountain I climbed."

I asked, "How old are you, John?" though I already knew the answer.

"Thirty-six," he said.

"Okay," I said. "Come back in fourteen years and, instead of visiting with old friends and looking at the mountain you once climbed, climb it."

John hesitated, stared hard at me and replied, "Yeah, I see what you mean."

If I'd had an attentive guide, any guide, I might have made it. Bonington had stuck to Dick Bass like glue. Mike Sutton volunteered to me that he felt he had gotten lucky when Wally Berg happened by, switched his oxygen tank, and increased the flow for him, giving him the strength and confidence to continue. I wasn't so fortunate, but I told myself 27,500 feet was higher than all but three mountains in the world and not many people, much less fifty-year-olds, get there without a seatbelt and cocktail service.

Walking down from Base Camp, I also had a long conversation with Hall Wendel, the guy who took the off-road-vehicle company Polaris public. Hall had not made the summit either and was planning to return the following year with Ed Viesturs, one of the best climbers in the world. He asked me to join them.

"Mike," he said, "it'll be just you, me and Viesturs."

"Hall, I've already told my wife Shelli I wasn't coming back here again—twice." I shook my head. It was over.

Back in Anchorage, adjusting to life without another climb to look forward to, I got a call from none other than Ed Viesturs, who said, "I talked with Hall Wendel the other day and he said you want to join the two of us next year on Everest."

I burst out laughing. "Ed, I said no such thing. I told Hall I'd have to get a new wife if I did, and I've worked long and hard at keeping the one I've got."

Life After Climbing

Shelli and I renewed our marriage vows on our tenth anniversary, September 17, 1993 in the beautiful old St. Oswald's Church in Malpas, England on the Welsh border. I was happy not to be celebrating my latest victory on a cramped mountaintop in bad weather with a handful of guides and acquaintances, but in the sunny countryside with friends and loved ones. My mother traveled all the way to England with us; Shelli's favorite uncle, Joe, her aunt Gwen, and her great-aunt Ferne were also there.

Her English relatives filled the pews as well as her best friend Deborah's parents, Don and Vivian MacInnes. Also there was Carl Birthistle, the Irish medical student we had met on our honeymoon. He'd been bartending in a pub we visited in Dublin and came over to tend bar at Chilkoot Charlie's the next two summers. It seemed everyone was there, from John Evans— my friend and assistant guide on Denali—to Jim and Maureen McCartin, good friends from my San Francisco college days.

As much as we had hoped to bring a child into this new beginning, my failed vasectomy reversal heightened the excitement, years later, when I got a call one Friday evening from a private detective who told me that a young man in Alabama wanted to talk to me. I had always wondered what had happened to the child I convinced Tiffany to put up for adoption only months after our wedding, even more convinced it wasn't mine when she agreed so readily—further evidence, it seemed, of dubious paternity. I had told Shelli about the adoption and we had discussed the call I assumed I would receive some day from an adoptee looking for his or her birth parents. And, of course, I had never been able to confirm one way or another whether the child really was mine or not.

"I'd love to talk to him," I said to the private detective on the other end of the line, "but could we wait until tomorrow night when my wife will be home?" She was visiting her Auntie Ferne in British Columbia. Arrangements were made for a call at 7:30 p.m.

When Shelli arrived early Saturday morning, on the drive home from the airport, I said, "I got the call."

She stared at me. "You mean THE call."

"Yes, THE call."

We counted down the hours until the appointed time—an opportunity for Shelli and me to have a relationship with a child that might reasonably be considered "ours."

The phone rang right on time. Paul was a very nice, well-spoken young man who had just gotten married. We spoke for over an hour. He volunteered he didn't have a very good relationship with his adoptive father, a fundamentalist Christian who operated a chain of retirement home facilities, successfully enough to own a private jet. Paul worked in a restaurant and said one day he hoped to be a restaurateur. Shelli and I were thrilled with the conversation and talked of plans to bring him up to Alaska for a visit.

After we hung up, Paul sent us a photo of himself by e-mail. At first glance I knew he was not my son. I told Shelli, "He looks like Bob Dengle, a bartender that used to work for me." He had dark hair, dark features and big hands. Tiffany and I both have fair complexions. Additionally, Paul didn't have the deep voice shared by my father, myself or my son Michael.

We decided not to say anything to my mother, who was almost ninety at the time, until we completed a DNA test. We did send the photo to my daughter Michele and her husband Jerry for their opinion. Jerry seemed to see some familial resemblance to the Gordon clan, so we withheld judgment and made arrangements for the test. We continued to communicate, and Shelli and I began the process of locating his mother while awaiting test results.

The results came back negative. Over the phone, Paul was obviously crestfallen.

Struggling to brace him a bit, I said, "I'll still treat you like a son. And we're trying to find your mother."

Tiffany didn't particularly care to be found since she apparently had encountered some financial hardships, but we found her nonetheless and put them in touch with each other.

In a weak moment I foolishly told Paul to give his mother my e-mail address and let her know it was okay for her to contact me.

Right off the bat, Tiffany e-mailed, "You're not man enough to admit that Paul is your son."

I shot back, "And you're obviously still fucking crazy to make such an assertion in spite of the fact that I, Paul, Shelli, the detective—and especially you—know he is not my child. Furthermore, if you are going to continue acting out in this manner, we are done communicating."

She replied, "I was just upset because Paul found you first."

This made no sense to me, but then I had already decided to cut contact.

She continued, "You were a major part of my life and I don't want to just let you go." It was spooky. I sensed a tentacle being extended.

I felt sorry for Paul, knowing his adoptive father didn't care much for him. He'll probably never know the identity of his real father; his mother told him she couldn't remember. The young man lived a long way from Anchorage, he was not my flesh and blood, and we had at least located his mother for him—for whatever that was worth—so over time we lost touch with one another. But at last the uncertainty was over—for me, at least.

In those years I still struggled with giving up my dream of climbing Mt. Everest and completing the Seven Summits. I surmise it was akin to a combat soldier trying to adjust to civilian life. I had thought that my success would put to rest everything I had left to prove to myself. I had failed to graduate university. I had failed two marriages and had seriously derailed a third. I had failed all my attempts so far to qualify for the Boston Marathon. And now I had a new notch on my failure belt, one that haunts me to this day.

Hall Wendel and Ed Viesturs did return to Everest in 1994 and, of course, reached the summit together. But even in my weakest moments, I was not inclined to accept Todd Burleson's open invitation, year after year, to return to the Himalayas. I felt he had let me down. Todd lives in Talkeetna, Alaska today and I still consider him a friend, despite Shelli's incredulity. I guess I've been on too many adventures, stood on too many summits and had too much fun with Todd to feel otherwise.

There were certainly days when I regretted declining Viesturs' invitation. In fact, I quietly communicated with Rob Hall about the prospect of returning with him in 1996, but dropped the idea when I discovered Susie Somebody might be part of the expedition. As it turned out, she went with Scott Fischer's expedition. Both groups were caught in the violent storm that year. Had I gone, I surely would have been involved in the disastrous events described in Jon Krakauer's *Into Thin Air.* The fate of my friend, Rob Hall, is well known because of the publicity generated by the size of the 1996 disaster. In May of that year, Shelli and I left our home early one morning for a flight to Seattle, before our copy of the *Anchorage Daily News* had arrived at our doorstep. I saw it on the plane. There was only one copy, which was read and passed along from row to row. On the front page was the story of the Everest tragedy and Rob Hall's death. I was crushed. It just didn't seem possible, but such a fate visited many of the friends I had made during my climbing days.

Gary Ball, Rob's partner in Hall and Ball, died from pulmonary edema near the summit of 26,796 foot Dhaulagiri in October, 1993.

Five years later, it was Sergei Arsentiev who, in the years following our successful expedition on Mt. Elbrus, had married a beautiful American girl named Fran and moved to Telluride, Colorado, where I visited the couple while on a trip searching for house bands. Not long after, they stayed with Shelli and me in our Woodside East condominium before and after climbing Denali together. During the winter of 1998, Sergei invited me to join him and Fran on a climb of the north side of Everest. Though I was tempted, I declined—thank goodness.

They both climbed the mountain without supplemental oxygen and Fran became the first American woman to summit without it, but she paid for the honor with her life. She started having trouble descending, eleven hundred feet from the top. Sergei went for oxygen and medication, but disappeared while returning to help her and was never seen again. A couple of other climbers tried to assist Fran in his absence, but gave up after about an hour because of her condition and circumstances, and continued down the mountain. If you become incapacitated at that altitude there's not much anyone can do to help you; they risk their own lives in even trying. It's called the "Death Zone" for a reason.

The following year, Alex Lowe died in an avalanche on Sisha Pangma, in Tibet, on October 5, 1999. He left behind a wife and three sons, all of whose photos he carried with him in the mountains and was always proud to show you.

A decade later John Evans, my assistant guide on Denali, died from a fall while rock climbing in Wales.

I stopped climbing before I was entirely ready, but I also stopped before I lost limb, life or wife. A full life has many false summits, and I've learned better how to navigate them. It seemed my best course of action adjusting to civilian life, leaving my dream of the Seven Summits unfulfilled, was to concentrate again on my business.

I purchased two more neighboring businesses, the Friendly Fireside Lounge and Hogg Brothers Café, turning them into an after-hours coffee bar for a while. They eventually became the Swing Bar inside Chilkoot Charlie's, a bit more up-scale from the rest of the establishment. It has been a very successful part of the operation, allowing for another dance floor and DJ as well as a perfect setup for private parties, though, sadly, the swing dancing fad that I personally enjoyed, only lasted a year.

Around that time we discovered Pete Ettinger playing out in the "boonies" in Canada. We were aware of Pete and had wanted to hire him previously, but he had been too expensive. Now, we found him on hard times, fronting a mediocre band in a small bar in a small town, a two to three hour drive from Vancouver, British Columbia. He looked very unhappy on-stage. When he took a break, we convinced him that we had some good musicians in Anchorage. Pete formed his own band from our local talent and has been playing the club successfully now for over twenty years.

But as much as I enjoyed the challenges and pleasures of growing my business, I couldn't look at a mountain without visualizing the climbing route, knowing I'd never be able to replicate the excitement, danger, challenge and adventure of climbing the big ones. Turning my back on climbing has been a hard thing to do in a state full of mountains. For a while, I tried my best to fill the void with my previous decade-old pastime: chasing the ever-elusive qualifying time for the Boston Marathon. But my heart wasn't in it anymore. When I started running, in 1979, Bill Rogers was regularly winning the Boston Marathon. I was a big fan of Bill's, and had been lucky enough to hear him speak in the old Central Junior High gymnasium when he visited Anchorage.

I had picked the Glacier Marathon twice in my qualifying quest, a race that started from the turnoff to Alyeska Resort in Girdwood, and proceeded through Portage, almost to the point where the highway starts its ascent into the mountains, and then looped back to the turnoff. The course was flat—the reason I chose it. It had a problem though. There was, and is, a crown in the highway, so when you ran out and back on the left-hand side of the road, your left foot fell farther than your right every step of the way. After running it twice with disastrous results I discovered that my left leg is two-thirds of an inch shorter than my right, compounding the problem.

On my first attempt, well on my way to qualification, I had to stop in Portage on the return, limping on a large blood blister on the ball of my left foot. I sat down on the left side of the road, totally distraught, in need of a ride back to the finish line.

On my second attempt, I felt an acute pain in my left hip at around twenty miles, had to slow my speed way down and managed to hobble across the finish line. Even with the injury, this race was my second fastest, but not good enough for a Boston qualification. Before the award ceremonies were over at the Indian House, the organizers called an ambulance to haul me back to Anchorage. As the paramedics put me onto the gurney, I screamed so loud I cleared the place out. The Seward Highway was under construction at the time and the temporary roadbed was the railroad tracks. I bounced most of the way back to town, railroad tie after railroad tie, with what turned out to be a stress-fractured left femur.

After I began climbing I still did a lot of running. I thought about running a marathon after returning from a big mountain like Everest. I would go to Nepal weighing one hundred eighty-five pounds and return weighing one hundred fifty pounds and in incredible cardiovascular condition—looking more like Bill Rogers than Mike Gordon. It seemed I should have been able to run a personal record with such timing, qualifying for Boston, but the calendaring just never worked out.

I have always been competitive, and though I played solid defense for the hockey teams at Anchorage High and the University of Alaska Fairbanks as a young man, I am by no means a gifted athlete. Consequently, I've preferred competing against myself rather than against others. I was not particularly good at distance running, but I am capable of long-range commitments and I can take a lot of punishment. I never wore headphones to listen to music while running. There's no need for artificial entertainment when you have earned that sensation that I call "effortless overdrive," where you feel you can run forever, your feet literally fly over the ground and an irrepressible smile breaks out all over your face. I preferred keeping my own company and would often come home with an alphabetical list of new ideas, such as recreating the Bird House Bar as part of Chilkoot Charlie's in 2003—the tenth bar in the place and our final addition.

Serendipity struck again. I was running the Chester Creek Bike Trail when the idea hit. I called Susan Delak, who had operated the Bird House after her husband was killed in a plane crash, until it burned down. Though a number of others had approached her, she agreed to sell me the rights to the name because she felt I would do a proper job of the restoration.

It fit perfectly into a space at the rear of Koot's that we had been using for a patio area with horseshoe pits—where Bill Jacobs had held his finger to my head. We consulted the extant as-built survey of the original bar and a scale model made by a Bird Creek resident, as well as lots of photos and videos. The fact that I had worked the place every weekend for a year didn't hurt either.

The Bird House had been everyone's favorite little bar. I was determined to make sure it was an exact replica. And it is, right down to the bumper stickers around the inside of the bar. Our crew at Chilkoot Charlie's, with the help of architect Jeffery Wilson, built the place and excitedly dragged me from my office nearby to have a look when they had at last installed the bar itself.

"The angle is wrong," I said. "It needs more of a slant to it."

Craig O'Hanlon, my property manager, said, "We can't do it, Mike. If we raise it on the outside end anymore you won't be able to see inside, and if we lower it anymore on the inside we'll have to tear the floor out and start all over."

"Start tearing," I said.

To my great satisfaction, no one has ever criticized the reincarnation, which features the stove from the old bar, singularly unaffected by the blaze. Shelli—and many others—have described walking into the new Bird House Bar as eerie, as if you're stepping out of a time machine and into the old, original bar on the Seward Highway. The Bird House was, in a sense, the parent of Chilkoot Charlie's—its idea originating there—and now Chilkoot Charlie's is the parent of the new Bird House, which is protected by a modern fire sprinkler system.

We moved our outdoor patio to the much larger open area behind the Swing Bar. We were fortunate to have that outdoor area in place when the Anchorage Municipal Assembly passed the smoking ban. I did not fight that ordinance like most in the industry, because I felt it was time for our employees and our patrons to breathe clean air. But I did fight for a level playing field. Had the private clubs been allowed to exempt themselves, it would have been disastrous for the rest of us, while completely undermining the intent of the ordinance. Thankfully, the assembly overcame the political obstacles and did the right thing.

The ideas for the expansions and the various themes at Chilkoot Charlie's were mostly mine, including the wood design on the front of the building. But the man who actually did the work of decorating the Russian-themed south side of the bar, the deck where the smokers now hang out, the Swing Bar and the wonderful wood design on the front of the building, was Joe Hamilton. Joe is truly a multi-talented artist who can work in any artistic medium, and with whom I have thoroughly enjoyed working over the years. We were a good team.

Who would ever have thought that a rustic little fifteen- hundred square foot bar in Spenard would end up setting national sales records for Coors, St. Pauli Girl, Corona, Captain Morgan's Rum, Jagermeister and Red Bull; that it would be listed in the "Top 100 Bars in America" by *Nightclub and Bar Magazine* for decades; or that, most proudly, it would lead the list of "The Best 23 Bars in America" in the May, 2000 issue of *Playboy Magazine*. I was so pleased I sent Hugh Hefner a gift. And what better gift for Hef than an oosik, accompanied by *Ode to an Oosik*? In his thank you letter he said, "Obviously, a walrus would be a hard act to follow."

Today I prefer the tranquility of retirement, enjoying the secluded surroundings of our home across Kachemak Bay in Halibut Cove. For years, Shelli had complained to me, her doctor and our therapist that she wished I'd slow down. Both assured her I would over time and I have, though it's taken thirty years. God, how I wanted to return to Everest! It didn't help that people were always asking me if I was going to give it another try. I knew I could do it, and moderation has never been my strong suit. I didn't give up on the dream until I'd grown too old and one day realized it was too late to be fulfilled.

Shelli and I spent our twentieth anniversary enjoying a weenie roast together on Eagle Beach outside Peterson Bay. We returned there for our thirtieth, sans weenies, since I haven't eaten meat or fowl in almost 20 years. Shelli has tamed the beast. It was her strength and perseverance that saw us through the hard times. Her belief in me, in spite of my failings, has made me a stronger, better person—focused on being a better husband and father, and returning to school to complete my education.

Shelli has said to me, "People don't change, but you actually did."

I'm proud of that. It wasn't easy. I have traveled a long and circuitous route, sometimes tortuous, making impulsive decisions—not all bad—and feel as if I have come full circle. I now realize that those same decisions came from a well of great inner confidence, despite my issues with low self-esteem that date back to early childhood. The first home I ever bought for myself wasn't a house, but a block of property on Sixth Avenue. When I started a business, I built it into the largest entertainment emporium on the West Coast. When I got annoyed with local government, I got myself elected to the Anchorage City Council. When I decided to start running, I headed straight toward the marathon, setting my sights on Boston. The first mountain I ever climbed—aside from Flattop—was Denali and then I immediately went after the Seven Summits.

I've done some terrible things in my life—some irreversible—and all I can say is that I've tried to atone for them. The last thing I would ever want to become is embittered, regardless of my setbacks, mistakes, failures or some of the injustices I might feel I have faced. I remain positive; I'm the undying optimist. I'm never jealous of the triumphs of others. I might be disappointed with myself or even a little envious of some, but success always inspires me.

I've grown to prize loyalty and honesty. I try to be fair and honest in everything I do, and I am a man of my word. I've spent almost my entire life growing up and doing business in Anchorage—you can't do that if your word is no good.

But I am flawed, and the hardest thing for me to confront is my history of infidelities. Where was the fairness and honesty there? I have been unfaithful to all three of my wives and, try as I may, I can't account for it. I don't know why I behaved so badly. I don't feel I owe Tiffany an apology. She did, after all, lie to me about the baby she was carrying. I do feel I owe Lilla one. My only excuse is that we had grown apart and I felt trapped in a relationship that was unfulfilling for me. The truth is I simply wouldn't, or couldn't, control myself. In the case of Shelli I have no excuse at all, and my infidelities to her have caused her (and me) more pain than all others combined. Though I am still a flawed human being, I have never strayed since my admittance of infidelity over twenty-five years ago.

About Shelli, I feel like the gambler Jack Weil, in the movie *Havana*, when he tells Bobby Duran, the wife of a prominent revolutionary with whom he has fallen in love—forcing him to choose between the man he is and the man he could be—"If I'd never met you, I'd have lived my life as a lie."

Afterword
Graduation (48 Years Late!)

In May of 2010, Shelli and I traveled south to visit Jim and Maureen McCartin in Bend, Oregon. Jim, one of my three roommates during my junior year at the University of San Francisco, had been diagnosed with prostate cancer. It was a surprise visit engineered by Maureen and me that had to be postponed once, due to the hospitalization of my mother. Originally, I had tied the visit to a ski trip to Utah, but I went to visit Mom at the hospital the night before I was to depart and made the decision to cancel my plans because it was apparent to me she would not last until my return. My mother, Ruth Isabell (Boisch) Gordon, died the next morning, March 23, at the age of ninety-six.

I spent some time alone with my mother's body, curiously unemotional, perhaps because her passing had taken years and had almost been a blessing when it arrived. I recalled the smell of her lipstick on the Kleenex she used to wipe my face when I was a boy, and the way she smiled up at me from her wheelchair years later, gushing, "You're so cute!" Once I delivered a whole case of Baileys liquor mini-bottles to her at Marlow Manor Assisted Living for Christmas. She made a noise I'd never heard before—"Huh! Huh! Huh!"— and immediately phoned Lucy, her friend down the hall, to brag about what her son had brought and invite her over for a nip. Mom was never a big drinker, but she loved Baileys, and she preferred the little bottles. She could upend them with her one good arm, like a wounded humming bird extracting nectar from a hanging flower.

It was a moment of reflection. I also recalled the many times I had returned home to Shelli, beaten and demoralized—wondering why I had bothered—after driving half an hour each way to Muldoon to visit with Mom, bearing a gift, card or flowers in hand.

Having just lost my mother, I was about to lose my college roommate and one of my dearest friends too. I was entering a poignant period in my life when friends and family were leaving faster than they were being added.

When we did make it to Bend, our visit caught Jim completely by surprise. I rang the doorbell of their lovely home and Jim promptly arrived, gazing through the cut-glass side panels of the door to catch a glimpse of the unexpected visitors. It took him a moment to figure out who was standing on his threshold before blurting, "Mike, Shelli. What are you doing here?"

"We're visiting," I said.

"But, where are you staying?" he asked.

"We're staying here."

Deer in the headlights! Maureen now appeared and the cat was out of the bag. With laughs all around, Jim acknowledged that he had been completely "had." The last time we had seen each other was in Wales, and I confess I was taken aback by Jim's appearance there in Bend. In fact, I had a hard time maintaining my composure because he had lost so much weight. Once over the initial shock it wasn't a problem because in every other respect, Jim was exactly the person I had always known, loved and admired.

The week we spent in Bend was as good as it gets. As two couples, we could not have gotten along better. From the hot-tub soak Jim and I shared in the mornings, to the rambling about Bend, the Rotary luncheon he and I jointly attended, to cocktail hours at the end of the day and the conversations that followed, the visit was thoroughly enjoyable.

Several days into the visit I happened to mention that I had written to the University of San Francisco to inquire about how I might go about completing my degree. I was disappointed not to have received a reply. Jim said, "What's your middle initial?"

"W," I said.

Shelli volunteered that my middle name was William, adding that the sole purpose of a middle name was so mothers could get the attention of their children without swearing or raising their voices.

Jim had graduated from the University of San Francisco in 1964 when I should have graduated, and he went on to spend twenty years in the U.S. Coast Guard. Upon retirement from the Coast Guard, Jim returned to USF for a master's degree in business administration and started a whole new career with American President Lines, now known simply as APL. He had spent many of those years living in the San Francisco Bay Area. Jim knew people at USF and had been a loyal and generous alumnus. I did not give any of this much thought, but when I returned to Alaska there was an e-mail from the University of San Francisco waiting for me.

The university, at Jim's urging, had embraced my needs. He had explained to the school, unbeknownst to me, that they should accommodate my desire to graduate and that they needed me as an alumnus. In response, I was provided with a liaison at the school named Tonya Miller. She was given the daunting task of finding my records, which were hidden somewhere off campus in the dusty archives of the university, and not conveniently accessible on a computer screen, tucked in with the records of students who had graduated. Amazingly, though, the records were located and being reviewed by the admissions office.

Tonya went about converting my credits from the anachronistic three-unit system to the present four-unit system; I needed only seventeen credits to graduate.

I had created a successful life for myself without a university degree, but it always bothered me that I had not graduated. I had regular dreams, or nightmares, about being back on campus at USF, always behind on my studies and always in search of my classrooms. Whenever the subject of education came up in a conversation, I would have to go into the story: "I was on the Dean's Honor Roll. I was a good student. I got married my junior year, my wife got pregnant the night of our wedding and I moved on with life."

Tonya now went to the department heads at USF to discuss the courses they felt I needed to take in order to complete a major in political science and a minor in philosophy. Meanwhile, she directed me to the school website and suggested I select classes in political science and philosophy that interested me. At Jesuit universities like USF, a philosophy course is required each semester to earn a diploma. They decided I needed two four-unit courses in political science and two four unit courses in philosophy plus one unit. I began selecting courses from the school website, including the philosophy of art, which sounded so interesting that Shelli said she wanted to enroll as well. Then word came down from on high that I needed a five-unit ethics course and a four-unit applied ethics course—taken sequentially. Oh, my God!

My decision to finish my schooling was, like all the other big decisions I had made in my life, met with some degree of disbelief. When I told my business manager, Doran, he looked up at me dismissively and said, "Well, you're going to be busy."

Deciding to run for the Anchorage City Council, to quit smoking, to run my first marathon or to climb Denali, I had always encountered the same reaction. I've come to the conclusion that when everyone thinks I'm nuts for deciding to do something, I must be on the right path.

I was terrified of taking seventeen units in one semester while running my business, rusty at the school thing after having not been to college in forty-eight years. But I needed to jam it all in like that so I could walk the stage in May in San Francisco, when Jim could be there—because without him, none of it would have happened. I couldn't put it off any later, considering his diagnosis.

My philosophy professor, Marvin Brown, e-mailed me more than a month before the semester started. He was not lecturing the two required ethics courses that semester, so he provided me with a syllabus for each class, as well as reading requirements and writing assignments. There was no mention of sequential anything. Elated, at this point I made a wise decision. I decided to apply myself to the five-unit ethics class and finish it before the semester started, which is all I did during that month. I did finish it, literally the day the semester began. Marvin called me from San Francisco to personally inform me of my grade.

Now the lectures began twice a week for each of my two political science classes, which were American Foreign Policy and Governments and Politics of the Middle East. Incidentally, this was a very interesting time to be taking these classes from Stephen Zunes, the Chair for Middle Eastern Studies at USF, since it was immediately following the self-immolation by Mohamed Bouazizi, the twenty-six year old street vendor in Tunisia, which kick-started the momentous events in Egypt and elsewhere in the Middle East that are now known as the "Arab Spring," which, incidentally, has never evolved into summer.

Tonya Miller arranged for a student to take a recorder to each class and forward the recordings online via Google Documents. Initially, it did not appear the system was going to work because there was too much background noise. We were in a learning curve for the university, the professor, my liaison and me. At Shelli's suggestion, Tonya asked Stephen Zunes if he would wear the microphone. It worked nicely, but I still could not decipher student questions and comments. I could hear the professor's answers, though, which was enough. I was just glad I could hear the lectures now— they were fascinating.

During the early part of the semester, I finished the applied ethics class by focusing on it as I had the ethics course. This was fortuitous because the reading, book report and term paper requirements from Professor Zunes were daunting. He gave bi-weekly objective quizzes to his students and, since I could not participate, he told me to "just write a page or a page and a half, single-spaced" on the reading material assigned each week. I ended up writing as many as fifteen to twenty pages because there was so much reading that I could have filled up "a page or a page and a half" by just typing the chapter headings and sub-headings. It was killing me.

I jokingly said to Shelli one day, "Honey, these college professors don't seem to think I have anything else to do!"

After a couple of weeks, I called Zunes to complain. He had not even received the result of my efforts, having suffered a computer catastrophe. He explained that the only reason he gave the quizzes was to make sure the students were completing the readings and that he obviously did not have to be concerned about me doing so. Thank God! After writing my mid-term papers I listened as my classmates were told of their scores, but had to wait two nervous weeks, pestering Tonya Miller regularly, to hear how I had done. It was a busy time for Stephen, giving interviews on radio and television, writing articles and traveling to Washington, DC, much less having to deal with his distant student in Alaska.

I was eventually rewarded for my efforts with an A in all four of my classes. Discussing my grade with Marvin Brown, my philosophy professor, by phone, he said, "Will you be attending graduation ceremonies in May?"

"Yes, I will," I said.

"I don't generally attend graduation ceremonies, but I'll be around," he said, which I took as an invitation to contact him.

I phoned Michele and Jerry and coordinated arrangements with Jim and Maureen so that we could all stay Thursday, Friday and Saturday night in the same hotel, the Queen Anne, a charming old hotel on the National Historic Registry. It was located next to Japantown, not far from the USF campus.

Settling into our rooms in the hotel, we all began preparing for our event that evening, the reunion of a group Shelli and I had spent three weeks with in China, Tibet, Nepal and Thailand the previous October. The trip had been orchestrated by Dick and Ann Grace of Grace Family Vineyards, St. Helena, in Napa Valley. The vineyard produces a small amount of exceptional cabernet sauvignon available only to people on their mailing list and affords Dick the ability to maintain a network of humanitarian missions located mostly in Tibet and Nepal. Dick and Ann travel there several times a year and frequently take friends along to visit the clinics, schools and monasteries they generously support. In October of 2010, we left for Asia with Marsha Williams, Robin's ex-wife; Peter Coyote, the actor and author, and his wife, Stefanie; Mike and Soek D'Allesandro, a young couple from the Seattle area; Pat Murray, Dick's cousin; and John Harper, the travel agent who came along for the Tibetan portion of the trip.

We enjoyed a festive evening at Marsha's home, located all the way out in the avenues of San Francisco overlooking the Golden Gate Bridge, and filled to the brim with the most tasteful and eclectic private modern art collection I have seen. Marsha's personal chef prepared and presented a wonderful meal with fine wines, and we lost ourselves in conversation with several of Dick and Marsha's Tibetan friends. I was thrilled to introduce Jim and Maureen, and Michele and Jerry to our new friends.

Friday morning, the six of us went to USF to pick up my cap and gown. The lady assisting me volunteered that she had worked with Tonya Miller for a couple of weeks at "bringing your school records into the twenty-first century."

"The school's computer did not want to accept your ancient course descriptions, numbers or credit hours, she told me."

"Well then, perhaps I could get a position here teaching Aristotle?"

Next I called Marvin Brown, who said he would meet us in front of the school bookstore at 1:00 p.m. In the meantime, Jim and Maureen wandered off, Jerry and Michele relaxed and Shelli and I purchased an entire wardrobe of USF clothing. Marvin arrived promptly at 1:00 p.m. and asked if we wanted to have a cup of coffee or walk down the street for a beer. We opted for the latter and found ourselves in a once-seedy location known as the Fulton Inn in the early '60s which had been nicely remodeled. We spent a wonderful couple of hours conversing with Marvin.

At one point in the visit I said, "Marvin, I hope you didn't drive all the way over here from Berkeley just to meet me," and he replied, "I did."

Marvin Brown is a brilliant man with a couple of important philosophical works to his credit. For him to make such an effort to meet with me was indeed an honor.

Shelli asked, "Professor Brown, how many students have you had like Michael?"

"None," he said.

I felt like I had come a long way in a few short months.

That Friday night, the three couples enjoyed dinner at a nearby sushi bar and retired early.

When I walked into the hotel restaurant on Saturday morning for breakfast a man approached me and asked, "Are you Mike Gordon?"

"Are you Rick Fischer?" I asked.

I had not seen my old USF roommate for decades. Rick earned a masters at USF and a law degree from Hastings, then moved to Washington, DC. He had lost his wife a few years before and had flown to San Francisco with his friend, Anne, for my graduation ceremony. A moment later I turned around and there was Rosie, the widow of the fourth roommate, Jerry Lombardi, a gentle soul who had recently succumbed to cancer.

What an unimaginable surprise! We were all lodged at the Queen Anne Hotel. Jim had not only managed to make it to my graduation, but had secretly arranged for Rick and Anne and Rosie to attend. I was overwhelmed by emotional gratitude. Forty-eight years later and there we all were together again in body or spirit.

It was a gorgeous day in the city. I could not have been happier to be back. After locating where I was to queue up, everyone else walked across campus to St. Ignatius Cathedral, where the ceremony was to be held. I hung out, feeling somewhat conspicuous, among the hundreds of kids, all of us in graduation garb. I watched the proctors in the crowd helping the young graduates fix their outfits and I thought, from looking around, that my hood was improper, so I got the attention of one and asked if she could assist me.

"Sure," she said. "I know who you are. You're that famous guy. Fifteen minutes before we depart for St. Ignatius I want you over there by that door, because I'm putting you in the front of the procession."

"Yes, ma'am," I said.

They led us all across the campus grounds to the stunningly beautiful cathedral, and I walked all the way to the front row, far right seat. My friends and family were seated directly across the aisle to my right. After the national anthem, during which I was the only graduate I could see that removed their mortarboard, and the speeches, I was first to walk across the stage and receive my diploma.

Handing it to me and shaking my hand, University President Stephen Privett, S.J. said, "You're the guy from Alaska, aren't you?"

"Yes, I am," I replied, smiling broadly.

I had been informed by the USF public relations people that I would be interviewed by Channel 5 television after the ceremony, so after we filed out of the cathedral I located the cameraman, as friends and family arrived on the scene. The guy from Channel 5 interviewed me and Jim, and we took some wonderful photos of family, friends and "the roommates." The clip "Mike Gordon graduates from the University of San Francisco, 48 years late!" was played in San Francisco that night, picked up by CBS affiliates and played all over the country, including in Anchorage. Overall, the University of San Francisco received the equivalent of $250,000 in free publicity.

The school's public relations department also interviewed Tonya and me for the alumni newsletter, which occupied a prominent location on the school's website. I was pleased that Tonya received well-deserved recognition for her efforts on my behalf, but in the end, the school administration removed all her comments. I was told it was because they did not want to shine a light on the fact that they had bent the rules in order to accommodate me. I was unhappy about this development and made my feelings known to the public relations people, who agreed with me. Whatever bending they did certainly did not diminish the amount of work that was required of me to graduate. So what if there is no such a thing as a five-unit ethics course and my transcript shows four units plus one unit? I asked Marvin Brown how he had gone about fashioning the five-unit class; he chuckled and said he had just added in "some graduate stuff."

Now Jim walked over and said, "We have one last surprise. I promise. We're going to have lunch with Father Lo Schiavo" (1925-2015).

We dined privately with the chancellor in his private dining room atop Lone Mountain, after first walking with him through the gardens that overlook the city and bay, including the Golden Gate Bridge. Lunch was provided by the chancellor's private chef, accompanied by a lovely Napa Chardonnay.

Father Lo was the only person, priest or lay, left at USF from the days that Jim, Rick, Jerry and I were there. He referred to himself as the "Last of the Mohicans," also because he was the last remaining conservative on campus. During the delicious meal, we discussed my last semester and encouraged Father Lo to spur the university in reaching out and accommodating others like me who might take advantage of classes offered on a long-distance independent-study basis in order to complete their degrees.

The last night in the city, Marsha placed a dinner reservation for the eight of us at Jardinière, a restaurant on Grove Street in which she has an interest. Without her "in" we would never have gotten a table, day of, on a Saturday night. It was the perfect end to a perfect adventure. The next day everyone went home with a great story to tell, including the college graduate and his wife.

When I realized the University of San Francisco was going to bat for me to find a way to graduate, I was so grateful, I cried and cried.

In fact, I became emotional throughout the entire experience, from beginning to end—even right now, as I type. There are simply no words to express my gratitude to both USF and to Jim McCartin, who succumbed to cancer on July 12, 2012, but not before Rick, Anne, Shelli and I visited him one last time in Bend. And, of course, I'm grateful to Shelli, for her moral support and for filling the role of editor while otherwise being ignored for months during my studies. I am very pleased that Michele and Jerry could attend such a milepost in my life and grateful to Marsha for opening her lovely home to us. And I am humbled that Rick, Anne, Rosie and Maureen thought enough of me to expend the time and effort to be there for my graduation. Lastly, I am proud of myself for doing what I did and doing it well. I would not trade the experience for having made it up the last 1,500 feet on Mt. Everest during my third attempt, and I no longer have nightmares about being back in school.

I'll go a step further. In the agony of not making the summit of Mt. Everest, I learned far more than I would have had I made it. Though I stopped climbing literally, I have never stopped figuratively. I have kept on climbing beyond Mt. Everest, to even higher pinnacles. Mt. Everest was another one of those false summits. It is no longer in the foreground; it's in the background. But surely there are more false summits ahead, as well as real ones, for I see a whole range of mountain peaks stretching to the horizon—as when you look at a range from the highest peak among them, or through the oval of an airplane window.